Enacting Platforms

Platform Studies
Nick Montfort and Ian Bogost, editors

Enacting Platforms

Feminist Technoscience and the Unreal Engine

James Malazita

The MIT Press   Cambridge, Massachusetts   London, England

The MIT Press would like to thank the anonymous peer reviewers who provided comments on drafts of this book. The generous work of academic experts is essential for establishing the authority and quality of our publications. We acknowledge with gratitude the contributions of these otherwise uncredited readers.

This book was set in Filosofia OT by Toppan Best-set Premedia Limited. Printed and bound in the United States of America.

Library of Congress Cataloging-in-Publication Data

Names: Malazita, James, author.
Title: Enacting platforms : feminist technoscience and the Unreal Engine / James Malazita.
Description: Cambridge, Massachusetts : The MIT Press, 2024. |
  Series: Platform studies | Includes bibliographical references and index.
Identifiers: LCCN 2023034695 (print) | LCCN 2023034696 (ebook) |
  ISBN 9780262548243 (paperback) | ISBN 9780262379069 (epub) |
  ISBN 9780262379076 (pdf)
Subjects: LCSH: Video games—Programming. | Video games—Design. |
  Three-dimensional display systems. | UnrealScript (Computer program language)
Classification: LCC QA76.76.V54 M35 2024 (print) | LCC QA76.76.V54
  (ebook) | DDC 794.8/1513—dc23/eng/20231012
LC record available at https://lccn.loc.gov/2023034695
LC ebook record available at https://lccn.loc.gov/2023034696

10 9 8 7 6 5 4 3 2 1

Contents

Series Foreword

How can someone create a breakthrough game for a mobile phone or a compelling work of art for an immersive 3D environment without understanding that the mobile phone and the 3D environment are different sorts of computing platforms? The best artists, writers, programmers, and designers are well aware of how certain platforms facilitate certain types of computational expression and innovation. Likewise, computer science and engineering have long considered how underlying computing systems can be analyzed and improved. As important as scientific and engineering approaches are, and as significant as work by creative artists has been, there is also much to be learned from the sustained, intensive, humanistic study of digital media. We believe it is time for humanists to seriously consider the lowest level of computing systems and their relationship to culture and creativity.

The Platform Studies series has been established to promote the investigation of underlying computing systems and of how they enable, constrain, shape, and support the creative work that is done on them. The series investigates the foundations of digital media—the computing systems, both hardware and software, that developers and users depend on for artistic, literary, and gaming development. Books in the series certainly vary in their approaches, but they all share certain features:

- a focus on a single platform or a closely related family of platforms
- technical rigor and in-depth investigation of how computing technologies work

- an awareness of and a discussion of how computing platforms exist in a context of culture and society, being developed on the basis of cultural concepts and then contributing to culture in a variety of ways—for instance, by affecting how people perceive computing

Acknowledgments

This book is the result of about ten years of research, collaboration, correspondence, excitements, and frustrations. Some small parts of it began as dissertation work, the results of which have been thankfully locked away in the digital basement of a library server somewhere. Most of the sensemaking throughout the next decade came about through conversations with my students and colleagues at Rensselaer, serendipitous Twitter search results, and—while surrounded by coffee mugs—half-working installs of old Unreal Engines, and cats.

Thank you to Epic Games and Unreal Academy, whose traveling workshops for games educators provided me with one of my first full dives into Unreal, leading me (perhaps unintentionally) to the thread I needed to tie together my developing thoughts about game engines, power, and theories of enactment.

Thank you to the Strong Museum of Play, whose Strong Fellowship program provided access to the *America's Army* archives that would shape chapter 1, and to the archivists and librarians there who geeked out with me about *ZZT* for three days.

Thank you to my faculty, committee members, and fellow graduate colleagues at Drexel for helping me navigate the first-gen student experience and come out the other side relatively unscathed. To Glen Muschio, for ten years of mentorship from my freshman year through my PhD, and for encouraging me to think more broadly about digital media than my technical classwork would otherwise have suggested. To Judi Storniolo, whose class I took because I thought it was about cults when in fact it was about culture, for pushing me to continue with anthropology nonetheless. To my adviser Doug Porpora, who scraped me off the pavement of grad school and got me out the door. I think you might think this project turned out to be an exercise in madness, but I appreciate your support all the same, and credit you for your rapid mastery of *Dungeons & Dragons*. To Wes Shumar, Mary Ebeling, Brent Luvaas, and Mimi Sheller for sticking with me. To Rachel Reynolds, whose feedback on my final seminar paper, "Jim, I don't understand your mind but I appreciate you," is lovingly burned into my soul. To Tyson Mitman for whiskey at Sheba. To Candice Roberts for everything else.

Thank you to my colleagues, supporters, and students at Rensselaer, who helped me shepherd this project and, frankly, my career to this date, to where it is now. To Dean Nieusma, who took on the hard task of taking a mildly traumatized half game designer/half cultural studies nerd and shaping him into a better teacher, scholar, and person. To Raquel Velho for your friendship, support, venting sessions in the hub, and mutual sanity checks. To Nancy Campbell for reading early drafts, and generally for helping me muddle through the mess. To Ben Chang, who let me hang out in the Games program as an unaffiliated, non-tenure-track STS lecturer, and then hired me on the TT and put me in charge of a third of it—and for supporting out-there ideas and initiatives about critical games graduate education and the future of games in the academy. To Silvia Ruzanka, Eric Ameres, Rebecca Rouse, Mark Destefano, and Kate Galloway for your time, reading, conversations, critical correctives, and overall generosity of mind and spirit. To Kim Osburn and Mary Simoni for your support, and for helping me navigate the hidden curricula and structures of university systems. To Lee Nelson, Alex Jenseth, Marina Fontolan, Jamie Steele, Yoehan Oh, Gabriel Medina-Kim, Matthew Hlady, and Jonathan Givan for your patience with me whenever I had to do "book stuff."

Thank you to my broader networks of academic support for your feedback, generosity, and general reality checks. To Ted Kim for your extensive work, reading, feedback, collaboration, and overall kindness to someone who randomly DM-ed you on Twitter. To Arianna Gass, Katherine Buse, and Peter McDonald for your time and careful reading of this work, for your critical eye, and for just in general being a kickass writing group. To Gillian Smith and Anne Sullivan for your advice, invitations to talks, networking, and counsel in navigating the social and disciplinary waters of games scholarship. To Colin Milburn and Ranjodh Singh Dhaliwal for conference conversations, journal collaborations, and hypemanship.

Thank you to my editorial team, both inside and external to the MIT Press. To Aure Schrock for your care, advice, close readings, and therapy sessions during your developmental editing process. I'm not sure how much of this would have seen the light of day without your support, and without the general knowledge that "hey, if this section is a mess, Aure will fix it!" To Noah Springer and the MIT Press team, who have made this process so easy and so smooth. To Ian Bogost and Nick Montfort, for supporting the manuscript even though I made you seem cheeky. To Eric Freedman, Aubrey Anable, and the anonymous reviewers of the proposal and manuscript, whose generous commentary and critical insight made this book richer than I could have on my own.

Finally, thank you to my family. To Jim and Sue Malazita, who always pushed me to do better—and for investing in my videogame and Magic: the Gathering habits, without which I probably would have become an engineer or something. To John and Maria Recco, Ianna Recco, and Simon Jia, who have continuously cheered me on for the past three years, taught me to garden to get outside, and supplied me with a steady stream of olive oil, cupcakes, and Taco Bell. To Belle, Gordy, Gus, Bea, Kitt, and Shelly, for the purrs. To Donna—even though you're a dog, you're basically a cat, and I really appreciate that about you.

To Gia, for your love, support, hype, and partnership in this and in everything we do. For always making me talk about the book at parties, thus sharpening my elevator pitch. For getting into videogames. For running marathons, working on the house, eating enchiladas, napping with cats, writing in cafes, walking in Athens. This book is for you.

Introduction

It looked amazing, and almost real. Which scared the shit out of me.

—Matthew Gault, *Vice*[1]

It's September 13, 2018, and Hurricane Florence looms off the South Carolina coastline. After intervals of waxing and waning strength as it soared northwest over the Atlantic, the storm had recently surged to its highest intensity. The next day Florence would bring sustained winds of 50 mph and torrential rains across the United States' southeastern seaboard and, over the following four days, would ravage the Carolinas and Virginia, contributing to rising water levels of 8–11 feet above sea level, fifty-five deaths, and over $24 billion in damage.

Five hundred miles inland, in Atlanta, meteorologist Erika Navarro stands on an emerald felt carpet surrounded by a circle of green walls hastily finished only the week before. As she begins her live broadcast for the Weather Channel, a motion-tracking system attached directly to the camera feeds her spatial coordinates to an array of NVIDIA graphics processing units. This computational array removes Navarro from her green closet and, from the point of view of her live broadcast audience, places her in a silver studio with large screens to her back. As she narrates Florence's potential impacts on coastal communities, the screens behind her zoom in and out across a gray map of the seaboard, where yellow, blue, and red splashes of data paint a cruel picture of impending sea level rise.

Forty-three seconds in, the image of Navarro's studio fades, giving way to one of a quintessential coastal Carolinian street. She stands in the road, where the lawns in front of terra-cotta-roofed houses weave themselves into cracked asphalt. The scene, crafted using Epic Games' Unreal Engine, has a surrealistic quality to it; Navarro's body, bathed in the characteristically overbright studio lights, blends seamlessly with a yellow-green sky, yet she seems unruffled by the winds swirling the digital foliage behind her. As she continues her narration of the flooding to come, water surges from the horizon line and floods the street, pooling around her (Figure 0.1). Curiously, the water avoids a six-foot circle at her feet. As the floodwaters continue their deluge, Navarro appears protected by an invisible cylinder, whose walls grow ever higher as the waterline travels to her waist. Sounds of creaking wood and crashing waves fill the audience's speakers, while Navarro talks about Florence's danger to cars, garages, and basements. She spreads her hands out to her sides and slowly raises her arms above her head. The water level follows her lead, eventually towering nine feet high. Faint silhouettes of fish can be seen in the murky waters, houses are completely submerged, and it becomes harder to pick out Navarro's voice from the deafening bass tones of the storm around her. From the dry safety of her cylinder, Navarro warns her audience of the deadly consequences of being caught in an area with a nine-foot storm surge. "If you find yourself here, you need to get out," she pleads, as the camera slowly rolls out to reveal a submerged neighborhood. The screen begins fading to black. "If you're told to go, you need to go."

0.1 Screenshot of the Weather Channel's coverage of Hurricane Florence using the Unreal Engine. (https://www.youtube.com/watch?v=qo1vSb_B1oo)

In the weeks following Florence's landfall, news and opinion outlets would begin dissecting the political, social, and infrastructural ramifications of yet another devastating US hurricane. As the days pass, more coverage turns toward the Weather Channel's digitally augmented broadcast. For some, the visual effects and cinematic techniques used showcased a new frontier in information reporting, with voices from the Weather Channel itself arguing that affectively engaging broadcasts have the potential to save lives. Others argued that such displays were merely more sensationalism in newscasting, a high-tech ripple effect of "if-it-bleeds-it-leads" journalism. *Vice*'s Matthew Gault, who watched the broadcast live from his South Carolina home, straddled the line, commenting on the broadcast's emotional power, but wryly questioning the benefits of that power for those on the ground: "Just what I needed as I buy crates of bottled water, store my garbage cans, and charge my generator: realistic images of impending destruction broadcast in high definition."[2]

Entangled at the center of the Weather Channel's Florence coverage is the Unreal Engine. The Unreal Engine is a "game engine," or a software platform used to streamline the development and publishing of digital games, and one of the most popular engines commercially available.[3] Game engines are complex arrangements of software that streamline the digital game development process. Some engines, like Twine or RPG Maker, are genre-specific authorship tools that, while flexible and extendable, are designed to produce the modal outcomes of their genre; Platonic ideals of interactive text-based narrative and role-playing games. Other engines, such as Unreal and its major competitor, Unity, are massive arrangements of codebases, toolsets, plug-ins, and corporate support networks designed to be flexible and reconfigurable. These engines' technical capacities include "top-level" game development tools like graphics processing and rendering, artificial agent and behavioral scripting, and physics simulation processing, as well as "lower-level" computational resource management systems such as multi-core threading controls, memory management, and multiplatform publishing. These engines are capable of being used not only to produce two-dimensional or three-dimensional games across multiple genres, but also to be used in the fields of architecture, product design, data visualization, and military and urban simulation, among others.

Beyond its use in games, Unreal is at the vanguard of a multiple industry-wide incorporation of gaming technology. Its real-time graphics capacities have been used for post-processed video, as seen above, as well as superimposed on live video, such as *Fox Sports*' giant "mixed-reality panther" that pounces around the Carolina Panthers' stadium during broadcasts. Unreal has been used for virtual production and in-camera effects, such as the Weather Channel's hurricane broadcast, and for live set replacement in Disney's *The Mandalorian* streaming show. Unreal's capacity for data integration and real-time simulation have seen the Engine used for architecture, physics simulations, and for military training purposes. As real-time networked virtual reality and digital conferencing tools—described by Silicon Valley hype men as the coming "Metaverse"— enter ever more into our post-COVID-19 lives, Unreal and technologies like it will be further woven into the fabric of everyday life. The Unreal Engine, like many contemporary game development software packages, must be understood as more than just a tool for game creation. As Stefan Werning argues, game engines are part of an ongoing digital platformization of everyday life, akin to the kinds of transformations Google and Meta (Facebook) have produced in information sharing and social connection.[4]

Unreal's impacts are evident not only in current events: Unreal occupies a unique position in gaming history, both as an engine and as an integrated platform. Unreal has drastically changed in form from its design in 1994 through today, and remains one of the most, if not the only, commercially successful and popularly used game engines to span nearly the entirety of modern PC/console-based gaming history. Early engines such as Sierra On-Line's Adventure Game Interpreter software[5] and idTech's *DOOM* Editor stopped being commercially relevant in the late 1990s, and Unity, currently the most popular game engine and Unreal's direct competitor, was released for Mac-only game development in 2005, only becoming the cross-platform development tool it is now in 2010.

Unreal began development in 1994, by programmer and game designer Tim Sweeney, building on and collecting prior rapid game development packages scripted by Sweeney and his company Epic MegaGames in the early 1990s. The Engine was formally released to the public in 1998 alongside the PC game *Unreal*, though select companies had licensed elements of the Engine for the development of their own games as early as 1996. Though the early version of Unreal was essentially a genre-bound engine—particularly good at making first-person shooters like the eponymous *Unreal*—its memory management, collision detection, and character animation tools were good enough, and accessible enough, to be used for an array of three-dimensional game development projects. Later versions of the Unreal Engine were released in 2002, 2004, 2012, and 2021, though the programming logics of the Engine are still heavily influenced by gameplay standards and aesthetic traditions of first-person shooter games of the 1990s and 2000s. As such, to study Unreal is to undertake a living media archeology; Unreal exists as a kind of strata of digital culture that expresses affordances, constraints, and qualities from across multiple eras of gaming.

Unreal is still owned by Sweeney, through his now-renamed privately controlled company, Epic Games, whose multiple divisions include Unreal Engine development, game development (most often using the Unreal Engine), the Epic Games Store (Epic's consumer-facing sales platform), and customer support and corporate relations wings. Epic experienced several monetary windfalls in the 2010s. In 2012 Epic received an infusion of $330 million from selling 48.4 percent of its capital shares to Tencent, a Chinese internet technology conglomerate, a sale that doubled as market entry into China as well as an embrace of the games-as-a-service (GaaS) model, wherein games are designed to continually generate revenue after the initial (sometimes free) point of purchase. The GaaS model led to Epic's second cash infusion from the commercial success of its game *Fortnite*, which was both developed using and whose updates contribute new functionality to the Unreal Engine.

From a game studies perspective, its breadth and scope make the Unreal Engine a complicated figure to pin down. One approach might be to deploy the lens of platform studies. Platform studies is part of the "material turn" in game studies, and affords an interpretive deep dive into the technical aspects of media, generally through reading the features and constraints of digital media creative software that influence the design decisions made through them.[6] Such a lens could highlight Unreal's changing material nature over time, as well as how game designers and users have played with and against Unreal's constraints to develop creative media.

However, given Unreal's multiple stakeholders, infrastructural engagements, and political and economic importance, to think of Unreal as a system of media affordances and constraints feels shallow. Further, as John Banks has argued in his ethnography of the Australian game development company Auran, game engines[7] are internally multiple. That is, they exist as collections of subsystems—graphics rendering systems, physics simulators, networking tools, and compilers—bound together by the engine's interface. They are positionally multiple as well, in that one's subject position in the game development pipeline creates vastly different experiences and understandings of the engine. Banks describes how the experiences of SAGE (Auran's internal engine) varied radically depending on where one was located in the company. Programmers experienced SAGE as a networked text editor for compiling code, while company executives regarded SAGE as a process of streamlining future projects and a potential revenue source from external licensing agreements. Artists navigated SAGE through a series of frustrating tensions between their specific technical needs and Auran's desires that SAGE be a "general-purpose" engine.[8] Casey O'Donnell has highlighted that game engines are quite literally multiple; modifications, modularizations, version updates, and corporate customizations have propagated to the point that claiming any distinct software or platform as *the* core engine is futile.[9] At the time of this writing, for example, I have no fewer than eight versions of the Unreal Engine installed on my home computer.

Science and technology studies (STS) scholar John Law has called these kinds of object assemblages *singularities*—single objects made through the coming together and adhering of multiple versions, interpretations, components, and stories.[10] In his book detailing the TSR2 British reconnaissance aircraft, Law describes the challenges of writing about singularities:

> An aircraft, yes, is an object. But it also reveals multiplicity—for instance in wing shape, speed, military roles, and political attributes. I am saying, then, that an object such as an aircraft—an "individual" and "specific" aircraft—comes in different versions. It has no single center. It is multiple. And yet these various versions also interfere with one another and shuffle themselves together to make a single aircraft.[11]

The analyst's job, according to Law, is to understand this *fractional coherence*, or the "drawing [of] things together without centering them."[12] Fractional coherence demands we understand how an object emerges and becomes stable out of multiple—and at times incommensurable—parts, objects, and stories. This endeavor is a recursive one. The stories that we as scholars tell about singularities contribute to and interfere with those objects' fractional coherence. We are entangled with our research objects.[13] As we shape these objects, they in turn shape our analysis; our gazes learn to follow similar analytical grooves and patterns, further stabilizing particular ways of drawing together these fractured objects.

Like Law's aircraft, game engines too are singularities. They are held together and made coherent as much by the stories we tell about them as by technology, politics, or commerce.[14] Much of the writing on game engines have read them as collections of tools, whose impacts can at times be felt by playing the games developed using them. Earlier game studies scholars drew a separation between the game engine and gameplay. Alexander Galloway, for example, described an engine as an "abstract core technology that, while it may exert its own personality through telltale traces of its various abilities and features, is mostly unlinked from the gameplay layered within it."[15] Contemporary writing on game creation software has highlighted more of these "telltale traces," which Benjamin Nicoll and Brendan Keogh have called an engine's "grain."[16] The grain—such as that encountered by a carpenter working with wood—does not necessarily determine the kind of product fashioned, but must be accounted for and worked both with and against. Most recently, Stefan Werning has argued for a dialogic reading of the grain or "poetics" of game engines that foregrounds the reciprocal relationship game makers have with the software tools they deploy.[17] While often game makers follow the design patterns that an engine calls for, Werning suggests, they also engage in moments of transgressive design. Their design choices may allow for moments of "unscripted" play—such as open-ended puzzles designed to allow a player to exploit an engine's physics simulations—or for "counterscripting," in which a game engine designed for one purpose is unexpectedly applied in another.

Whether the engine is conceptualized more akin to wood or to tools, a similar tone echoes across all these engine stories; though an engine is abstract and multiple, it retains a sense of immutability. This immutability is not deterministic, in that the game engine defines gameplay. But there is a kind of "bubble up" effect, in which the qualities of the engine become more influential or knowable—even if through resisting them—via playing or designing games.

The implicit logics here coincide neatly with platform studies' classical "bottom-up" layered ontology of digital media, in which the hardware and software's affordances deeply shape media content. We can also see why engine companies like Epic may prefer a narrative like the one told in games studies research; it posits that a game's potential is at least partially based on the engine used to produce it. These scholarly narratives make sense, particularly from the point of view of a contemporary player-consumer. Changes in licensing agreements, free trials, and an abundance of freeware and open-source development software have broadened consumer access to game engines. Working with game engines now is certainly easier than in the early 2000s, when Unreal licenses cost hundreds of thousands of dollars. Players experimenting on their own, game design students working in small teams, or professional indie and AA developers can now experience an engine as an immutable, semi-structuring force on game design. These spaces—home offices, classrooms, university research groups, or small/midsized creative teams—are also where social scientists and humanities scholars are most likely to encounter game development software.

The stories we tell about game engines aren't necessarily wrong, but they do include an inherent positionality. As feminist science studies scholar Sandra Harding has argued, an observer's subject position shapes the object of study.[18] Capital, for example, is a major situator of the materiality of game engines. For major studios and well-funded projects, the game engine is as malleable as the game to be produced, meaning game and engine are trapped in a recursive relationship.[19] This recursion is doubly evident in a product like the Unreal Engine thanks to Epic's unique dual role as both a commercial engine developer and a game developer. For smaller designers, the "grain" of an engine must be selected for (i.e., the choice of engine depends on the kind of game to be made, and what engine best affords that style of gameplay) or resisted. For larger developers, the grain must be accounted for in design, to account for both material and structural constraints, as well as produce the desired gameplay. In other words, the grain of the engine is, in part, *determined by the imagined game or interactive scenario to be produced though that engine*. The speculative future bleeds into the present; the layers model articulated by platform studies captures only one small slice in game development time. That moment happens when the engine developers have settled on the features needed for their desired designed experience, right before that experience demands new and unexpected features, thus resulting in changes to the engine.

Eric Freedman highlights the need to bring to game studies an analysis of how game engines emerge through the convergence of spaces, individuals, infrastructures, power. Citing Paul Dourish, Freedman calls for "a more situational notion of convergence . . . as the game engine is a site where historical, social, and political concerns and determinants are brought into temporary alignment."[20] While platform studies analyses have done considerable work in advancing our capacities to interrogate and interpret the more technical layers of digital texts, the method has also been criticized by feminist and critical race scholars as artificially bracketing out the embodied and structural conditions of the digital, thereby risking a fetishization or concretization of the technical apparatus.[21] Our position in relation to game engines is more than our relations to infrastructures and to capital; it is also part of the broader coproductions of race, gender, epistemology and identity.

As such, an analysis of Unreal Engine must then do two things: first, it must deal with the Engine as a fractional coherence—as an ever-extended set of materials, texts, culture, and knowledge, and, yes, games—that cohere together to produce different alignments of the engine. There is no singular Unreal Engine to study; rather, Unreal is multiply enacted:[22] it becomes configured and reconfigured over time through material practices, discursive utterances, and infrastructural entanglements. Second, understanding

Unreal as an enacted object means our analysis must always be grounded in an interrogation of systems of power. Where we stand in analyzing the engine, and who we stand with, is a part of producing Unreal.

To do this, I argue for the need to synthesize platform studies with the work of those who are in the best position to identify its gaps: writers in intersectional feminist technoscience studies. Feminist technoscience studies has long questioned the bracketing of identity, culture, and power from the analysis of scientific and technological systems.[23] This has included not only a push to further examine the identities of scientific practitioners and those of their subjects,[24] but also broader calls for complicating and blurring the lines between the "cultural" and the "technical,"[25] and for an analysis that stays with, rather than attempts to resolve, the uncomfortable tensions that come with acknowledging one's partial and situated being within the world.[26] Drawing on Annemarie Mol's theories of enactment, feminist technoscience studies also acknowledge flexibility and fluidity, that our world is ever shaped by our own practices within and through it.[27] Intersectional feminist technoscience studies, as exemplified by scholars such as Catherine Knight Steele[28] and Ruha Benjamin,[29] further acknowledge how raced, gendered, embodied, and queered positionalities are also produced with and through technology and technical practices. Game studies scholars such as Kishonna Gray (who coined the framework of "intersectional technology),"[30] Jennifer Malkowski and TreaAndrea Russworm[31] and Amanda Phillips[32] have already made steady inroads into examining the intersecting productions of gaming narratives, technologies, and broader configurations of identity and power. Following these scholars, as well as Banks, Freedman, and Law, I leverage intersectional feminist technoscience studies to extend platform studies, showing how through the Unreal Engine we enact configurations of epistemology, agency, gender, and race: how they all "come to *be* in a relational, multiple, fluid, and more or less unordered and indeterminate (set of) specific and provisional practices."[33] An enacted, practice-oriented turn within platform studies allows games scholars to better view the humanity that lies at the heart of all technical formations, and to grapple with the inherent instability of the platforms we so desperately try to make stable.

Histories and Intersectional Feminist Critiques of Platform Studies

In *Codename Revolution*, the second book in the MIT Press Platform Studies series, Steven E. Jones and George K. Thiruvathukal write that the Nintendo Wii "only *invokes* a *feeling* of simplicity. . . . The Wii, like other computing devices, is actually a relatively complex system."[34] The same could be said of the object of platform studies itself; much like its objects of study, it becomes more slippery the more you engage with it. Platform studies is simultaneously a methodological approach and an anti-method, a disciplinary intervention and anti-disciplinary, open-ended and fluid, ontologically and epistemologically rigid. It too is enacted in ways that can both highlight and obscure power.

A diverse array of platform studies scholarship focuses on the technical "platformization"[35] of media, the body, and the social world writ large. While, recently, social media platforms such as Facebook,[36] Twitter,[37] and Google[38] have garnered much of the empirical attention, researchers have also analyzed medical platforms, governmental technical concerns, and capitalism itself as platforms for social and technical action. Topics of concern include the relationships among platform developers and users, the construction of platforms and communities by their user groups, the impact of moneyed interests in the development and deployment of platforms, and the production of race, gender, ability, and hegemony with and through media platforms. In these platform studies, the software and hardware components of a system are only partial qualities of its material being, which are both more enacted and more widespread than seen at first glance. As such, this platform studies work often intersects with infrastructure studies, studies of large-scale sociotechnical systems, and anthropological or sociological studies of labs, developers, and technologies-in-practice, and can be commonly found within social media studies and in internet/new media studies, and in media-focused science and technology studies.

The games-centric model of platform studies is first concerned with an empirical focus on the computational platforms—often, but not exclusively, understood as hardware—that "underlie"[39] creative media work. As such, it often manifests as a deep dive into the technical aspects of media, generally through explorations of how the affordances and constraints of platforms influence the creative decisions made through them, a peek "under the hood" at what drives creative digital media. While this brand of platform studies work, including that by MIT Press Platform Studies series editors Nick Montfort and Ian Bogost, often highlights digital gaming hardware platforms like the Super Nintendo and the Atari 2600, it is neither hardware nor gaming exclusive. Other work in this scholarly community has covered software media production platforms, such as Macromedia/Adobe Flash;[40] non-gaming or gaming-adjacent hardware platforms like the S-C 4020;[41] or non-digital game "hardware" such as the card-stock paper used to print the *Magic: The Gathering* collectable card game.[42]

Though these communities of platform studies can sometimes be found grouped together in literature reviews, and certainly do have inter-citational networks, these communities are divided by more than just their empirical focus; they have different disciplinary *takes* and political and ontological *stakes*. Conversely, the social media/infrastructure model more often frames the platform as a part of—even a secondary outcome of—broader social and political processes. The analytic focus, then, is more the unfolding process of platformization: how social and technical forces coproduce worlds where platforms and their logics become naturalized, how what it means to be human becomes remade through sociotechni-cal apparatuses. The game studies associated model, on the other hand, has come to be more interested in the technical apparatus of the platform itself; though the contours of this object may change over time, it is held relatively stable as the central orienting empirical focus of the research project.

Lars Konzack's initial sketch of platform studies proposed a method-ological and ontological framework for holistic studies of digital games, one that divided games into seven layers for analysis.[43] These layers are stratified, in that the qualities of each layer can be understood through—though not reduced to—the qualities of the underlying layers. These layers, from bottom to top, are hardware, program code, functionality, gameplay, meaning, referentiality, and socio-culture. In this model, as the game analyst moves "up" layers, she also moves from concretely defined material properties (and from hardware to software) to phenomenologi-cal actions to human meaning-making practices. Moreover, these layers are enacted across what Konzack described as two "levels": the "virtual space," or the game-defined logical space within which the game takes place (Konzack uses the example of a chessboard), and the "playground," the phenomenological site of play that includes bodies, players, places, culture, and the game equipment itself.

Nick Montfort refigured Konzack's seven-layer model into the "five levels" model[44] that has now come to operate as the de facto topographical backbone of platform studies. This model, from bottom to top, is struc-tured (1) platform, (2) code, (3) form (or sometimes form/function),[45] (4) interface, and (5) reception and operation. These layers have since been commonly understood, respectively, as (1) the hardware and/or soft-ware that allows the game to run, (2) the lines of written and textual code that make up the underlying "programming" of the game, (3) the game-world instantiated by the executed game code, (4) the tools and inter-action options that allow the player to manipulate and interact with the gameworld, and (5) the player- or community-inscribed meanings and interpretations of the game. Montfort is more forthright than Konzack about the stratified relationships among these layers:

> Lower levels enable and constrain what happens in higher levels. Players can only assign meanings to images if there are images presented in the interface, which can only happen if the game form affords something to present using images, which can only happen if that game form is realized in code, which can only happen if the code runs on a platform—specifically, a platform that supports graphics.[46]

Further, Montfort redistributes Konzack's "socio-culture" layer as a "context" bubble around all five levels of this newer model, arguing that culture "surrounds and interacts with"[47] a game at each level. Konzack's virtual space layer, too, falls away, as virtual space becomes subsumed into the "form" layer of analysis. Despite some later criticisms that platform studies is exclusively focused on computer hardware,[48] Montfort's earliest definition of the "platform" level acknowledges that software, too, can be a platform: "a game that runs on Windows XP has that operating system, not just Intel-compatible hardware, as its platform."[49] Further, Montfort argues that platforms themselves can be "modular as well as layered,"[50] with hardware and software elements like peripherals, plug-ins, extensions, updates, and versioning complicating any notion of a concrete and unchanging platform. Thus, though Montfort's model is still exclusively focused on digital games and their platforms, that focus adds empirical nuance to Konzack's original model, which more strictly delineated the responsibilities of hardware and software in digital games.

In excising and redistributing the sociocultural as a sphere surrounding the five levels of a game, Montfort's model integrates what Paul Dourish describes as the "positivist model" of context[51] into the roots of platform studies. Here, context is stable and delineable from discrete objects or actions that take place "within" that contextual space. Notably, this model of context eliminates the need for the "playground" layer of analysis from Konzack's model, as the physical play space as well as the bodies and identities of players themselves become subsumed and consumed by the *ur*-bubble of context. Examining the Unreal Engine through this model might frame Unreal as a stable object that is used in different places, by different people, in different social and cultural spaces. While the outputs of the Unreal Engine may change because of its different use across diverse spaces, the Engine itself would be characterized as relatively immutable, aside from temporal changes such as updates and the introduction of modular peripherals.[52]

Montfort's model becomes concretized into the foundations of platform studies at the 2007 Digital Arts and Cultures conference in Melbourne, where Montfort and Ian Bogost first coin the term "platform studies" itself (at least in the games community). Montfort and Bogost would go on to helm the editorship of the MIT Press Platform Studies book series, releasing their own book, *Racing the Beam: The Atari Video Computer System*, in 2009. Though, as of this writing, thirteen books have been released through the Platform Studies series, Montfort and Bogost's *Racing the Beam*, a deep dive into the Atari VCS, remains one of the most-cited and paradigmatic examples of a platform studies work. In *Racing the Beam* Montfort and Bogost forward a new definition of platform as "whatever the programmer takes for granted when developing, and whatever, from another side, the user is required to have working in order to use particular software."[53] Platforms can be built on or contain other platforms, as in the case of a Facebook API requiring Facebook, which requires platforms and extensions like Thrift, Varnish, and React, which require operating systems, and so on. Epic Games, for its part, specifically defines Windows and Linux as platforms that support the Unreal platform.[54]

In a later clarifying essay,[55] Bogost and Montort borrow a multipart definition of platforms from Marc Andreessen, the co-developer of the Mosaic web browser: "A 'platform' is a system that can be reprogrammed and therefore customized by outside developers—users—and in that way, adapted to countless needs and niches that the platform's original developers could not have possibly contemplated, much less had time to accommodate."[56] And, later, "The key term in the definition of platform is 'programmed.' If you can program it, then it's a platform. If you can't, then it's not."[57]

Though in theory a broader definition of platforms could allow for platform studies to have a further reach, Bogost and Montfort have stood firm in defining platforms in the "computational sense,"[58] rather than in the social media or large-scale sociotechnical system senses analyzed by communication and STS scholars. These efforts go as far as to enroll the figure of the game developer in their definitional alliance: "Current video game developers," Bogost and Montfort write, "have a very clear idea of what 'platform' means, and use the term in the same way that we do and that Andreessen does."[59] Further, they argue, the programmable and computational as platform "is certainly, overall, the most relevant [definition] in the history of digital media."[60]

However, despite the significant amount of definitional and technical language at play above, Bogost and Montfort are also, at best, ambivalent when it comes to having a metaphysical argument about what is or isn't a platform, even going as far as to sidestep the question itself. They argue,

There are many ways to slice platforms. . . . The question of whether something is or isn't a platform may not ever have a useful answer, by itself. We could ask whether the Web is a platform. . . . Is *World of Warcraft*? *Second Life*? LambdaMOO? Certainly we can think of all of these as platforms, since they have APIs. But the real question should be whether a particular system is influential and important as a platform. Something is a platform when a developers consider it as such and use it; that activity can be more or less culturally interesting. Rather than asking "Is it a platform?" we might ask "What interesting or influential things have been developed on the system?" and "Does the system have unique or innovative features as a platform?"[61]

As such, the general impetus of platform studies thus far has coalesced less around exploring the empirical and conceptual questions at play when demarcating an object as a platform and more around engaging with any object that can reasonably be called a platform. This tidying definition, however, has epistemological and political consequences. While Konzack grounded his seven-layered model as part of a methodological project—how to develop a more rigorous and holistic description of games and digital media—Montfort frames his five-leveled one as an act of analytical focusing: a delineating of discrete parts of a game in order to highlight those that have been understudied in games and media studies. Montfort notes that his own layered model of digital media is almost beside the point:

> The most important point I hope to make here is that, whatever specific model is used, certain low levels that critics have neglected or glossed over can be important to understanding games, and these levels can be usefully explored by scholars.[62]

Whereas Konzack's model is about building an ontology to narrate the interconnected material-discursive elements of a game, Montfort's presumes an underlying ontology to make an argument: no matter the model, games have "lower levels" that the "upper levels" are indebted to, games cannot be fully understood without studying these lower layers, and game studies scholars have not spent enough time studying these layers. This claim dovetails with those made by critical scholars such as Lisa Nakamura, who has recently agreed that the humanities and interpretive social sciences have tended to spend less attention on hardware and materiality than on texts and culture.[63]

This may feel like a mundane point. After all, all methodological practices have ontological and epistemological assumptions built into them, and plenty of scholarship operates by identifying gaps in existing literatures. But this move is important, as it sets the stage for the current platform studies moment: the platformization of platform studies via both highlighting and burying the very object of "platform."

In her feminist analysis of platform studies, Aubrey Anable identifies that the levels model itself produces consequences, namely the bracketing of culture and technology that platform studies attempts to resolve.[64] In her work highlighting embodied and affective dimensions of games and play as a countermand to game studies' focus on procedurality and code,[65] Anable notes that games studies has often framed the debates between the focus on "hardcore" mechanism and the focus on narrative or representation as one of depth/surface—often cast as, what occurs on the screen or in the story is an effect of the "deeper" underlying structures of code. The positioning of digital media as layered, Anable argues, "spatially reinforces dubious claims in digital media studies that identities and their representations are merely 'surface effects' of a deeper and more significant technological structure."[66] For feminist media scholars, platform studies thus reproduces earlier raced and gendered academic tensions in film theory, media studies, and STS, that a focus on the capacities of the technical apparatus displaces or undermines examinations of human agency and power in sociotechnical systems.[67]

Anable, citing Lisa Nakamura, also argues that platform studies tends to overlook the embodied, gendered, and racialized labor conditions and practices that constitute the platforms studied. This is especially prescient because of the major role—both historically and presently—played by poor communities, indigenous communities, and communities of the Global South and East Asia in mass electronics production.[68] "The laboring bodies of electronics assembly," Anable writes, "are the actual platforms— the underlying and usually overlooked foundation—on which our digital creativity and expression depend."[69] This analytical reorientation does important political and ontological work. It resists and queers masculinist and technocentric narratives of technological progress and production, centering the roles that labor and bodies—particularly those of poor women and women of color—play in the materialization of electronic platforms. They are, both Anable and Nakamura write, the foundation of the foundation. This continual bracketing occurs in spite of work by scholars like Anable, Nakamura, Wendy Chun, and Cadence Kinsey to continually blur and question the existence of the technical/social gap. The bracketed model of technological development, as Tara McPherson has argued, has been epistemically platformed into the humanities' own critical lenses and methodologies.[70]

The "platform" under interrogation in these debates, I argue, is thus not any specific concept of hardware or software, but rather the "platforms" of the humanities and games studies themselves. It's telling that despite the importance of the five-layer or five-level models in the history of platform studies, this model is rarely invoked methodologically in platform studies work. Montfort himself explains that platform studies "isn't a methodology or even a method," but rather "simply [a] way to *focus* an investigation of computational media."[71] Methodology is downplayed in favor of a broader critique of the humanities and social sciences: that these fields are too focused on the narrative and cultural dimensions of media and technology, and that analysis of the technical dimensions of media are at best underthought and, at worst, actively derided.[72] The layers model does act as methodological direction and empirical grounding for platform studies.[73] But, moreover, it acts as a *situator*, in that the layers/levels model produces situations that allow certain kinds of knowledge practices to come into being—in this case, that of a demarcated textual and technical inquiry in the humanities.

Enacting Platforms

It matters how we tell our stories of game engines; our analytical tools situate ourselves in relation to our objects of study and determine in part how those objects can be thought through. As Thomas Apperley and Darshana Jayemane argue, the muddled object of the platform "can be turned inwards to examine the individual components of a platform, and just as easily outwards to focus on the organizational structure that allows the platform to be produced . . . allowing [the platform] to perform the role of a center around which other relationships may be traced and examined."[74] Casey O'Donnell, invoking John Law, argues that, in platform studies work, "much of the theoretical platform is never hinted at. . . . The lifeblood of a platform studies text is its own platform; the assumptions made by the researchers. These assumptions are the system through which material is made sense of and put into motion."[75] In other words, O'Donnell argues that too often in platform studies our scholarly standpoints remain unspoken and uninterrogated, the boundaries of our objects of analysis become taken for granted, and our interrogations of these complex objects fall back on familiar disciplinary, theoretical, and interpersonal divides: narrative versus system, text versus technology, deconstruction versus description. Which parts of game studies are studying surface effects, and which parts are studying the "real" depths underneath?

To quote anthropologist Marilyn Strathern, "What is to count as figure and what is to count as ground is not a definitive matter at all, and here the values to be attached to particular phenomena are unpredictable. Figure and ground promote, we might say, unstable relationships."[76] What counts as readable surface and as plumbable depth depends as much on our positionality as scholars as it does on the object of our interrogation. Apperley and Parikka argue that "in the process of 'doing' platform studies, a uniform platform is produced."[77] What platform is "under the hood" of a game at any given moment is not a pregiven reality. It is always produced alongside power, matter, and meaning.[78] Platforms are enacted.

At the heart of platform studies, then, are questions of mattering.[79] What matters in the production of digital media? What matter are platforms made of? Are platforms culture materialized, or does culture arise in response to material affordance and constraint? How do platforms come to be matters of concern for humanities scholars? Whose theories matter in the study of technological artifacts? How do raced and gendered bodies come to matter with and through platforms? How do we keep our focus on broader systems of power and oppression while remaining close to the trouble of technical practices? How do we keep looking for the big in the small?

Merging platform studies with feminist science studies can maintain the technical intimacy with the Unreal Engine in ways that are aligned with software studies and platform studies, while also taking seriously critiques of platform studies, especially those made by science and technology studies, feminists, critical scholars, and cultural scholars. As Anable has argued, a feminist approach to platforms studies would "look to where the perceived boundaries of platforms break down and blur."[80] We can turn to science and technology studies, which has long been unraveling the boundaries of nature/culture, gender/bodies, technology/society, and objectivity/subjectivity, to help platform studies resolve our surface/depth and technology/culture tensions.

Though examinations of feminist STS will be woven throughout the book, my primary conceptual thread comes from Annemarie Mol and her use of "enactment." Developed alongside her collaborations with John Law, Mol's theory of enactment acts as a way of tracing how real objects—in her case study, the disease atherosclerosis—are brought into being in multiple, sometimes conflicting, ways through sociomaterial practices.[81] Diseases, technologies, even human bodies and practitioners, Mol argues, exist differently at different times and in different spaces, even as they are ostensibly stable: "objects come into being—and disappear—with the practices in which they are manipulated."[82] Objects, and reality, are enacted.

Mol embarks on an ontological project that intertwines the careful attentiveness of Latour's actor-network theory[83] and his tracing of the interconnectedness among people and things, with the critical insights of Judith Butler and their highlighting of the processual performativity of bodies, subjects, and objects.[84] As Mol argues, ontologies:

> inform and are informed by our bodies, the organization of our health care systems, the rhythms and pains of our diseases, and the shape of our technologies. All of these, all at once, all intertwined, all in tension. If reality is multiple, it is also political. [85]

Moving beyond the "layers" ontology of prior platform studies work and toward a model of enactment, better allows us to analyze how the Unreal Engine exists as an always-unfolding intertwining of technologies, bodies, governments, industrial systems, and politics. In tracing Unreal, this book takes a double tack: first, in a familiar approach to platform studies, each chapter in this book centers an aspect of the Unreal engine that could be easily rendered as "technical." This includes Unreal's early development history, an analysis of its interface and coordinate systems, its programming languages, and its graphical rendering systems. However, each topic is also read through central concerns of intersectional feminist technoscience studies: the enactment of technology and militarized masculinity, the forced alignment of working bodies with industrial infrastructure, questions of the location and forms of gendered agency, and the coproduction of race and racialized bodies with systems of knowledge and power. Throughout the book, I explore how the Unreal Engine comes to be materially and culturally enacted with and through various productions of epistemology, gender, race, and power.

Chapter 1, "Seeing Like a Soldier: The Coproduction of Engine and State through *America's Army*," examines Unreal's entanglements with the military-entertainment complex, which influenced the Engine's development history from 1995 to 2005 and contributed to broader changes in the games industry.[86] Particular attention is first paid to Epic's partnership with the US Army in the development of *America's Army*, a game-qua-recruitment tool that focused on training players of the first-person shooter genre in basic military tactics and in military culture. In this chapter I argue that a game engine and the games made with it are mutually constitutive and, in Unreal's case, entangled with broader parts of the militaristic state. *America's Army* had a double production with the Unreal Engine—not only did programmed functionality for developing *America's Army* become hardwired into the standard design toolbox of the Unreal

Engine, but the combination of Unreal and *America's Army* also coproduced ways of seeing and inhabiting the world, particularly when it comes to the double-production of masculinity as violent and as coolly rational. Players learned at once how to embody the divergent Hollywood and US military affective visions of being a soldier.

Further, through archival materials provided by the Strong Museum of Play, I argue that the partnership between Epic and the US Army was more than one of technical and marketing convenience. Rather, the US Army sought in Epic a willing partner to provide backroom connections with the entertainment industry and with arts and humanities scholarship, and Epic sought in the US Army the opportunity to be scaffolded across government operations and, thereby, to become the de facto game engine of the US government. These mutual expectations were codified into the military's licensing agreements for Unreal, and were reinforced through personnel movement, including US Navy researcher and *America's Army* lead Mike Capps's ascent to Epic's presidency in 2002.

The book then enters two arcs: the first examines Unreal's role in coproducing bodies and their orientations and agencies, as told through feminist and queer scholarship. Chapter 2, "Orienting Z: Interfaces and Coordinate Space as Unreal's Bodily Proxies," examines the role that coordinate space and ludic space play in the epistemological orientations of Unreal. Drawing on queer philosopher Sara Ahmed, I argue that Unreal's interface and coordinate systems, as exemplified by the Z axis, play important roles in orienting the user's body and mind to Unreal. In mathematics, the Z axis is used to extend the two-dimensional "X-Y" plane into the third dimension, providing the capacity to more accurately model physical objects in Cartesian space. In software, however, the direction of Z is contextual, depending on the presumed orientations of X and Y. Depending on the software platform, Z may face upward, toward the top of the user's screen, or outward, to and from the user themselves. This orientation derives from understandings of the idealized user's bodily relation to their work: are they "looking down" onto a space, as an architect might when designing floor plans, or are they "looking through" space, as an animator would when drawing frames for an animated film? Space in Unreal works both ways, and as such participates in the attuning of game designers and those in other disciplines—such as architecture and engineering—to imagine their disciplines through the visual and embodied language of play.

Chapter 3, "Elizabeth and Threads of Kismet: Agency as Queer and Affective Entanglement in *BioShock Infinite*," traces the development of the Elizabeth character from 2013's *BioShock Infinite* and the game's 2014 downloadable content (DLC) expansion, *Burial at Sea 2*, both of which were developed using Unreal and its Kismet visual programming system. Elizabeth was multiply enacted by her development staff, sometimes treated as a mangle of code, sometimes as a collaborative designer, sometimes as an independent agent, and sometimes as a glitch, a piece of broken code. These shifting enactments of Elizabeth were more than just representational—they had material impacts on the development of *BioShock Infinite* and its sequels, not only resulting in large changes to gameplay, but also playing a double role in changing both the game's narrative arc as well as the game's text. Elizabeth tears and stitches together boundaries and realities across the game's enactment, and becomes materially, narratively, and agentially core to producing the multiple worlds of *BioShock Infinite* for its creators.

Elizabeth becomes a lens through which game studies can bring feminist literary understandings of entangled agency into platform studies. Rather than framing agency as an agonistic contesting of power—player versus game, agent versus world—Elizbeth represents an intra-active kind of agency, one that emerges through the weaving of Unreal's Kismet programming and that recognizes Elizabeth as an agent distributed across and through *BioShock*'s programmed world.

The second arc of the book traces what I call "white photorealism," or the coproduction of race, power, and knowledge, through Unreal's photorealistic rendering systems. Chapter 4, "Epistemic Prestige in Unreal's Physically Based Rendering," explores Unreal's physically based rendering (PBR) system and its "Materials Editor," its particular construction of the relationships between light, color, surface, and the viewing subject, and how those technical elements intersect with histories of race and visual art. PBR is a popularly growing method for real-time rendering and digital art production, and one that claims to better model real-world lighting phenomena than traditional CGI techniques. PBR "shaders"—the properties and operations that give a digital object its screen appearance to the viewer—build in controls that systematize the physical properties that a digital object is supposed to represent, such as its mineral composition, the roughness of its surface, and the color the surface reflects to the eye. Hailed as a more "rational" rendering technique, Unreal's PBR has been used as a measuring stick for "the real" and as a stand-in for truth claims, such as in a collaborative project between Epic and NVIDIA that attempted to prove the 1969 US moon landing via a photorealistic, PBR-based real-time re-creation of the scene. However, PBR's narrative is a fantasy, in terms of both its adherence to physical reality and its universality. Through media studies scholar André Brock and feminist science studies scholar Chanda Prescod-Weinstein, chapter 4 explores how PBR "works" due to its alignment with multiple kinds of whiteness: that of the raced and gendered practices of physics, and that of the raced and gendered practices of cinematic aesthetics. PBR, I argue, does not represent a universal physical world, but rather one that preferences white perspectives and vision.

Chapter 5, "The Raced Histories of MetaHuman Creator's Skin, Shine, and Melanin," continues this argument, demonstrating how Unreal's PBR shading system acts as a text that produces embodied forms of race and racialization—this includes well-known issues between contemporary film/photography/video recognition and darker skin and the game development industry's decades long de-prioritization of Black skin and hair, but also production of understandings of Black "color" and melanin, as argued by Prescod-Weinstein. Of particular attention will be Epic's Meta-Human Creator project, which Epic promises will be the future of modeling and rigging photorealistic virtual human bodies. MetaHuman works by using neural networks to blend photogrammetric image captures of real persons, mixing and matching them together onto a universalized 3D character model. However, though Epic and the MetaHuman developers argue the photograph-based models represent the human body's "ground truth,"[87] historical anti-Blackness baked into the cinematic apparatus combines with Unreal PBR's "metalness" workflow, which binds visual representations of shine and reflectivity with metal, to cause failure when rendering melanated skin. Chapter 5 demonstrates how Unreal participates in broader historical enactments of melanated skin and Blackness as derivations from whiteness, and how those derivations are assembled within Unreal at both the aesthetic and material levels. In both the capturing and rendering of skin, whiteness becomes doubly enacted as both a universal body containing all others, and also as an unmarked body, removed from the mess of the social and the political world.

To conclude, I trace the role that Unreal aims to play in the future of gaming, including in the shaping of the "metaverse." Unreal is now inseparable from national and international systems of capital, a fact made more evident by Epic's second major shift, the allowing of a $330 million ownership purchase by Tencent, a Chinese media and internet communications conglomerate. The ongoing platformization of Unreal has resulted in a figure-ground swap: creative and design elements of the Unreal Engine are now being repurposed into gameplay and player-led content creations assets in *Fortnite*. Dispersing Unreal's creation and monetization affordances into games has technical, legal, and political ramifications that have metastasized in the form of multiple ongoing lawsuits between Epic Games, Google, and Apple over the rights of media platform distributors to monopolize access to software and hardware platforms. Epic, I argue, is using Unreal to produce new kinds of resource materialities:[88] new embodied, material, and legal ways of creating and extracting value from its users. Unreal thus serves as a platform for legal battles and games creation, while being simultaneously transformed into content to be served through games-as-platforms—games that were themselves made using Unreal.

This book thus combines feminist STS with platform studies not only because of the broader analytic need, but because Unreal itself demands it. Understanding Unreal's history, practices, and entanglements with power highlights the limits of thinking in terms of surface/depth and content/culture binaries. We move into a future where game engines are increasingly the eye of a hurricane of capitalistic, militaristic, raced, and hegemonic practices. Platform studies must attend to power to navigate through that storm.

Lieutenant Colonel (LTC) Casey Wardynski flipped through the faxed brief
on his desk. It was a typical gray early November day in upstate New York
at West Point, where he served as a professor of economics. The draft in
front of him represented a culmination of his efforts over the past year; it
was an official proposal from West Point's Office of Economic and Manpower Analysis (OEMA) to leaders in the US Army for $300,000 to make
a videogame. It was autumn of 2000, the day before George W. Bush would
lose the popular election to Al Gore, only to see a conservative Supreme
Court hand Bush the presidency. It would be another eleven months
before the 9/11 terror attacks on US soil gave Bush and his vice president,
Dick Cheney, leverage to launch the "war on terror"—a war fought as much
to revitalize jingoistic ideologies in the American consciousness as it was
to secure oil pits in a desert on the other side of the world.

Recruitment had waned in all branches of the US military since the
end of the Gulf War. While some analysts framed the sagging numbers
as a deliberate policy choice or the result of a collective hangover from
the Cold War,[1] the lieutenant colonel thought differently. Wardynski
was convinced that the biggest motivation to attract highly sought-after
demographic of sixteen-to-twenty-two-year-old young men was consistent, lifelong, positive associations with the US military. And for Wardynski, while media propaganda and individual recruiters could help build
a vague sense of interpersonal military connection or national pride
within young potentials, no recruitment was more efficient or effective
than the presence of a combat veteran in a young person's life. Fathers,

grandfathers, uncles, cousins, and elder siblings could share stories, demonstrate deep fraternal bonds, and—importantly—provide empirical evidence that joining a combat corps does not necessarily entail death, permanent physical injury, or PTSD. Family members could also instill in potentials the seven basic LDRSHIP values of the US Army: loyalty, duty, respect, selfless service, honor, integrity, and personal courage.[2] For all of the hyperviolent military cinema that inundated US audiences during the 1980s and 1990s, the US Army wanted obedient, disciplined soldiers—not Rambo wannabes.

The problem, as Wardynski understood it, was that there hadn't been enough wars recently to continue the familial cycle of recruitment. Or, at the very least, there hadn't been enough *good* wars. Veterans of the Great War had helped drive recruitment for World War II. Veterans of World War II in turn attracted young men to the "police actions" of the Korean War. Now, however, Americans were left with what he saw as distorted visions of war, muddled by both time and the media. Vietnam had been a mess; ambivalent political support at home rapidly turned to outright disgust as televisions aired nonstop footage of maimed soldiers and civilians on fire. The inflations and recessions of the 1970s, combined with increasing cultures of austerity in government, meant fewer resources for these men to rebuild their lives. Veterans faced increased chances of homelessness, alcoholism, and traumatic disorders that were quite visible to family members. They grew bitter toward a government that they felt had abandoned them. Besides, for Wardynski's purposes, Vietnam was just *too long* ago; generations of American men had grown up whose only knowledge of war was one fought behind desks and through economic sanctions and proxy battles, not one where honorable US boots were on the ground.

The 1991 Gulf War had the opposite problem; it was too short, too overwhelming, and too technological. Too easy. The forty-three-day invasion of Iraq was monstrously imbalanced. The US-led six-country coalition lost 292 soldiers out of nearly one million, and only 147 of those losses were combat-related, whereas indigenous Iraqi forces suffered an estimated 20,000–35,000 deaths.[3] The US media coverage of Iraq had painted the war as a marvel of the technological West over the third world—a triumphant declaration of the United States' post–Cold War position as the supreme empire on the planet.[4] The war was portrayed as so smooth and "push-button" easy that public commenters in the early 1990s had even taken to calling it "the Nintendo War."[5] If some saw such narratives as a kind of international bragging rights, Wardynski saw recruitment problems. Could men excited by the image of techno-cowboy adventurism be molded into effective, team-centered soldiers? When cybernetic wars can be won with so little manpower, why would anyone but the most gung-ho feel called to serve?

The solution, Wardynski thought, was videogames. The idea of incorporating electronic gaming technology wasn't new to the US military. Just months after the release of *Battlezone*, an independent group of retired US Army generals contracted Atari to modify their 1980 vector-based arcade shooter into a training simulator for gunners who manned the tank-like Bradley Fighting Vehicle, resulting in what would colloquially be called Army Battlezone or Military Battlezone.[6] The US Navy, CIA, and US Secret Service also had their own virtual training environments, powered by internally developed simulation technology. But training simulators, almost by design, were boring. They were clunky, with limited graphical capacities, uninterested in engaging an audience in an emotional or affective way.

What Wardynski had in mind was different: a game, developed by experienced game designers from the entertainment industry, using the latest in commercial game development technology and distributed for free online. The game would introduce young men to army careers, encourage them to join social "clans" (whose members included veterans), and allow them to experience the excitement of "real-world" combat scenarios. Importantly for Wardynski, the game's design logics would refute playing techniques popularized by contemporary first-person shooters like *DOOM* and *Quake*. There would be no running-and-gunning; players attempting to Rambo through a level and ignore their teammates would drag down their "fireteam," or team of players. Players who engaged in "griefing" behavior—intentionally sabotaging or killing their own team—would first be officially warned. Consistent griefing behavior would lead to the player's IP address being banned from the game. Most crucially, players would not advance through the game according to their kill count, but instead by demonstrating commitment to a gamified version of the US Army's LDRSHIP tenets. The game would attract many different kinds of players, but those who stayed and advanced to become a core part of the game's community—those players would have army potential.

A few years earlier, Wardynski had reached out to Dr. Michael Capps and Dr. Mike Zyda, computer science professors at the MOVES Institute (Modeling Virtual Environments and Simulation) at the Naval Postgraduate School (NPS) in Monterey, California. Together, Wardynski, Zyda, and Capps—who served as principal investigator on internal and external project documentation—had assembled Wardynski's vision into a concrete proposal for the Army Game Project (AGP). The proposal described two first-person shooter games with military-career-path simulators, and they had successfully lobbied the administrative chain of command for funding. Capps and Zyda had already made names for themselves in the 1990s developing training simulators for the armed forces. Along with other gaming contemporaries, they were leading a push for tighter collaborations between the US military and the games industry.[7] Wardynski didn't much like Zyda, who he thought was bombastic and self-serving. He was annoyed with Zyda's growing influence in the project, as Capps slowly drifted away from the development team. Still, Zyda had been an effective coleader and had assembled a stellar team of game designers, and Wardynski was out of time; he had to settle on a software development environment and begin building the project.

Wardynski flipped to the second-to-last page of the faxed proposal. In accordance with government funding guidelines, the AGP team had to provide a comparative list of different vendors who could supply a game engine and offer an "objectively formed" suggestion of the best vendor. Capps and the MOVES team had developed a list of eleven criteria that their game engine and vendor must meet. Their criteria included traditional factors of computational effectiveness and cost, but also social factors, such as the capacity for the vendor to effectively embed the AGP team into the commercial entertainment games industry. Wardynski's eyes moved over columns at the bottom of the page, where Capps had cross-compared six different companies against the US Army's eleven criteria. Only one column had all seven criteria checked: "Epic MegaGames: Unreal."

Engine Stories

Wardynski's Army Game Project would be released to the public on July 4, 2002, as *America's Army* (*AA*), a game that would later boast over 9.7 million registered players and spawn numerous updates, sequels, and spinoffs.[8] *AA* would also be the first game developed on Unreal Engine 2 (UE2), a collaboration widely hyped across the entertainment industry popular press and within the US government.

This chapter offers a historical view of Unreal, its early development period, and its influence on the entanglements with the game industry and the state. However, rather than reinscribing a tool-first or "tech boys in their garages"[9] history of Unreal, I instead offer another kind of story. As discussed in the introduction, game engines are "fractional coherences,"[10] heterogeneous juxtapositions of multiple parts, objects, and stories, none of which serve as a central object. How we as analysts tell the story of game engines determines in part that engine's boundaries, qualities, and political enmeshments.

This story is told with and through the games made with Unreal—and that made Unreal. The origins of Unreal through the games developed through it reveal the uncertain boundaries of the engine—how it crosses and blends across entertainment, technology, culture, and legal infrastructures—as well as provides evidence for the coproduction of games and engines. Rather than following platform studies' traditional layered model that implicitly positions engines as historically prior and materially determinant, this chapter highlights how games and engines come to be, and come to be understood, only through one another and through their participation with the state and militarized masculinity.

There are many games—and combinations of games—that one could use to tell Unreal's early history. Games like *ZZT*, *Myst*, *DOOM*, and *Quake* are inseparable from both *Unreal* the game and Unreal the Engine. Not only did these games influence one another's aesthetic styles and programming decisions, they also shared development staff, technology, and state and government connections. *America's Army* manifests as part of these games' cultural and institutional legacy, while also revealing how government institutions seduce the populace to normalize war through games. Unreal cannot be disentangled from nation-building and wartime recruitment.

Culturally, *America's Army* was part of a renewed fusion of the North American games industry and games culture. The late 1990s and early 2000s were a political inflection point for games. Public discourse about the potential violent impact of games on children's psyches had reached a zenith. The popular press and Senator Jeff Sessions, then chairman of the US Senate Judiciary Subcommittee on Youth Violence, linked first-person shooters *DOOM* and *Duke Nukem 3D* to the 1999 Columbine High School shootings.[11] Sessions echoed earlier 1990s congressional investigations, which suggested the need to regulate "realistic violence" in games[12] that stemmed from reactions to titles like *Mortal Kombat* and *Night Trap*. *America's Army*, on the other hand, was interested in turning young boys into practitioners of violence, rather than in shielding them from it. Wardynski and the Army Game Project team were keenly aware of the game industry's penchant for valuing over-the-top gore and violence, as well as of the potential public outcry against *AA*. Wardynski would attempt to solve both these issues at the same time by enrolling the games industry, media critics, and scholars into to production of *AA*.

Unreal would serve as the vessel for these institutional threads. Its very multiplicity allowed Unreal to serve orthogonal goals during *America's Army*'s development, marketing, and release. Technologically, Unreal provided common ground for the government-contracted developers at MOVES, the game design community, and game modders, who were familiar with Unreal through UnrealEd, Unreal's level editor, which came bundled with copies of Unreal-developed games, and its accompanying Unreal Script programming language. After the game's release, the military, veterans, fans, and *AA*'s designers collaborated to iteratively change the game, produce new levels, create new recruitment opportunities, and connect militaristic ways of seeing and making space with designerly ways of knowing.[13] The soldierly perspective became familiar in the hallways of game development.

Further, licensing a game engine also let clients access valuable labor. As Eric Freedman notes, depending on the terms of contract and money invested, licensing can also grant access to an engine's developers.[14] In the case of Unreal and *AA*, the Unreal licensing agreement would go even further, entangling Epic and the US Army in an array of promotional, institutional, and infrastructural components of the entertainment world and governance. In turn, Epic would provide the US government access to the entertainment industry, including the E3 Expo in LA and cultural capital with the gaming community. Institutionally, Unreal and Epic Games would be brought into branches of the US government through personnel moves and licensing agreements. The most prominent move was Army Game Project lead Mike Capps stepping down from MOVES in order to become the president of Epic Games. The licensing agreement between Epic and the US military also hints at the potential for broader collaborative efforts, including sublicensing clauses that could have make the Unreal Engine the de facto game engine of the US government. However, as this chapter will detail, funding and licensing impropriety from within the *America's Army* team led to the government backing away from institutionalizing Unreal.

The tale of Unreal and *America's Army* is also archivally and methodologically compelling. Much of the source material for this chapter is drawn from the *America's Army* collection at the Strong Museum of Play in Rochester, New York. This 2018 collection, which had not been accessed before this book project, contains game development materials that are notoriously difficult to acquire, including the full licensing agreement and contractual obligations between the US government and Epic Games, US Army internal memos, PowerPoint presentations, and documentation dating back to the Army Game Project's inception in the mid-1990s. It includes the entirety of Project Co-Director (and eventually director) Mike Zyda's email correspondence within and among the MOVES team, the US Army, and Epic Games, as well as with the various academic and public collaborators contacted by the US Army to help manufacture public consent[15] for the game. These correspondences help me tell what feminist media studies scholar Tara McPherson calls a "lenticular" history[16] of Unreal—a history that uses multiple, overlapping lenses to understand how a particular technical object can be simultaneously read as a mechanical artifact, an institutional process, a cultural text, and a collection of interpersonal partnerships and rivalries. Unreal and *America's Army* not only enacted one another, but also shaped broader cultural understandings of game engines and the military-entertainment complex.

America's Army has attracted much prior attention from games scholars. They've been attracted to the game's success, the publicity assault from both the US Army and Epic, and the general analytic juiciness of a propagandistic military partnership with the games industry. At times the game has stood in for the military-entertainment complex[17] or for illustrating the broader subgenre of militaristic and tactical first-person shooting games.[18] For other scholars, the game has highlighted new forms of the manufacturing of militaristic consent among the US citizenry,[19] and even outright shaping of militaristic subjectivities within audiences—the conversion of the game player into future solider.[20] Anthropologist Robertson Allen even spent six months in 2006 in the field with Wardynski and the developers of one of the *AA* sequels, at a time when the project was transitioning away from MOVES and toward AAA developer Ubisoft.[21] Unreal is often mentioned in these analyses as a background element that helps explain *AA*'s massive commercial success. David Nieborg, for example, describes Unreal Engine's relationship to *AA* as an "advanced, commercial, off-the-shelf game technology . . . that affords the Army a perpetually updated and versatile platform to provide high-fidelity simulations."[22] Tim Lenoir and Luke Caldwell paint Unreal as the period's "most advanced game engine . . . featur[ing] brilliant graphics."[23] Allen similarly describes Unreal as,

> crucial commercial middleware . . . [that] was critical to the game's
> initial success, as version of the Unreal Engine form the basis for a
> great number of popular games and it is a development tool with which
> both hard-core gamers and game developers are generally familiar.[24]

That the Unreal Engine is mentioned at all across many of the scholarly investigations of *AA* is a double testament to Epic's and the US Army's dual marketing strategy. Not only was it less common in humanistic game studies scholarship of the early 2000s to detail the technologies involved in games creation,[25] the "Unreal Engine" had also not yet publicly stabilized as a product to be marketed and delivered. *America's Army* was not produced on a stock version of the Unreal Engine. Its underlying software was the Unreal Warfare Engine, a spinoff/sequel to the Unreal Engine designed for Epic's unreleased title, *Unreal Warfare*, a multiplayer shooter game that would eventually be used as a prototype for 2006's *Gears of War*. Unreal Warfare—the engine—would be incorporated into a software suite collectively dubbed Unreal Engine 2. In fact, at the time of *AA*'s production, there was no "stock" Unreal Engine—just collections of modular pieces of software that were compiled differently for each product and client.

The Unreal Engine was not merely a middleware tool that afforded *AA*'s creation. Rather, *America's Army* and the Unreal Engine were mutually constitutive, in both material and discursive terms. Materially, the technical and gameplay capacities of Unreal and *AA* were formed in a recursive relationship with one another. In discursive terms, *AA* and the US government shaped contemporary understandings of the Unreal Engine. Unreal and Epic Games are not just characters in the story of *AA*'s development—they are fundamentally entangled with it, and through that entanglement produced the still-enduring public imagination of game engines themselves.

"Recruiting Generation Y"

America's Army was grandly announced at the 2002 Electronic Entertainment Expo (E3)—one of the largest consumer game industry events in the world—with tanks stationed outside of the Los Angeles Convention Center. Inside, enlisted soldiers rappelled down ropes from the ceiling every two hours, landing astride an American flag in front of photographers. Staff from both the US military and Epic Games were on hand to answer press questions and pose for photos. Flanking them were CRT monitors draped in "desert-camo" style tarps and plastic shells, each running an early build of the game.

AA certainly benefited from the still-fresh 9/11 US jingoism, including a Democratic "opposition" party that operated in lock step with Bush administration military ventures and a press corps that largely parroted White House press statements.[26] Even so, *AA*'s public relations strategy was shockingly effective. The US Army had anticipated pushback by working with the notoriously inscrutable games industry of the early 2000s to identify key partners across the entertainment industry, academia, and journalism that would be friendly to their cause. When faced with what little public resistance there was by members of the press corps, the *America's Army* team was disarmingly forthright about their recruitment intentions for the game. Wardynski and his surrogates wryly embraced the "propaganda" label hurled at them. *AA* showed up at major games industry events like E3 and was frequently featured in games press. The US Army partnered with museums and institutions of higher learning to co-curate exhibitions and events chronicling the historical relationships among the arts, humanities, and the military. These partnerships culminated in a polished Game Scenes event sponsored by Stanford at the Yerba Buena Center for the Arts in 2004. Meanwhile, Epic Games widely distributed a press release detailing the US Army's licensing of the Unreal Engine, alongside hype quotes from Wardynski, Capps, and Mark Rein, Epic's vice president:

> It's an honor to be working with the U.S. Army and to have our engine selected as the technology solution for the game's development. Our mission is to constantly improve the gaming experience, and with our latest engine, both traditional and non-traditional players in the industry can join us on this crusade." said Mark Rein, vice president of Epic Games. "The development team on this has been top notch, and we can't wait to see everyone's reaction at E3."
>
> Our selection of the next generation Unreal Engine was the most important decision we made when charting our development path for 'America's Army.' The Unreal engine has allowed us push our graphics and realism beyond the state-of-the-art," said LTC Casey Wardynski, originator of the "America's Army" concept and manager of the development program.
>
> Dr. Michael Capps, development team lead, said, "Our team was certainly excited about working with the Unreal technology—but the support and feedback Epic's team has given us, from the early design stages to last-minute optimization, has been truly invaluable."[27]

Unreal helped Wardynski and Capps sell *America's Army* to two audiences. First, they targeted the American gaming public, who typically associated government-produced games with clunky edutainment-style civics lessons. Second, they seduced the check writers within the US military, who needed to be convinced that development of a new recruiting tool wouldn't require financing an entirely new computational arm of the army's marketing department. Unreal satisfied both these requirements. Epic Megagames was known by players and the gaming press for producing quality first-person shooter games with high-fidelity PC graphics. Meanwhile, Epic's reputation was growing among game studios; by 2000, six different studios had licensed the Unreal Engine to produce their own games, and Epic's client list was only expanding. The successful external use of their engine, coupled with Epic's dedicated technical support for teams licensing Unreal, helped convince military higher-ups of the fiscal feasibility of the AGP, while the deluge of Epic-Army partnership advertisements showcased *AA*'s gamer street cred. Unreal also better enabled Capps to recruit industry veteran game designers to his team at MOVES, lured by the promise of working closely with the engine. On its part, Epic was excited about the development team and served to refute stereotypes about janky government tech. The Epic contract was not only lucrative—$300,000 US, with potential additional charges built into the licensing contract—it also allowed Epic to purchase valor. What better way could a gaming company contribute to the post-9/11 war effort than by embarking with the US Army on a joint "crusade?"

When reading through the Strong Archives, internal email threads, or public press releases, you quickly learn that LTC Wardynski has a fondness for telling the origin myth of the *America's Army* project. Several figures have taken center stage in this tale as the game has unfolded over the past twenty years (the *AA* online servers were shut down in 2022). John J. Rambo, Sylvester Stallone's titular hero of the *Rambo* film series, was regularly invoked throughout the 2000s—though more to internal older US military members than to *AA*'s target younger recruits—as an example of the kinds of combat fantasies the AGP was interested in erasing. Also regularly featured is Wardynski's thirteen-year-old son, whose bored response to the US Army's website in the mid-1990s was used by him as a stand-in for the disposition of all members of Generation Y (Millennials). The Army Game Project was Wardynski's attempt to forge a middle ground between the extremes of soldier-as-action-hero and soldier-as-bureaucrat. He'd produce an image of a fun and exciting, yet profoundly violent, life that still played by the government's rules. As such, *AA* was a part of the ongoing reforging of American militaristic masculinity in the twentieth century, which Judy Wajcman argues was the Janus-faced production of masculinity as violence, anger, and bodily domination, à la Rambo, and masculinity as the rational, calculated master of the social and physical world, à la the Manhattan Project mathematicians and engineers.[28]

Early drafts of the Army Game Project (AGP) reflect this muddling of emotional valence and bureaucratic decision-making. The first internal documents pitching the Army Game Project to the US government appeared in late 1999, in a series of drafted PowerPoint presentations that read like a rogues' gallery of the 1990s military-academic-entertainment research establishment. The first presentation, "You're in the Army Now!," dated October 4, was coauthored by Wardynski, Zyda, and John Hiles, a developer with ties to both the Naval Postgraduate School and Maxis Games, creators of *SimCity* and *The Sims*, and proponent of the applicability of

SIM-like games to national health, military, and economic security.[29] The second, "Recruiting Generation Y," dated October 23, features Wardynski and Dr. Michael Macedonia, a PhD advisee of Zyda's and a military simulation fundraiser and researcher who was instrumental in building institutional bases for games and militarism in the US academy.

Macedonia had long-standing connections with the US military. He served in Desert Storm as an electronic warfare combatant and was the son of Ray Macedonia. Ray Macedonia was a West Point faculty member who led the charge to incorporate simulation technologies into training in the 1970s and was described by James Der Derian as "one of the Army's best wargamers."[30] By 1999, Michael was the chief scientist at STRICOM (US Army Simulation, TRaining, and Instrumentation COMmand),[31] a new simulation and training technology R&D wing of the US Army headquartered in Orlando, Florida. Through his role at STRICOM, Macedonia had spearheaded the development of both the Institute for Creative Technologies (ICT) at USC and the Institute for Simulation and Training (IST) at the University of Central Florida, where he would later serve as assistant vice president of research.[32] Like MOVES, both the ICT and the IST were designed as simulation and computer graphics research enclaves within higher education that could be supported via military funding. They were also strategically located near two of the biggest entertainment hubs in the United States: Hollywood/Disneyland/Los Angeles and Disney World/Orlando.

Taken together, these two internal presentations provide insight into how Wardynski was pitching games for militarization to the US government. "Recruiting Generation Y" is the broader of the two, leveraging the figures of Rambo and Wardynski's son to advocate for the US military moving into the entertainment sector. The history of the technical and political partnering of the entertainment industry—particularly cinema and Hollywood—with the international military industrial complex is a long one, dating back to at least *Birth of a Nation* director D. W. Griffith's work for the British War Office during World War I. The AGP documents, however, are notable for their amalgamation of entertainment and *simulation*. Simulation was nothing new for the military, as wargaming has been ever present in organized warfare.[33] Digital simulations like the aforementioned *Battlezone* had been used for combat training since the 1980s, meaning AGP wouldn't even have been the only game in soldiers' memory to use commercial first-person shooter technology. *Marine DOOM*—a modified version of 1994's *DOOM II* that featured a team of four Marines storming a bunker—spread through the ranks via official and unofficial military channels in 1996. However, these simulations were often boring, and, more importantly, they were often used only internally for training purposes or to boost morale. AGP deftly combined what were at that point two separate wings of US military intelligence: outward-facing recruitment, and internal-facing training, simulation, and data collection. It was *Rambo* meets Honeywell.

Reflecting its dot-com-era sensibilities, the document broadly labels the syncretism of entertainment and simulation as "interactivity." Interactivity here is multimodal, and the PowerPoint included a pitch for a US Army Adventure Van—a traveling tractor trailer with virtual reality rigs, gaming stations, paid recruiters, and locally recruited veterans who could run high-tech recruitment tours around the country. Incidentally, though this pitch was unfunded in 1999, army and navy recruitment Adventure Vans and Cinema Vans would be touring the country by 2008. They drove alongside an expansion of the van concept in the Army Experience Center, a 14,500 square feet *America's Army* branded VR and AR experience, which occupied a converted movie theater at Franklin Mills Mall outside Philadelphia.[34] Digital games, however, by far dominated the document as the future of interactive recruitment and training.

Digital gaming was important to the AGP pitch team for two main reasons. It demonstrated potential for technical and promotional collaborations with established entertainment companies, and it showed how to introduce surveillance and psychological operations into recruitment practices. On the entertainment side, the details of working with commercial software now, twenty-five years later, sound familiar to anyone who has sat through a meeting championing the cost and efficiency benefits of outsourcing your organization's internal data management systems. Wardynski, Macedonia, Hiles, and Zyda all tout "dynamic" development. With an entertainment company handling the back end and software development, the AGP team would be free to devote their time to content development. According to AGP, custom content would prevent the game from feeling technically or politically stale; new levels and gameplay modes could be constantly designed and deployed, and new hostile combatants rapidly created to reflect the US enemy of the week. External corporate partners could also connect the game to the broader public, as they had experience in marketing, emotional appeals, and visual rhetoric that the US military couldn't hope to match. To provide their higher-ups with evidence of prior success, Wardynski and Macedonia regularly pointed to STRICOM's successful partnerships with the entertainment industry, including their close business and personal connections with Sony Entertainment, Electronic Arts, and Maxis Games, as well as with military contractors Janes Information Services and MAK Technologies.

The military's use of the gaming industry would go beyond simple platform development, however. Hiles, Zyda, and Wardynski imagined digital gaming as the beginning of a new mass infrastructure for recruitment—infrastructure that would include both new distributed recruitment practices as well as new telecommunications technologies like the internet. Web technologies and marketing in this document are consistently bundled together. They are together referred to as "the AOL Approach," referencing the 1990s internet service provider giant America Online's marketing strategy of mailing out free floppy disks that included their web client software and a short-term free trial subscription. AGP would mimic AOL by sending free copies of their games across the United States, providing free servers for players, and introducing persistent nudge points that would direct traffic to the army's more formal recruitment apparatus, such as their website and recruitment centers. This distributed approach was highlighted for its potential to recruit rural boys—a highly desired market with high enlistment percentages and a group that was a logistical nightmare to target through traditional recruitment methods. Traditional recruiting stressed in-person interactions in central locations like high schools and shopping malls that were easily managed in urban and suburban communities. However, recruitment required either a higher monetary investment in rural areas—more recruitment officers distributed in more places—or traveling officers to cover a territory as large as an entire state. Framing AGP as an internet service provider afforded an opportunity for rural boys to interact online with recruitment officers and veterans, who would be paid to play the game and build rapport with its playerbase.

The AGP team has never been shy about its role as a propagandistic device. Public-facing interviews with developers and representatives have glibly referred to the game as "propaganda with a purpose"—media always propagandizes, so why not produce propaganda that promotes the values of honor and integrity in the US military?[35] Internally, the AGP pitch refers to the power of digital games as an explicitly "hypnotic"[36] force. First, in a vulgar materialist sense, it promises that games' interactivity was inherently interesting, so they served as a natural venue for propaganda and suggestion. That is, players would be so excited and engaged that they would create positive associations with "nudges" to actions, including navigating to a redesigned army recruitment website. Second, hypnosis is framed in a sense akin to Csikszentmihalyi's "flow." When well-balanced, the call-and-response nature of an interactive environment will lure players into a loop that suspends their experience of space and time.[37] The presentation promised that young men would become psychically enmeshed with the game—meaning they would spend more time in the army's headspace, developing positive associations with the military and learning to see the world as a soldier.

It's a dubious claim, that games produce hypnotically propagandistic narratives that shape young minds according to the desires of a game's design team. Even Csikszentmihalyi's still-dominant heuristic of flow has begun to show cracks, with recent examinations comparing the concept's core assumptions with wrongheaded models of society and the human mind espoused by eugenicist and anticommunist thinkers in the twentieth century.[38] In fact, much of the pitch documentation across the archive reads as magical thinking. Some of it was typical techno-hype, such as AGP's promised ability to measure solider IQ based on an uncited reference to "past research [which shows IQ] correlation to reaction time."[39] Other parts of the pitch were more fantastical. In another attached document, speculative fiction written by Colonel Matthew Caffrey tells the story of a future, Mumbai-born pope prayerfully reflecting on how the AGP project deradicalized anti-US Indian militants, improved Chinese-Taiwanese relations, and defeated Stalinism.[40]

Despite the boldness of these elements, there is little change in rhetoric or tone between the internal pitch documents and the formal request for funding, also titled "You're in the Army Now!" This proposal, submitted to Patrick T. Henry, assistant secretary of the army for manpower and reserve affairs, requested $13.6 million from January 1, 2000, to September 30, 2005, and was authored by Wardynski, Hiles, Zyda, and Michael Capps, who would serve as the principal investigator and project lead. Aside from Macedonia's absence and Capps's presence, the only major differences between the internal and formal AGP pitches were a rhetorical change from "hypnotizing" to "compelling"—an email exchange shows project leadership thought the term was too loaded—and a more detailed cost breakdown of game development costs, with $200,000 specifically earmarked to license a commercial game engine to produce the game.

Notably, the Unreal Engine makes no appearance in these early documents. The two game engines pitched—Disney's PANDA (Platform Agnostic Networked Display Architecture), and Numerical Design Limited (NDL)'s NetImmerse engine—were not closely associated with the mainstream gaming entertainment industry, to the point where one could question whether they were "game engines" at all. PANDA (later released as the open-source Panda3D), was Disney's in-house 3D environment editor for its DisneyQuest virtual reality rides, a now-defunct arm of Disney's parks division; NDL was mostly known for its work with the government and industrial CAD sectors.[41]

In the funding request, the AGP team claimed that these non-gaming game engines stood out because of their technical and design flexibility: "Unlike many commercial engines, [both] can be used for a wide variety of game styles."[42] However, given how the remainder of the project would progress, it seems likely these early engine pitches were more about doing interpersonal favors or relying on established social networks than about seeking technical flexibility. The Disney teams in LA and Orlando had prior connections with ICT and IST, respectively. NDL's largest client at the time, Interactive Magic, was founded and owned by retired Lt. Col. John Wilbur "Wild Bill" Stealey, a former pilot and Air Force Reserve instructor who had previously collaborated with the US military on simulation technology. Similarly, the integration of the Unreal Engine into the AGP would depend as much on interpersonal and political maneuvering as it would on Unreal's technical affordances.

The Army of the Potomac

At the time of the Army Game Project (AGP) pitch, Epic Games and their Unreal Engine were considered a rising star in the games industry. *Unreal*, 1998's sci-fi first-person shooter (FPS), had set new graphical and gameplay standards for the genre. The next year's multiplayer follow-up, *Unreal Tournament*, was named Game of the Year by several gaming press outlets, and has sold over one million copies since its release. Both games were developed using *Unreal*'s game engine, which according to Cliff "Cliffy B." Bleszinski, one of *Unreal* and *Unreal Tournament*'s two lead designers, had seen few changes or updates since the first game's release.[43] By the time of AGP's interest in using the engine in 2000, *Unreal*'s source code and level editor—the software packages that would become the first Unreal Engine—had been licensed by thirty-five external developers for the cost of around $500,000 per full source-code accessible license.

Unreal and the Unreal Engine have often been framed as responses to the growing ecosystem of PC first-person shooter games in the early 1990s. The typical story is they followed on 1993's *DOOM* and 1996's *Quake*, both developed by id Software. Coverage from gaming magazines at the time wondered whether *Unreal* would finally be the game that became the "*Quake* killer," and the underlying rendering and physics technologies embedded in the Engine were regularly compared to those in *Quake* and *DOOM*'s sequels. Tim Sweeney—one of Epic's two founders, its CEO, chief technologist, and still the major face of the company—and other *Unreal* developers would lean into this narrative as well. They noted how *Unreal*'s ambient and direct lighting algorithms were light-years ahead of those in

Quake. Even very early in *Unreal*'s development, around 1994, Sweeney had realized that the technical and gameplay standards of these game-world "superstars" were "actually beatable."[44]

Across multiple interviews, however, Sweeney, Cliffy B., and *Unreal*'s level editor, Juan Pancho Eekels, cited two other games as *Unreal*'s major inspiration: Cyan Worlds' first-person point-and-click adventure game *Riven* and Sweeney's first game, the text-based graphical dungeon explorer *ZZT*.[45] *Riven* and its predecessor *Myst* were slow-moving adventure games known for their beautiful pre-rendered CGI environments and video cutscenes. They pushed the *Unreal* design team to create lighting systems and environmental renders that could process wide-open terrain and skylit vistas—which were uncommon in the hallway-runner style FPS games of the day. The Unreal Engine's lighting models, which allowed for different hues and shades of color to be cast as part of the software's lighting model, were also inspired by *Myst*. Sweeney even credited *Myst* as the technical advancement that convinced the team to settle on *Unreal*'s visual style. Two of the most famous level maps in *Unreal*—the SunSpire and Nyleve's Falls—were directly cited as being technically and aesthetically modeled off *Riven*'s beauty and scope:

> The game *Riven* was a HUGE inspiration for me [Eekels]. It managed to create an atmosphere I have never seen duplicated in a game after it. . . . I strive to get to that level of world making. . . . [*Unreal*'s] Sunspire map was, at that time, the largest level ever made. It went well outside the boundaries of UnrealEd's (the game's map editor) building area. Come to think of it, it had a phallic quality to it. . . . [Nyleve's Falls] made a point that, yes even an fps shooter can have romantic overtones in where for just a moment you can be lost in a virtual world and stare at it in wonder. Then you can go blow everything up and kill the little Nalangaroos hopping around. Yes![46]

The Unreal Engine has always straddled the line between meditative graphical beauty and a boyish appetite for action and destruction. It's the kind of technical/aesthetic sweet spot that demonstrates *Unreal*'s capacity to render both indoor/hallway and outdoor/terrain environments, as well as advanced lighting—some of the most appealing technical features for the Engine's early licensees.

ZZT's inclusion in *Unreal*'s inspirations may be more surprising than *Riven*. Still, it serves to highlight the coproduction of *Unreal*, the Unreal Engine, Epic Games, and the gaming industry at large. Though Epic's business was thriving due to both its game sales and its engine revenue, Sweeney had long argued that the Unreal Engine's modular and easily portable code were not designed with other companies and licensees in mind. Rather, the "editor-centric"[47] workflow—in that one can create gameworlds and navigate the Engine without needing to be an expert in low-level computer programming—and comparatively low barrier to entry that the Unreal Engine provides were intended to appeal to players and modders, not gaming companies. Sweeney credits the player- and modder-centric approach of *Unreal* to his early shareware success with *ZZT*:

> "ZZT served as a conceptual blueprint for Unreal," Sweeney said. "A game engine with a high-productivity, what-you-see-is-what-you-get tools pipeline, bundled with a programming language aimed at simplifying gameplay logic."[48]

The text-and-color-block-based dungeon explorer *ZZT* was Sweeney's first published game, developed while he was an undergraduate mechanical engineering student at the University of Maryland. The game was published by Potomac Computer Systems; Sweeney named his company after his parents' residence in Potomac, Maryland. *ZZT*'s popularity came not from its graphics, but from its extensive level-editing tool and creation systems. The level editor was coupled with a custom object-oriented programming language, ZZT-OOP, named in a nod to the bespectacled and bearded rock band. ZZT-OOP let users modify the core behaviors of *ZZT*'s combinable components. Taken together, the level editor and ZZT-OOP allowed for a surprisingly deep level of customization and creativity. The online bulletin board service (BBS) sites of 1991 and 1992 were littered with free custom levels and games based on *ZZT*'s codebase.[49]

ZZT's 1990s production and distribution model would foreshadow that of Unreal twenty years later. *ZZT* followed the "shareware" model of software distribution popularized in the 1980s and 1990s by game developer Apogee Software. Users could download shareware software for free and donate to the development team if they found the software useful or enjoyable. Non-internet users at the time could also mail checks and request hard copies of software; Sweeney's first employees at Potomac were his childhood friend Carolyn Smith, who handled accounting and shareware fee processing, and Sweeney's father, who would receive checks mailed to his home and send out floppy disk and CD copies of the game. BBSs were so central to ZZT that even the game's name itself reflects their importance; "ZZT" is not an acronym, but rather a series of letters chosen to make sure that the game would consistently appear either at the very top or very bottom of BBS download lists, which were typically arranged alphabetically.[50] Players who built their own levels and shared them on message boards increased *ZZT*'s popularity, meaning BBSs and online distribution systems became key to *ZZT*'s monetary success and popularity. Potomac and other popular games shareware distributors of the 1990s profited from a similar, though smaller scale, platform distribution model as media companies of the 2020s.[51]

By 1994, when Sweeney started programming the software and editor spaces that would become *Unreal* and UnrealEd, Potomac Games had changed its name to Epic MegaGames. Sweeney joked that it was a "scam" to make the company seem bigger than it was: "'Epic . . . Mega . . . Games'—yeah. Of course, it was just one guy working from his parents' house."[52] Sweeney, still in college at the time, partnered in 1992 with Mark Rein, a self-described "loud" sales executive who had become interested in computer games' business potential, and had recently split from *DOOM*'s id Software following salary disputes.[53] From his office in Waterloo, Canada, Rein would become responsible for standardizing Epic's sales practices and attracting key early hires like Cliffy B. The team had achieved moderate successes with 2D platformers like *Jazz Jackrabbit* and *Jill of the Jungle*, and with the sci-fi-themed *Epic Pinball* in the early 1990s. But they had yet to see the level of commercial success that would skyrocket the company into direct competition with major players like id Software. *Unreal* would be Epic's gambit.

Unreal took five years to develop, a process that emotionally and financially stressed Epic's team. Development had emptied Epic's coffers, forcing members of the team—including Rein and a still-teenage Cliffy B.—to max out personal credit cards in support of the project. Epic's talent pool was geographically spread across North America and had mostly worked remotely, slowing down production and driving up telecom costs. Epic decided to temporarily relocate to Waterloo for the duration of the *Unreal* project, a move that irritated some on the design team. Many of the problems were caused by the entangled nature of the game's development; Epic wanted *Unreal* to both be a commercial success and demonstrate their newly developed expertise in 3D graphics technologies. *Unreal*, in other words, had to sell itself, its underlying engine, and Epic MegaGames as a whole. But a 2012 feature by *Polygon*'s Chris Plante notes that by the beginning of 1998, *Unreal* was a shambled mess, and the team had to start attenuating its ambitions:

> Levels and a weapon were the first to get cut, but the coding language, UnrealScript, along with a map editor, UnrealEd, were kept at Sweeney's insistence. His first game, *ZZT*, had found unexpected success

by allowing for easy modification. Players of *Unreal* would have the same opportunity.[54]

Sweeney and Epic decided that they would rather release a smaller *Unreal* to eventually release a larger UnrealEd. The move proved prescient. *Unreal* was a critical and commercial success upon its May 1998 release. Its gameplay was fast-paced and smooth, and the engine elements that Sweeney had prized—the lighting models and the ability for players to develop their own levels and mods—were celebrated by the industry and players alike. The game's publisher, GT Interactive, released an official strategy guide for *Unreal* that featured the typical descriptions of levels, backgrounds, and enemies. It also served as an introduction to UnrealEd and UnrealScript, since it included engine tutorials, code snippets, and best practices for designing levels. The guide also included interviews with *Unreal*'s designers, who led a PR campaign that both amplified their own growing celebrity and sharpened *Unreal*'s three-point commercial pitch: the game is boyish and fun, the game looks great, and the engine is easy to develop on.[55] Of the guide's twelve developer interviews, eight mentioned the lighting system and level editor as the best parts of the game. By the time of the game's 1999 sequel, *Unreal Tournament*, Epic (with the new stream- lined name "Epic Games") was flush with cash and awards. Their design- ers and level editors had emerged as figures in popular culture. Though UnrealEd had been designed for players and Epic's internal design team, external development companies had also begun licensing the engine. Epic began taking its modern-day shape as a hybrid game developer, soft- ware manufacturer, and entertainment industry trendsetter.

Enlisting Unreal

Though the Army Game Project (AGP) pitch had been provisionally approved earlier in the year, by October of 2000 the army and the MOVES team still had yet to select a game engine. Ironically, the importance of using an "off- the-shelf" game engine in the pitch to the military was itself becoming a roadblock; the promised engine needed to do too much. Though MOVES was staffed with highly competent computer scientists, they were still a small team. They included fewer than a dozen workers at the project's start, and no more than twenty developers at their team's height in 2004. While shipping a professional game with a staff of twelve to twenty devel- opers was not totally unheard of in the early 2000s, most of the MOVES team were graduate students, and very few had worked on digital games for entertainment before. John Hiles had worked in the games industry, but his connections with the daily operations at MOVES were tangential. His own development experience was in simulation games, which were vastly different in programming, aesthetics, and scope than what the *AGP* was pitching. Mike Zyda was a faculty member and researcher; he had led development teams before at the Naval Postgraduate School and had a strong record for securing grant funding but had no commercial game shipping experience. Michael Capps, a VR-for-military-training researcher who had assumed the principal investigator and director roles on the AGP, had an entrepreneurial spirit and ambitions to found his own software companies post-MOVES, but was still in an early stage of his career.

The MOVES team had promised the army that a commercial engine would paper over these structural problems. A professional engine could, in theory, streamline programming and reduce development time, allowing for the MOVES team to focus on game content instead of on building physics simulations and rendering pipelines. Game engines were also still largely inaccessible to the broader gaming public, whose appetite for game development had been whetted through their interactions with level designers like UnrealEd. Level editors act as "lite" versions of game engines; most of their interfaces are the same as the engines that professional level designers and game programmers use, but they had limited ability to modify core game behavior and import external assets. MOVES had hoped that licensing a professional game engine could alleviate their labor shortage, with many first-person shooter game modders leaping at the chance to be paid for their design work. The team was excited about making more professional software and gaining the added benefit of being able to cosplay in a military-adjacent space.[56] Further, since game engines were still tightly coupled with the games they were developed to create—Unreal with *Unreal*, idTech with *DOOM* and *Quake*, and Build with *Duke Nukem*—MOVES hoped that their selection of engine would itself help sell their game to the broader gaming public.

By October 2000, none of the engines under consideration in the initial pitch had met their ideal criteria, and the MOVES team was beginning to panic. While the development team had experience with the aforementioned PANDA and NetImmerse Engines through their academic-military-simulation collaborations with ICT and IST, neither had enough users to excite potential development teams, nor sufficient public credibility to excite gaming audiences. Support and technical problems loomed as well. As both PANDA and NetImmerse were largely developed for internal development only, they did not offer the kinds of external support networks and staff that the MOVES team would need to complete the AGP. From a technical perspective, though both engines were praised in the initial funding pitch for being flexible enough to produce multiple types of games, what the MOVES team needed was the *opposite* of flexibility. They needed an engine that would force them to produce an entertainment-quality FPS[57] game, while offering just enough developmental wiggle room to incorporate gameplay styles for the army.

Ever the salesman, Mark Rein had heard of the Army Game Project after the project's approval in early 2000. Epic Games was coming off the successful release of *Unreal Tournament*, and the Unreal Engine was beginning to gain a reputation in the development community as a powerful tool for first-person shooter games. But securing the US military as a client for the development of its own mass-marketed videogame was a tantalizing opportunity. It could help advertise Unreal as a useful tool for "serious" games as well as for play, while politically benefiting from the ongoing national militaristic and imperialistic high in the post–Gulf War United States. Further, if the AGP game proved to be a successful recruiting device, the US military and US government could potentially be secured as long-term—and lucrative—clients. Rein reached out to Capps to advocate for Epic.

The initial meetings were, apparently, a disaster, and Epic's collaboration with the army almost never happened. There were immediate personality clashes between Rein's bombastic salesmanship and Capps's more managerial and strait-laced persona. In an interview with *Polygon*, Capps recalls those initial conversations with bemused annoyance:

> [Rein] and I are oil and water personalities, he's a salesman, and I'm sort of a programmer and a manager. . . . He actually really turned me off, and it was somebody else at Epic who called and said, "Seriously, here's what we can do. What's it going to take to make this deal work?"[58]

While there is no direct record of who that "somebody else at Epic" was who repaired the deal, emails from the Strong Archive point to Jay Wilbur. Wilbur had spent the early 1990s as the CEO of id Software during its *DOOM* heyday and was poached by Epic in 1997 under the official title of "Imperial Advisor."[59] Wilbur would serve as the lead negotiator, business manager, and, later, enforcer, between MOVES, the US Army, and Epic. He was offhandedly mentioned in an email from Capps as the person to "originally discuss and later architect the deal"[60] with the army alongside Capps.

The licensing agreement between MOVES and Epic Games, authored by Capps and Zyda, likely with assistance from Wilbur and Rein, both read as dry administrative documents, though each is packed with revelatory information. Corporate and governmental licensing agreements in the gaming industry are notoriously difficult to access, and many employees with a knowledge of them are bound by strict nondisclosure agreements, making it difficult to even study them. Their surprise presence in this archive is a bit like finding buried treasure. Most important for our purposes, each highlights a multidimensional understanding of game engines and platforms by Epic and the US government. The underlying material technology of a platform is important, but so too are the instructional, political, and cultural relationships entangled with and through that platform.

Vendor request forms exist to justify specific material needs of a project to government funders, and why those needs cannot be met by internal resources. These forms also provide a measure of cost-effectiveness. When a government entity requests funds for external partners, they are expected to conduct a market survey that compares costs and capabilities of various private entities, and then suggest an ideal vendor based on these metrics. However, since the requestor is the one to design and justify these metrics, it is easy to write the statement of work required so that your preferred vendor is also the only vendor that appears viable. The metrics here showed a certain favoritism toward Epic and Unreal. In the November 6 vendor request statement of work, MOVES outlines eleven properties that their game engine must have in order to ensure the success of AGP. These properties span technical, institutional, and economic needs:

Engine Requirements:

1: The game engine must support the seamless blending of indoor and outdoor terrain; realistic indoor and outdoor lighting calculations, including shadowing and dynamic lighting; and rules-based artificial intelligence for autonomous players.

2: The game engine must offer a developer-accessible scripting layer for the generation of new game objects.

3: The game engine must support client/server networking for at least 30 simultaneous players.

4: The game engine must be specifically designed to support first-person perspective games.

5: The game engine must be packaged with level authoring software.

6: The game engine must operate and compile out of the same codebase on the following platforms: Microsoft Windows, Sony PlayStation 2, and Linux.

7: In order to ensure appropriate product quality and maturity, the contractor and its game engine must have the following experience:

7a: At least two titles built atop the engine, and developed by the contractor, must have sold over 1,000,000 units for the PC platform.

7b: The contractor must have developed and published at least one title atop the game engine for the following platforms: Microsoft Windows, Sony PlayStation 2.

7c: The engine must have been used for the development of at least three published computer games *not* built by the contractor.

7d: Authoring software for the game engine must have been used by third-party developers to build at least 500 levels not included in any commercial product.

7e: The contractor must have experience with videogame software launches having an installed user base of 10,000,000 units.[61]

Coupled with this list was an assessment table that compared the ability of six different available game engines (including major competitors id and Valve) to meet MOVES' needs. Of the six, only Epic's engine matched with all eleven criteria.

It's not hard to see why Epic came out on top. While criteria 1 through 6 are reasonable technical demands to be made of an FPS engine, the technical needs (7a–7e) align with how Epic had been advertising the benefits of its engine since *Unreal*: high quality indoor/outdoor lighting coupled with a robust level editor and scripting language. The sub-elements of criteria 7 read as straight from an Epic Games press release; 7a almost literally does. Epic Games was not shy in the early 2000s about promoting their millionth copy sold of *Unreal* and *Unreal Tournament*. It is questionable at best why one million copies sold of a game made by the engine's developers would be a required metric for success.

The army was desperate for the AGP to reach a wide audience and also be accepted by the gaming public. The technical-cultural properties of the engine needed to accommodate AGP's rapid popularization. One of the major distinctions of Epic's Unreal Engine from its major competitor at the time—id Software's "id Tech" engine—was its ability to simultaneously compile game source code to consoles and personal computers. Multiplatform compilation is not a trivial matter. Game consoles and personal desktop computers have substantially divergent hardware and software architectures, particularly as consoles' hardware becomes outdated. While PCs were the dominant hardware platform for FPS games in the 1990s, console gaming hardware was rapidly catching up in terms of computing power—at a lower price point and maintenance cost than the most high-powered PC gaming rigs. Thus, Unreal's ability to reach consoles at low production cost would ensure that the AGP could reach more gamers. Crucially, they were the *right* gamers—boys whose low-income families could afford only a console, not a PC.

While the army and the MOVES staff wanted to ensure that their engine of choice would be easily used by their development teams, they also wanted to replicate *Unreal* and *DOOM*'s success in letting external modders keep the game relevant after release. Requirement 7d—that third-party developers had used the engine to make at least five hundred levels "not included in any commercial product"—is an explicit reference to the modding community. The army did see an inherent risk in using player mods, as they were deeply worried about the proliferation of non-military-developed maps and gameplay designs that did not represent army values or "Army-approved realism."[62] Still, they saw the modding community as an important development and PR asset.

Further, Capps and MOVES came to understand the Epic Games team was an asset entangled with Unreal. The December licensing agreement in part reflects the kinds of standard licensing language described by Freedman; it gave access to both the engine technology and its developers for technical support and updates.[63] At the discount price of $300,000 (normally $500,000) and an ongoing developer support cost of $100,000, Epic agreed to license its Unreal Engine to MOVES. The agreement explicitly defines the Unreal Engine as

> The proprietary computer software program known as the Unreal engine, including all Epic owned, commercially available platform ports and any improvements, enhancements, updates, fixes and other changes thereto through the most current version of Unreal Warfare.[64]

We can again see here that "game engines" are multiple, in terms of fractional components, updates, and improvements made to the engine over time. They are also multiple, because divergent instantiations of an engine exist each time a new game is made (in this case, the unproduced *Unreal Warfare*).[65] However, the licensing agreement also included a contractual obligation for Epic to introduce MOVES and the US Army to major gaming publication and hype venues, as well as to provide "no less than 20 hours" worth of labor to facilitate connections with "Electronic Entertainment PR."[66] One of the major outcomes of this facilitation would be the *America's Army* grand reveal at E3 in 2002. For its part, Epic Games required that the final product of the licensing agreement would feature an introductory splash screen advertising that *America's Army* was made with Unreal, and the company and its staff would stand alongside the US Army when *America's Army* was announced and publicized. Interestingly, Epic also ensured that it could nullify its PR connections with the army, including the splash screen and public exhibitions, if they determined that the resulting game didn't meet industry standards. In true gamer fashion, Epic didn't want to be associated with a game that sucked. Finally, Epic agreed to grant MOVES sublicensing capacities (around $150,000 per license) of the AGP version of the Unreal Engine to other developers working within the Department of Defense and Department of Energy—a move that would later kickstart a chain of events leading to MOVES' dismissal from the AGP.

It's evident that Capps, MOVES, and the US Army valued the Unreal Engine for far more than its technical and gameplay capacities. Unreal was seen as connective tissue hidden in the background, which could recruit production-ready developers and connect the army with valuable promoters and press opportunities. This idea worked better than perhaps the MOVES team could have ever anticipated. Capps and Zyda were right in their instinct that using Unreal would attract talented members across the game industry, academia, and the modding community. They could be highly selective when hiring their programming team. Project manager Alex Mayberry was brought on after having worked at Electronic Arts and mastered 3D previsualization and prop creation for Hollywood blockbusters. Programmer John Gibson was a Christian metal musician turned game modder whose small team had won a license to the Unreal Engine following a Best Unreal Tournament Mod contest held by Epic.[67] Using the Unreal Engine allowed the MOVES team to work shockingly quickly for such a relatively small operation that had to navigate military red tape throughout the development process. The timeframe of licensing the Unreal Engine to the now-infamous *America's Army* E3 reveal was a period of s months.

The game also was a popular and commercial success. According to MOVES, by six months after *AA*'s release, the game already had 1.3 million registered users, 800,000 of whom had completed the "basic training" levels of the game that allowed them to participate in online play. *AA* averaged 1.1 million "missions played" per week, and players had logged 600,000 hours of playtime.[68] Wardynski was enjoying his time in the spotlight as well; he became a regular spokesperson for the project in both traditional media outlets and in the gaming press, was the go-to point person within the Department of Defense for advice on using videogames for training and simulation, and was invited by companies like Sony to give presentations to their research and development divisions about how to best collaborate with military entities. MOVES and Wardynski were networking with the research world as well. When Tim Lenoir and Henry Lowood, two historians in Stanford's History and Philosophy of Science Program, reached out to MOVES asking to feature *America's Army* in a "history of military technology" curated event, they leaped at the opportunity. Together, Stanford, Wardynski, and MOVES produced a recreation of the E3 set at the Yerba Buena Art Center in San Francisco, as well as a coedited booklet featuring essays from Wardynski, Zyda, Lenoir, and Lowood that contextualized the historical and technological importance of *AA*.

Behind the PR bumps, Epic Games partnering with the US military also provided important technical and institutional benefits behind the scenes. Epic continues to advertise *America's Army* as the first game to be produced using Unreal Engine 2, the first major update to and consolidation of the suite of software packages that comprised earlier versions of Unreal. However, this claim about Unreal 2 isn't quite true, or is at least not that simple. As seen in the licensing agreement, *AA* was built on Unreal Warfare, a heavily modified version of the Unreal Tournament engine. The Warfare engine was then heavily modified by MOVES staff for *AA*, and adjusted by Epic games for their own game development and research projects. These independent modifications regularly caused breakdowns when new updates to the Engine were released by Epic, leading to panicked emails between MOVES developers and Epic programming staff.

But beyond standard game development pains and version control nightmares, MOVES and the US Army did advance the Unreal Engine forward technically. As evidenced by the sublicensing agreement, the US Army knew that, if successful, the technology developed through the AGP could serve other branches within the military service. If *America's Army* raised recruitment numbers, why not produce an *America's Navy* or an *America's Air Force* using the same base technology? Beyond recruitment, the newly developed engine could also be repurposed for training exercises, new forms of internet-powered communication and meeting spaces, battle planning and tactics, and risk simulation. Scaling up the engine, however, would also involve either scaling up MOVES—an already institutionally complicated matter, given MOVES' close association with the US Navy—or building mini-MOVES across multiple military branches and intelligence services. Either option would be enormously expensive. The engine would need to be as "plug and play" as possible. The more standardization and automation built into the engine, the less labor would be required to program new games and levels, and the more efficiently the US military could scale it up. The military didn't need just a game engine, it needed an infrastructure.

Among the more difficult programming and design problems the MOVES team encountered was meeting the requirement for "Army-approved realism." It was arduous to realistically simulate *AA*'s combat physics and create lip-sync and character animation for the game's basic training and specialization training levels. The army wanted to make sure that its weapons and vehicles realistically reacted in non-cartoonish ways, and Unreal's sci-fi-inspired internal physics simulators were not necessarily up the task. They also wanted to present their training materials respectfully; most of the videos and dialogue in *AA*'s training sessions weren't performed by actors, but rather were recorded trainings and presentations of real enlisted servicemen and -women. These videos and recordings would also need to be periodically updated, and proper lip-sync and character animations are time- and artist-intensive processes.

To solve these problems, the MOVES team secured military funding to purchase two external software packages: MathEngine's Karma physics engine, and OC3 Entertainment's Impersonator. Karma, an update over Unreal 1's base physics systems, was particularly adept at handling vehicle-based combat. Impersonator provided easily editable character animation toolsets and came equipped with an automatic voice-to-lip-sync generator. This allowed MOVES to have lip-sync animations applied to their character models driven mostly by voiced audio files, rather than animated totally by hand. These additions, however, weren't confined to the MOVES version of the Unreal Engine. Rather, Epic would integrate these two software extensions into the base Unreal Engine. Karma became the standard physics engine for the entirety of Unreal Engine 2's life cycle. Similarly, Impersonator was incorporated as the default character animation and lip-syncing option in Unreal Engine 2. These packages not only improved the physics and animation capabilities of the base engine, they also lowered the technical barriers to others using it. These packages also foreshadowed Unreal's continuing platformization—increasing levels of automation and standardization introduced through a combination of technological advancement and corporate acquisitions. Framed in such a way, rather than understanding *AA* as built on Unreal 2, it might be better to say that Unreal 2—and the Unreal platform as a whole—only came to be through *America's Army*.

Technological advancement and platformization weren't the only benefits to Epic from their collaboration with MOVES. While Epic had been growing in scale and scope, their corporate culture hadn't changed much since their early days developing *Unreal* and *Jazz Jackrabbit*. There were no set hours, developers could come and go as they pleased, and there was no middle management or central coordination service to speak of. Mark Rein was often in Canada or San Francisco, and Tim Sweeney was still more interested in programming than leadership; according to Plante, UnrealEd's lead programmer was known for coming in at odd and unpredictable hours.[69] The already short-staffed team was stretched thin, as their focus was divided between making their own games and providing technical support for Unreal Engine licensees. They needed more labor power, and someone who could instill a better sense of organization and corporate structure. Rein found someone who could provide both in Mike Capps.

On July 4, 2022—the same day that Wardynski and MOVES were celebrating the launch of *America's Army*—Capps was in Cary, North Carolina. Unbeknownst to the AGP team, he was negotiating a new employment opportunity. After leading the *America's Army* project for three years, Capps left MOVES and the Naval Postgraduate School to become CEO of Scion Games, a subsidiary company under Epic.[70] One year later, Scion would merge with its parent company, and Mike Capps would be named president of Epic Games.

License to Kill

"Mike, this just is not your day."[71]

The email that appeared in Mike Zyda's inbox was sent by Jay Wilbur, Epic's "Imperial Advisor." Zyda had stepped into Mike Capps' role as MOVES' principal investigator on the *America's Army* project almost a year ago to the day. Capps had left the team after giving a week's notice, while many of the *AA* staff were running a victory lap at SIGGRAPH—a major international computer graphics research conference—finally able to publicly discuss their two-year development experience working with the US military. The quick transition in leadership had damaged morale and, more importantly, had left major administrative gaps. Capps had served as the central connection point between MOVES, the broader Naval Postgraduate School (NPS), the US Army, and Epic Games, which included managing funding and contracts. Since his departure there had been a litany of misplaced emails, missed payments, and missing documentation, and it had largely become Zyda's job to put out all these fires. The contract with Epic was turning into a conflagration.

At issue was the sublicensing agreement written into the MOVES-Epic Unreal contract. This seemingly mundane addition was designed to allow for other government entities to use elements of *America's Army* for other internal, noncommercial purposes, such as training, simulation, or research. However, *AA* and Unreal were so entangled that developers would at least need access to UnrealEd and Unreal Script in order to make any additions to the games. Any more substantial changes would require the ability to modify the by-then bespoke version of the Unreal Warfare Engine used at MOVES. Access requires licensing, which requires funding. MOVES and Epic had come to a mutually beneficial sublicensing agreement: entities within the Department of Defense (DoD) and Department of Energy (DoE) could sublicense Unreal directly from MOVES for $150,000—a price cut from the $300,000 that MOVES paid Epic, and a steep discount from the $500,000 it would normally cost to license the engine. Though the money would go directly into MOVES' coffers, Epic benefited from further institutionalizing Unreal within the US government; the more trainings and simulations that were based on an internal version of Unreal, the more likely the government would be to license future versions of the Engine once *AA* Warfare was out of date. Epic had restricted what the sublicense contained; users of MOVES' license were allowed to access only the version of the engine that MOVES had developed, and not the source code of the Unreal Warfare engine itself. This is an important distinction, as while MOVES could modify the engine to suit their game needs, sublicensees could not. Their products were bound to the gameplay and technical decisions made by MOVES staff for *AA*. Further, since sublicensees were working on a version of the Unreal Engine that was several iterations removed from Epic's version, and since Epic wasn't receiving any monetary compensation from the sublicense, sublicensees were prohibited from contacting Epic for development support or training.

Recalling John Law, the sublicense agreement in the Epic-MOVES contract codifies Unreal's "fractional coherence." Unreal became multiple.[72] Different versions of the software existed in tension with one another, not only in terms of differing and diverging codebases, but also in terms of access. What was locked for some users was open for others, depending on their position within a sprawling network of license agreements, military research centers, and entertainment industry production houses. The boundaries between game and engine continued to blur. As *America's Army* gained popularity, requests for sublicenses stopped referring to the software as "the Unreal Engine" and instead as "the Army Engine." Even within MOVES, *AA* programmers began making legal and technical distinctions between "pure Unreal" and "Army Unreal." Depending on the communication, Unreal's ontological status shifted between a discrete, local phenomena and an abstract, underdefined collection of software.

As Unreal's material and legal realities began multiplying, so too did its usefulness to MOVES. While Unreal was once framed as necessary technical and cultural connective tissue, the growing popularity of the sublicense had turned Unreal into a vital source of capital. An email between Zyda and *AA* project director Alex Mayberry equated each $150,000 sublicense to hiring a new programmer at MOVES, creating an incentive to sublicense as often as possible while stretching the definition of "eligible." It's unclear how many sublicenses were granted in the period from *America's Army*'s release to the less-than-amicable nonrenewal of the Epic-MOVES license in late 2004, but it seems that the opportunities were plentiful, as Capps and Zyda fielded requests every couple of months. The license requests came from a variety of locations, including the US Air Force, the US Navy, the US Secret Service, and West Virginia University. At the very least, the air force and the Secret Service began building levels in the *AA* UnrealEd level editor, and MOVES had obtained a special source code sublicense with the Los Alamos National Laboratory (LANL), the former weapons design facility for the Manhattan Project, now a Department of Energy national security research center. Unbeknownst to the MOVES team, LANL had also licensed Unreal in 2000 as a part of their VISIT (Virtual Interactive Simulation and Inspection Tool) program, a virtual city simulator for testing equipment to detect hostile nuclear weapons and other weapons of mass destruction. Not wanting to duplicate government efforts, LANL reached out to MOVES to consolidate their technology, support, and licensing costs.

All told, by 2003 there were several versions of *AA* and the Unreal Engine lurking in various arms of the federal government. Furthermore, the consolidation with LANL had convinced Zyda that MOVES could serve as the exclusive vendor and support of Unreal for the DoD and DoE, if not eventually most of the military and research arms of the US federal government. To Zyda's understanding, this also included granting *AA* Unreal sublicenses to external contractors—including West Virginia University and major DoE contractor E&S Environmental—who would partner with the DoD or DoE. Such exclusivity would position MOVES and NPS, through the *AA* Unreal Engine, as both the central service provider and infrastructure underpinning entertainment and virtual simulation for the US government. If Epic had agreed, there would be potential for the Unreal Engine to become more than a tool used by federal contractors, but rather deeply entangled with the state.

However, such license exclusivity was not Epic's understanding, to say the least. Misunderstanding the terms of the sublicense contract, E&S had reached out to Epic directly demanding developer and training support, which had alerted Jay Wilbur and Mark Rein to Zyda's rather broad interpretation of the Epic contract. After intermediation by Mike Capps, Wilbur and Rein decided against suing Zyda or initiating breach of contract proceedings, and instead offered a sternly worded email clarifying Epic's understanding of the contract—that sublicenses were available for internal use only—and cautioning Zyda against misrepresenting MOVES' exclusivity for federal uses of Unreal or from sharing confidential Epic documents. Less than three months later, Zyda sent a confidential copy of the Epic-MOVES contract to external military contractors BBN Technologies (later Raytheon) and MAK Technologies, each of which were interested in the *AA* engine. In response, Wilbur began legal proceedings against MOVES and the NPS, and Wardynski stepped in to salvage his pet project.

The next few weeks were a flurry of emails between MOVES, Epic, and the US Army. They would fundamentally break the relationship between MOVES and the military, as well as change the future of *America's Army*. Zyda accused Epic of trying to renege on the original contract, claiming that Wilbur and Rein had realized the sublicense was a potential gold mine that they had been foolish to give away. Wardynski accused MOVES leadership—Zyda and Mayberry, but also stretching as far back as Capps—of being consistently incompetent with payments, licensing, and development. In a postmortem memo to the secretary of the army, Wardynski argued that Zyda had been trying to use sublicenses to build capital for spinning off MOVES from the NPS into its own for-profit military contracting company; that programming and development teams had been regularly behind schedule and over budget; and that the Epic-MOVES contract was illegal from the beginning, as Mike Capps was not a legally empowered contracting officer of the army, and yet had been the signatory on the contract. Zyda, in his own emails and postmortem memo, accused Wardynski of attempting to sabotage MOVES so that the colonel could shift development funding away from NPS and toward new startup companies run by Wardynski's old army buddies. Zyda also characterized Wardynski as a bipolar figure, one who would go from "charming" to raging between meetings, and whose constant demands for changes to *AA* delayed production and negatively affected team morale.[73] According to Robertson Allen's fieldwork, there were also rumors within the AGP development team that members were secretly being assigned for-profit work for other game companies like Activision, while MOVES pocketed the revenue that came from double-dipping from both army and private funding to pay the same employee.[74]

Epic, for their part, seems just to have wanted a stable contract and a narrower sublicense provision. The army just wanted the whole dispute to be done with. Heads had to roll—the army made Mayberry the NPS scapegoat and fired him in the middle of a development team meeting—but there was enough evidence of corruption and funding misappropriation from all sides, including from other branches of the US military, that the army was content to not pursue further punishment.[75] The Epic license—upgraded to ditch Unreal Warfare and instead incorporate the newly released Unreal Engine 3—was transferred to out of MOVES/NPS and to the US Army. By 2007, the *America's Army* project was completely privatized, with AAA developer Ubisoft taking control over future development of the game's sequels and spinoffs.

Conclusion

The story of *America's Army* would continue,[76] and the Unreal Engine would still be used for the development of the game's sequels. Versions of the game would be released for PC and multiple generations of both Microsoft's Xbox and Sony's PlayStation. Though the game's popularity and critical acclaim had peaked by the late 2000s, the *AA* servers hosting online play were only shut down on May 5, 2022, two months short of the game's twentieth anniversary.[77] The major players on the MOVES side had long since moved on. Capps continued his presidency of Epic Games until 2012 and attempted to found smaller companies in Silicon Valley focused on AI and corporate management. Mike Zyda is now a faculty member at USC, where he continues to lead projects combining entertainment technology with military training and simulation. Wardynski retired from the army in 2010 as a colonel, but was tapped by the US Trump administration in 2019 to serve as the assistant secretary of the army for manpower and reserve affairs—the same office he had pitched the Army Game Project to twenty years earlier. After resigning from the position just before the start of the US Biden administration, Wardynski announced his run for Alabama's fifth congressional district as a Trump-styled "America First" Republican, succeeding Mo Brooks. He was crushed in the Republican primary by eventual seat winner Dale Strong.

Epic would never again be as institutionally and technologically intertwined with the game as it had been in the early 2000s. The company had matured and grown, and with that growth came further centralization and institutionalization. Individual licensees outside of Epic's own game development had less upstream impact on Unreal's development than when the development team was smaller. Epic's and Unreal's joint destinies are now intertwined with the popular platform game *Fortnite* as well as with Tencent, the Chinese megacorporation that purchased over

40 percent ownership stake in the company in 2012. Only Tim Sweeney himself now has more of a say in Epic's operations than Tencent.

The detachment of Epic from *America's Army* would not be the end of Epic's entanglements with the state and the university, though *AA* still marks a high-water point for Unreal's potential to serve as the gaming infrastructure of the US government. Epic still partners with multiple other companies for training and simulation development, including SoarTech, a military education contractor that originated at University of Michigan's AI Laboratory.[78] In 2012 Epic launched the Unreal Government Network, a collaboration with former *AA* developers, to develop an expedited cost and licensing system for government and military contracts.[79]

The story of Unreal and *America's Army* serves as a nexus point for understanding the coproduced role of games, software, and broader legal and institutional infrastructures. *AA* represents both the military's embrace of and rejection of the cultures and mechanics of 1990s first-person shooters: the US Army needed the affective ludic and graphical elements of *Quake* and *Unreal*, but needed them threaded through their self-understanding of a rationalistic and systematic military system, populated by disciplined and committed soldiers. On the other side of the relationship, Epic and the games industry writ large needed money—the kinds of windfall money that can be found only in ongoing licensed military-government contracts—and a broader cultural legitimacy in the wake of the moral panic around games in the 1990s. Game companies, and Epic particularly, benefited from a broadened public understanding of the roles that the games industry could play in society.

As we turn to the remainder of this book, which highlights more the gendered, raced, and queered productions of knowledge with and through Unreal, it is important to restate that the infrastructural entangling of game engine and the militarized state produces gendered effects as well. Unreal and the US Army's response to the moral panic of violent video-games in the 1990s was not to argue that games did not influence their players, nor was it to socially neuter the games industry. Rather, games were reconfigured as a co-participant in the matter of proper, state-sanctioned gendering. Games and gaming technologies had the potential to transform boys into proper men: not the reckless and hypermasculine Rambo, but the coolly computational and analytic soldier. Following Sara Ahmed, we could say that a broader societal goal of Unreal and *AA* was to enact a mass "straightening"[80] of young men. Straighten up their bodies and their approach to conflict and they become an ideal soldier for the new wars of the twenty-first century. Straighten up their understandings of proper male socialization and they become culture warriors, ready to reject the parodic and homoerotic portrayals of the action hero that flourished during the Reagan era.[81]

To the state, then, games and game developers become reconfigured from purveyors of senseless violence into partners in the war against terror, collaborators with university-affiliated laboratories and think tanks, and instruments for instilling discipline, honor—and proper straight masculinity too—in children and teens. Unreal was not just an engine, and Epic Games was not just a company—they were purveyors of ideal masculinity; they were citizen-soldiers.

Queering Orientation and Agency

Whenever I teach Unreal, there is an inevitable moment in the semester when a student will turn their head to stare at their screen sideways. Their brow furrows, and I see them quickly press the "undo" hotkeys on their keyboards. A couple of mouse clicks are followed by another head tilt and undo press. Again. And again. Finally, a hand raise.

When I walk over to the student's computer I see a 3D asset, created in a separate modeling software package, which has been freshly imported into Unreal. The object—for the sake of this chapter, let's say a table—is on its side in a fetal position on Unreal's world grid. No matter how many times the student reimports it, the table still lies askew. Worse, *every* other object the student imports *also* appears on its side—and no other student's project has a similar problem. Unreal, it seems, has it out for them.[1]

The student pulls up their model in its original home, the 3D modeling program Autodesk Maya. The table stands there, resolute, on its four legs. The student the next seat over has modeled her own table in a different program, McNeel Rhinoceros (Rhino). Her own version of the table stands tall in both Rhino and Unreal, oriented properly despite its translation across programs. She looks at her fellow student's sideways table and shrugs: "Mine just works."

With Unreal, Maya, and Rhino now open across multiple screens, I point both students to the lower left corner of each software's "perspective" viewports. This is the interface element that displays the three-dimensional scenes with appropriate dimensional scaling, approximating what the scene would look like in "real-world" space. In the corners of those viewports lies a tiny multicolored figure—rendered as a ghostly cube, a series of perpendicular lines, or a spherical gumball—that orients users to the Cartesian space of the software's design world. These "gizmos" all conform to the broadly accepted color conventions of the medium. The X, Y, and Z dimensional axes are respectively rendered in red, green, and blue hues. As the students compare the three windows, they notice that the colors don't quite match up. In Rhino and Unreal, the gizmo extends a blue vector toward the top of the 3D scene—the Z axis is pointed up. In Maya, a green line, the Y axis, is the vertical spine, while the blue Z axis points outward, along the ground, into depth space and away from the viewer. The three different software packages have two fundamentally different orientations of user space.

Without taking care in exporting from Maya or importing into Unreal, Unreal will directly reference Maya's spatial coordinates—the numerical values of X, Y, and Z—for the table when rendering the object in Unreal's coordinate grid. Unreal has no understanding of a table and its proper orientation relative to a floor or a sitter. It only recognizes the array of three-point coordinates that represents the location of each vertex in the model's polygonal mesh. Since Z and Y represent different spatial axes in Unreal and Maya (each, inversely, "up" or "out"), directly porting one coordinate system into the other will result in vertices along Maya's Y axis (up) rendered along Unreal's Y axis (out). To the viewer, the table is pivoted on its side when moved from one software to another.

This a relatively easy fix—a user could simply use Unreal's "Rotate" tool to reorient the table upright. However, they would have to do this rotation for every object imported into the scene. The additional rotational math on the object could lead to unexpected results later, such as when applying physics or texture mapping to the table. The better solution is to handle this spatial discrepancy at the time of import. If the user indicates to Unreal that it is importing an object from a "Y-up" software, the import function will transpose that object's Y and Z coordinate data, leading to a "clean" transliteration from Maya to Unreal that allows the object to behave as a typical user might expect. The table will emerge upright.

The student checks a single box in Unreal's import settings, and upon reimport, the table works as expected. The next exasperated question that I get is, understandably, "Why aren't these software packages all the same?"

This chapter explores that question and its implications for the relations among digital space, orientation, knowledge, and the body. I argue that 3D visualization programs—ranging from game engines like Unreal to architectural and engineering CAD programs—use 3D space to epis-temically and industrially "orient" the user. Unreal and other forms of 3D modeling and animation software produce a doubly oriented body. First, the body is oriented epistemically, by aligning the user's understanding of space with that of industry and labor. Different industries, however, have different desired spatial orientations of their workers. In order to "succeed" in industry, workers must first align their bodies and minds with that of the factory floor, whether that factory floor be a literal machine shop or the virtual factories of game development. They must learn to see their spatial conditions of labor as the natural and normative way of navi-gating the world. Second, the body is oriented through software proxies of the ideal body within the interface itself. In the case of Unreal, the ideal game developer's orientation of space can be traced back to first-person shooter gaming communities in the 1990s and their experiments with "optimal" keyboard and mouse-based interactions in 3D space. Rational optimization and experimental playfulness become entangled, a quality leveraged by Unreal to integrate game engines into more "serious" indus-tries such as the automotive and architectural sectors.

Unreal's orientations thus configure and reconfigure laborers' under-standings of space and of their role in broader networks of production and industry. Here Unreal shares similar kinds of pedagogical qualities with the games produced through it. For example, Brendan Keogh traces how games train players in embodied literacy—the bridging of bodily action with ludic and representational action, or the capacity to simul-taneously occupy both physical space and ludo-narrative space.[2] Citing James Ash, Keogh argues that games attune us to their embodied and nar-rative worlds.[3] As Keogh highlights, when an in-game character asks the player to "press F1 to open your inventory,"[4] not only are we trained how to use our hands and the keyboard to activate a certain action, we are also trained how to mingle diegetic and non-diegetic prompts. Though spoken by a character within the story of the game, the call to press a button on our keyboard is not a moment of narrative disjuncture that breaks the "fourth wall." It is instead a teaching moment to unite our physical and virtual bodies. The game cannot be effectively read or played without that unity. We can extend this games analysis to game *engines* as well; to become liter-ate in Unreal is to become attuned to how playful logics and computational logics of the body and space become muddled.

Users are not, however, configured by software alone. Like the case of my students above, laborers are oriented through massively distributed educational systems; everything from university classrooms to online videos and tutorials to community hubs to industry-sponsored outreach and training events. Both Unreal's epistemic framework and bodily expectations become distributed across time and space, and across technologies and educators. Unreal's orienting of users, however, is certainly not uniformly experienced or adopted. Users shift back and forth across embodied and epistemic software norms, leading to moments of experimentation, play, breakdown, failure, and productive friction with ludic space.

This chapter examines three intersecting pedagogical moments that orient or disorient Unreal's users to their bodies and their labor. First, through Dylan Mulvey and Sara Ahmed, the chapter sets the conceptual groundwork for how software practices embed normative understandings of the body into their interfaces, and why those interface methods play a central role in shaping the user's engagement with digital space. This shaping goes beyond considerations of ergonomics and user experience and toward the epistemic, to how users come to know 3D space and their bodily relationship to it. Second, the chapter moves into moments of user pedagogy, and how Unreal's interface and tutorials foreground the body and kinematics of a 1990s FPS player, Dennis "Thresh" Fong. Thresh's popularization of the WASD keyboard-and-mouse interface among shooter players in the 1990s has become a standard interface configuration throughout gaming. WASD is an awkward fit with many CAD and modeling programs, due to their splitting of 3D space into embodied versus mathematically optimized viewports. To bridge this gap, Unreal's pedagogical materials encourage users to playfully pivot their understanding of 3D space into a more gamelike one, and to orient themselves to that new understanding of 3D space by imagining themselves as playing a videogame. In order to successfully orient themselves to Unreal, users must align their own bodies with that of Thresh's. Finally, this chapter returns to the Z axis as an orienting figure, to explore how broader cross-disciplinary educational contexts use and abstract the human body in order to orient their students to 3D space. This is often done through "handedness," or by encouraging the user to use the metaphor of their own bodies' bilateral symmetry to properly align themselves with 2D and 3D space. These handed "rules of thumb" conflict when students have to transition between ludic and engineering orientations of space, leading to conflicting relationships with their own bodies and how they interact in space. Thus, even when neither avatars nor direct user interfaces are onscreen, the body and our relationships to it are ever present, ever-contested within digital space.

My students' experiences with Unreal's Z-axis are certainly not unique; their frustrations are so common in the games and graphics industry that they are often made points of fun (see figure 2.1). Apocryphal tales of the axis have wound through the game development community over the past twenty years. One commonly accepted story reinforces the role of labor and industry in orienting the user to their object of work: modeling software that presumes an animation use case—that the users will create motion graphics for a two-dimensional screen—and will require a Z-out/Y-up orientation; the Z axis operates as the user's eyeline, extending "through" the screen to guide perspective distance scaling. Animation software thus mimics the "Albertian window" and classical Western forms of perspectival drawing,[5] including the common mathematical translation of the window to a two-dimensional, XY Cartesian coordinate grid. Conversely, modeling software that presumes an architectural or manufacturing use case will feature a Z-up/Y-out orientation. The Z axis still serves as a stand-in for the user's eyeline, but the user's body is hunched over a drafting table, looking down onto floorplans and manufacturing schematics. Again, the XY Cartesian coordinate grid serves as a default vehicle for translating spatial experience into mathematizable space. However, rather than mapping a window, the XY grid maps the floors of homes and factories.

There is at least some truth to this tale about gaming's divergent axes. Despite their similar user interfaces and toolsets—and despite an overlapping developmental genealogy—3D modeling software developed for gaming/animation and those developed for manufacturing have starkly distinct mathematical and ontological orientations. Each derives from assumptions about the transmigration of content created within them. 3D models rarely stay confined to the programs used to create them. They are assets, always designed to serve a broader organizational, institutional, or material whole. 3D models are built to move into gaming worlds, where the laws of physics are often warped in service of compelling and entertaining gameplay.[6] They enter pre-rendered animation, where models become twisted and contorted in order to meet directorial needs on a frame-by-frame basis. They also are brought into manufacturing, where physical precision is so important that *imprecision*—micro faults and misplacements that exist on any given factory floor—must be preemptively accounted for from within modeling software. These and other uses demand we reverse engineer modeling software and shift the software's default assumptions about what is "important" in any given

Freya Holmér
@FreyaHolmer

...

okay WHO STOLE MY GIZMO

SOMEONE took it to the kitchen, and then had the GALL to place it Z up

7:42 AM · Sep 28, 2022 · Twitter for Android

2.1 Tweet by Freya Holmér (@FreyaHolmer) making a joke about the Z-axis orientation on their 3D printed gizmos (the blue axis, typically corresponding to "Z," is facing up) (https://twitter.com/FreyaHolmer/status/1575088463891771392). Reprinted with the permission of Freya Holmér. Copyright © Freya Holmér 2022.

model—physical accuracy? rendering speed? mesh density? The Z axis, too, of any given modeling program must align in space and time with a model's larger destiny.

The material and institutional networks that enact 3D software are so different as to loosely spread these programs across a genre spectrum. At one end are programs, commonly grouped together as "3D graphics" applications, which orient toward animation and games. They often feature Y-up world spaces and prioritize aesthetic flexibility and mesh efficiency, typically at the expense of physical replicability. At the other end are programs lumped together as computer-aided design/computer-aided manufacturing (CAD/CAM, or simply CAD).[7] CAD software favors physical construction and accurate physical simulations, including material stress and fracture testing. In this genre of software, the vertical Z axis corresponds to the orientation of manufacturing equipment, which ranges in scale from large mechanical arms in a Toyota factory[8] to the winching gears on a 3D printer. Programs like Rhino fall toward the middle of this software axis and have less predictable Z orientations.

Epic CEO and Unreal's original programmer Tim Sweeney himself adds weight to the bodily-institutional explanation for Unreal's Z axis. In a conversation across Twitter and Epic's Unreal Community Forums, Sweeney confirmed that the world space orientation for Unreal was taken from the software package 3DS Max, a prominent 3D modeling program.[9] In the early 1990s, during Unreal's initial development, 3DS Max (then known as 3D Studio) was among the more popular modeling programs used by the animation and games industry, due to a lack of alternatives and 3D Studio's robust (for the time) mesh editing tools. 3D Studio was designed as a catchall tool for more visually oriented graphics work, including animation and architecture. It modeled itself on architecture's Z-up world. *Unreal's* (the game) modelers worked primarily in 3D Studio, leading to Unreal (the engine) inheriting architecture's axes. Not until the late 1990s would Maya—3D software specifically designed for animation and gaming—supplant 3DS Max as the major industry standard, bringing with it Y-up as animation's default orientation. By this time, Unreal's core mathematics were already established; its core spatial orientation was transformed into a living archeology of a prior generation of game development. It is also probable, though impossible to confirm, that Sweeney's education as a mechanical engineer—a disciplinary paradigm dominated by a Z-up world—and not as an artist or animator, influenced his coordinate programming of the original Unreal.

The body and its relations with labor, institutions, and infrastructures, then, do play core roles in the spatial orientations of the Unreal Engine and 3D software, whether that body be human or machine. However, these interrelations tell a more complicated story than one simply about industry standards. From a user's perspective, Unreal's bodies and spaces are always in constant reconfiguration and realignment. To produce a deliverable product through Unreal, a design team must negotiate an interrelated chain (or "pipeline") of spatial translations and orientations, each link designed to make the gameworld sensible to different bodies and infrastructures. Like the translation of a 3D model to the factory floor, each overlapping digital construction of space (world space, object space, screen space) indicates a different occupied subject position in both space and time during the development, rendering, and (in some cases) manufacturing pipeline. To use Unreal is to become entangled within its multiple orientations and spaces. Further, as Unreal's role in the games industry has ebbed and flowed over the past three decades, its spaces, orientations, and operations have themselves gradually accrued ontological sediment: Unreal retains core code architectures and the bodily norms of play from gaming's past, is reconfigured by new industry and material standards in the present, and contains experimental features that attempt to both predict and guide game development's future. Not only are developers forced to navigate embodied orientations across a rendering pipeline, they also travel through time, as different spatial calculations embodying Unreal's layered strata of game design's past, present, and future.

Within the spatial world of Unreal, the XYZ coordinate system and the embodiment of the user operate as what Dylan Mulvin has called "proxies"—figures, objects, and narratives that "stand in" for the real world during moments of scientific practice or regulatory decision-making.[10] Through their representative power, proxies produce new realities. They shape future scientific and legal work, as well as bind together knowledge workers around common figures and myths. Mulvin centers his analysis on embodied proxies that are designed to stand in for human labor and presence during abstracted technical and managerial processes. In so doing, Mulvin argues that these human-delegate proxies share the following qualities:

> *Proxies are bodily*: this is visible in the work of measurement and training that relies on finely tuned embodied and relational practices.
>
> *Proxies are both sticky and permeable*: though proxies are built as laborsaving devices to stand in for worldly phenomena, they inevitably carry and leave traces of their cultural milieus and the places where they've traveled.

Proxies rely on suspended disbelief: the scientific and technical expertise underlying them is formed and repeated through scenes of performance, where participants must act as if a stand-in were the real thing for the purposes of getting work done.[11]

We can already see traces of how the Z axis operates as a proxy, following Mulvin's tripartite definition. Working with Z in Unreal, and in 3D modeling more broadly, depends on disciplinary training that allows a user to relate their work to the broader conditions of industry, accept the implicit values and orientations built in to Unreal's construction of space, and simultaneously believe that Unreal's spatial configurations are computational simulacra[12] and visual, mimetic techniques of capturing of the physical world. Further, Mulvin argues that proxies operate both epistemically and communally. Insider stories and humor—like Sweeney's feeding into the "animators=Z-out, architects=Z-up" mythos and the visual humor of Z axis wars—highlight how the Z axis functions as a proxy tool for community formation. "[Like] inside jokes, there is an affective dimension to the cultural work of proxies," Mulvin notes, "we recognize others through their recognition of our shared references."[13] Proxies cross and complicate material, cultural, and institutional boundaries. Connecting the body to the Z axis—and spatial orientation more broadly—affects how games and platform studies can conceive of virtual embodiment. Games studies scholars have performed extensive analyses of the role of the bodily avatar in game space, its capacity to represent and distort the bodily narratives, its material and cultural constructions, and its connections to assumptions and standards of the body holding the controller. Orientations-as-proxy highlight how the body and its assumed activity, as well as the game controllers and other methods of playfully interfacing with digital space, are distributed and ever present in game spaces, even when there is no avatar or non-player character in sight.

My primary formulation of orientation comes from philosopher Sara Ahmed, who centers embodied orientation in her project of queer phenomenology. For Ahmed, queer orientations include, but extend beyond, sexual orientation. We come to know and to produce both the body and our own subjectivities through our relations in space; the objects to which we "reach out," and the bodies and minds we use to reach. Each "impress" on one another, participating in a dance of mutual shaping.[14]

Ahmed argues that our bodies, our identities, and our subjectivities are produced through our orientations in-and-of space. Ahmed threads the phenomenological work of Kant and Merleau-Ponty through feminist and queer theory, suggesting our bodily and spatial experiences are as founded in epistemic structures and affective yearnings as they are in the material world. Reflecting the affective sensemaking of 3D space experienced by my students at the beginning of the chapter, Ahmed speaks to her own identity, as oriented around and by her home writing table:

> It is here I will gather my thoughts. It is here that I will write, and even write about writing. This book is written on different writing tables, which orient me in different ways or which come to "matter" as effects of different orientations. . . . How important it is, especially for women, to claim that space, to take up that space through what one does with one's body.[15]

Writing and knowledge practices, for Ahmed, remain entangled with their sites of production. The intimacy of being oriented, of feeling "at home"— as though you have the agency to take up your space—is what allows writing to flow. Further, Ahmed's interest in bodily orientation helps reconnect the body to itself. While film and screen phenomenology has long understood the body through the eye—that our location within and orientation to visual media can be understood through our situated gaze—Ahmed returns the rest of the body to the equation. This is done not only through a recognition of the material impressions made on the body by objects and spaces, but also through "handedness," as in being left-handed or right-handed. Our demarcations of "left" and "right" in space reflect our (normatively assumed) bilateral symmetry, and how we "reach out" to how we navigate and understand our local space shapes core parts of our subjectivity.[16] As this chapter explores, the apocryphal stories of the animation-architecture split in Z fail to take into account how hands act as proxies in coordinate space, both in terms of determining axis directions and in terms of labor.

While Ahmed's is a philosophical project, in that it brings queer perspectives to bear upon the mapping of the body in its relation to space, it is first a political one. Ahmed notes that the spatial forces of orientation affect different bodies and subjects differently, particularly so for queer and raced subjects. Cultural and bodily practices work to naturalize hegemonic constructions of space: white and straight subjects occupy space in ways they are "supposed" to, and are oriented toward the correct bodies and desires. So too for the world's production of some bodies as abled and others not, whose bodies are configured as productively normal and whose are not. As Ahmed describes it, normative spaces abhor slants: those whose bodies and actions don't fit, such as queer subjects, are those who have "failed orientation."[17] It can be dangerous to not adhere to the spatial standard; spaces both work to straighten bodies and work for straightened bodies. They demand a kind of embodied and ontological conformity, while also providing those who conform the capacity to better exist within and extend through those spaces.

It would be irresponsible to say that the kinds of embodied and disciplinary straightening employed by the Unreal apparatus are of the kind or scale enforced every day on queer, nonwhite, and disabled persons. However, bringing phenomenological theories grounded in queer perspectives to bear upon game engines allows us to highlight how moments of disorientation, breakage, and alienation also serves as productive and engaging "teaching" moments. In the case of my students, the tilted table disrupts their orientations of virtual game space. For some, this leads to a deeper understanding of the virtual world systems they inhabit, opening new kinds of creative possibilities for playing with and against their tools of production. For others, it leads to an alienating disorientation—the fear of punishment by a computational system whose logics they cannot fully glean. Further, though this chapter does not deeply engage with questions of marginalized subjectivities, its reading of Unreal's enactment of spatial, embodied, and mathematical orientation resurfaces throughout the remainder of the book. Where bodies reside, how they are distributed, and the logics that orient Unreal users "how to see" are all imbricated with gender and race and produce virtual bodies that must conform with normative, white masculine epistemic space.

Where to Start: Synthesizing Play and Production through the Body

For all their tool tips, game engines and other 3D visualization software can be overwhelmingly disorienting for new users. Opening a default Unreal 4 scene for the first time, for example, presents users with a prebuilt scene of a table and chairs, alongside multiple panels and windows featuring software plug-ins, asset folders, VFX generators, and internal data visualization tools. Disorientation-through-scale is coupled with disorientation-through-scope; not all tools that game engines offer are meant for every user or every discipline. The potential multiplicities of game engine and user capacities has become even more evident since the early 2020s, when companies like Epic and Unity began "platformizing"[18] in earnest. They expanded their core mission from just game development toward operating as a crosscutting 3D and digital simulation tool for multiple industries, including entertainment, cinema, architecture, automotive design, urban design, and crowd simulation. Unity has chosen a multi-software approach, similar to that of Adobe or Autodesk, in which developers pick and choose from an ecosystem of interconnected applications. Conversely, Epic has chosen to offer all potential users a single software package—Unreal—and make that package as reconfigurable and customizable as possible. Unreal's power derives from the user's ability to carve agential cuts[19] through the software, picking and choosing from various packages to import. Unreal users assemble their own Unreal milieu through a combination of their role in the production pipeline (often) within the context of a broader game development organization or business. The first steps of working with contemporary versions of Unreal occur outside of the software itself.

To attract new users and industries, Epic takes multimodal approaches to orienting the user. These approaches are threaded across social, material, and textual milieus. They include educational outreach campaigns and multiday in-person and online workshops, and disciplinary presets and configurations within Unreal that will auto-import specific technical extensions and auto-populate default scenes with activity-specific actors and settings. Epic also produces a vast array of online documentation and video tutorials, most of which are regularly updated when new features or versions of the engine are rolled out. Following Steve Woolgar, we can understand these tutorials effectively as extensions of the Unreal Engine itself.[20] They act to configure new engine users, in terms of their capacities to act within Unreal, in terms of producing expectations and narratives about how the engine is supposed to work and what the user's bodily and labor relationship to the engine is. Further, Epic's unique status as both a consumer-oriented tool developer and game developer allows them to bring the hybridization of play and production to bear in orienting their users.

Epic's official "Your First Hour in Unreal" tutorial for Unreal 5, produced and narrated by Epic instructor Mathew Wadstein, begins not with the Unreal interface, but with the Epic Games Store.[21] The Epic Store is akin to a blend of consumer e-stores like Google Play and the Apple App Store. It also resembles creative software ecosystem launch hubs, such as the Unity Hub, the Adobe Creative Cloud Desktop Launcher, and the Autodesk Launcher. The Epic Games Store provides users with access to new games and applications, and add-ons to both, in the form of mods, downloadable content, extensions, and plug-ins. Meanwhile, it serves as the launching portal for both games and creative tools. *Fortnite* and the Unreal Engine, for example, live next to one another in the Epic Games Store, reinforcing Epic's broader strategy of blurring the line between play space and production space.

Unreal's software continues to orient the user to a synthesis of ludic and production space. After navigating through the Epic Games Store to manage Unreal version installations, Wadstein brings his audience into the formal bounds of the engine through a showing of a prebuilt third-person game demo scene. User experience and viewpoint is the first thing addressed. Unreal's viewport dominates the software's visual frame and serves as the primary interface for designing Unreal's gameworlds. Wadstein notes how the Unreal designer exists as a camera within Unreal space. After pivoting the camera around its origin point—the "center of gravity" to which an object in digital space is anchored—Wadstein walks the designer through navigating in space: "If you've ever used a first-person or third-person game, you may be familiar with the WASD keys for movement."[22] The tutorial's camera shifts around the space, as Wadstein's fingers manipulating an unseen and unheard mouse and keyboard, present just outside of screen capture.

The first minute of the "First Hour" Unreal tutorials provide a glimpse into the most important part of learning a game engine: constructing how to imagine oneself in the software's space, and how to orient one's body to it (see figure 2.2.). Unreal's viewport isn't a neutral representation of a gameworld-in-construction. Rather, it's a "view from somewhere," grounded in a body, as a digital marker in memory that mimics a cinematic eyeline. It is a continuation of a long history of player experimentation

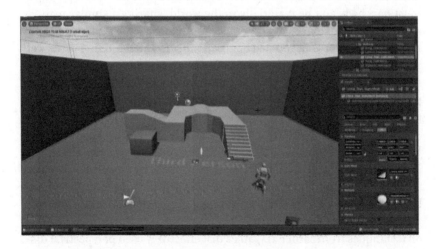

2.2 Screenshot of the opening minutes of "Your First Hour in Unreal," showing the Unreal viewport, navigational systems, and the difference between world space and object space (https://dev.epicgames.com/community/learning/courses/ZpX/your-first-hour-in-unreal-engine-5-0/OEa/unreal-engine-creating-your-first-project).

with first-person interactive play, always entangled with a body behind the keyboard and mouse.

Cinematically, we could interpret the viewport as quite literally collapsing the cinematic apparatus with the viewing subject. It allows a virtual camera—and its attendant qualities such as focal length and light exposure control—to stand in for the designer, enabling their movement throughout a space. This interpretation would be thin, however, without the incorporation of embodied and historical practices. Incorporating WASD navigation—the control combination that typically places the left hand on the W, A, S, and D keys on an Anglo-QWERTY keyboard, controlling movement, and the right on a mouse, controlling the direction of a camera—point to an intent to orient the designer's relationship to Unreal as a player is oriented to a gameworld. Additionally, this ludic production represents an active choice to break from and later infiltrate the spatial and disciplinary bodies of prior CAD software. Through the platforming of ludic interfacing with production software, Unreal shapes how designers situate themselves and their labor (and that of other bodies) within contemporary 3D space. As Vivian Sobchack has contended, cinema works only while connected to a body and situated in physical-cultural-epistemic space. In other words, we understand the film itself as having a kind of vision, a capacity to view, prehend, and shape the audience. "This act of viewing," Sobchack argues, "implicates both *embodied, situated* existence and a *material* world; for to see and be seen, the viewing subject must be a body and be materially in the world, sharing a similar manner and matter of existence with other viewing subjects."[23] The viewer's experience in a theater is negotiated between the film and the audience, as well as by the material conditions of existing as a body among others within a theater space. Similarly, being oriented by Unreal also incorporates the practices and histories of postures, finger taps, and hand crossovers that coproduced Unreal's spatial interface.

The practice of WASD movement arguably extends back to the 1970s. However, it was popularized by competitive *Quake* player Dennis "Thresh" Fong during the golden age of PC first-person shooter gaming,[24] a golden age that of course included the original *Unreal*. Early-1990s "2.5D" shooters, like Id's *Wolfenstein 3D* and *Doom*, used two-dimensional maps to generate 3D levels. They rendered flat tiles perpendicular to the "floor" map, drawing on techniques from earlier 2D games that effectively used perspectival distortion to imply depth space.[25] One of the downsides to this technique was that the player could rotate the virtual camera only along the vertical axis—turning to the left and to the right. The popularization of 3D, full-motion games like *Quake* brought the capacity for "free look," or the divestment of the virtual camera from a single rotational axis, allowing the player to rotate the camera spherically around a single point of origin. Free look also separated the player's movement from the player's vision; a player character could be instructed to move to the left or the right, while the camera could be held straight, introducing new movement possibilities such as "strafing"—moving sideways while looking forward.

The new combination of independently moving both the player-character and the player-camera led to an explosion in different keyboard/mouse/trackball setups ("configs") in competitive play. Players hoped their custom configs would give them an embodied edge over their opponents. Thresh credited his *Quake* config to playing against his brother, who broke the player bases' keyboard-only conventions by using a trackball to move the camera. Thresh's incorporation of the mouse into his *Quake* config, using his right hand on the mouse to control the camera and his left hand on the WASD keys to form an "inverted-T" four-directional control axis, greatly improved his play. His media presence and popularity among *Quake* players had an outsized impact on the mass adoption of his config. By the late 1990s, FPS games such as *Quake 2* and *Half-Life* would include WASD as one of several preset configs players could choose from, and *Daikatana* adopted WASD as its default control scheme. By the mid-2000s the control scheme had migrated outside of the FPS genre; games journalist Tyler Wilde argues that WASD as the default control scheme in 2004's successful massively multiplayer role-playing game (MMORPG) *World of Warcraft* concretized the config as gaming's assumed navigation system.[26]

Thresh's personal style of keyboard navigation would slowly become naturalized as the assumed default bodily orientation for game developers as well. WASD navigation first appeared in the Unreal Engine with 2006's Unreal 3/Unreal Dev Kit (UE3/UDK). It was introduced as an optional navigational scheme, not the default setting; UE3/UDK retained the original Unreal Engine's mouse-centered navigational system. Users could left click and drag to pan the virtual editor camera in space, right click and drag to rotate the camera around its free-look origin point, and hold both mouse buttons and drag to raise and lower the camera vertically. The older mouse-oriented navigational control was suited for Unreal's quad-plane viewport—a standard visual setup across animation, CAD, and modeling programs that features four windows aligned in a two-by-two grid. Three of these windows typically represent orthogonal viewpoints (or "wireframe") blueprint-like views from the top, side, and front of an object that ignore perspectival distortion. While not visually appealing, orthogonal viewports are useful working spaces for constructing multidimensional objects, as they can ensure that the edges and vertices of 3D models are

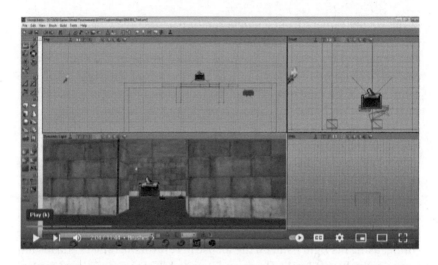

2.3 Screenshot of a tutorial of the Unreal 2 Editor, which features the quad-plane (three wireframe orthogonal views and a single rendered perspective view) default user interface, in contrast with UE4 and UE5's synthesis of ludic space as both input and output (as seen in figure 2.2) (https://www.youtube.com/watch?v=elgH38wgBZU&t=133s).

correctly aligning in space (see figure 2.3). Orthogonal viewports are so useful in engineering and architecture software that the fourth plane—the "perspective" plane that features the capacity for full graphical coloring and shading, as well as appropriate perspectival and Z-axis distortion—is often treated more as a presentation plane than a working plane.[27] In other words, the perspectival plane becomes constructed as the "final" window through which the results of CAD work can be made translatable to clients and managers. The orthogonal, abstracted planes remain the meaningful fields of vision for engineers and architects.

At the time that UE3/UDK incorporated WASD, contemporary tutorial videos and documentation noted the new control scheme but described it as a secondary or specialized navigational mechanic. It was primarily seen as useful for game modders who first crafted levels for 1998's *Half-Life*. Its packaged level editor/builder—sequentially named "The Forge," "World-craft," and, most popularly, the "Hammer Source Engine," depending on what version of the editor one was working with—used *Half-Life*'s WASD config as the default engine navigation system.

WASD (and subsequently, Thresh's body) would fully become Unreal's standard with UE4's release in 2014. Not coincidental was UE4's total divergence of Unreal's user interface away from the quad-plane standards set by UE1, 2, and 3 and toward a single-plane viewport. The single plane maximizes the perspective view in the interface while transforming it into the primary workspace—a major deviation from both past and present animation and CAD standards. Notably, Unreal's viewport is real-time rendered, and not a pre-rendered visualization. The perspective viewports of animation software such as Maya provide only a rough estimate of the visual end product of artists' work. Not only must the elements in the viewport go through the computationally expensive and time-intensive rendering process to process the artists' work, it is also generally assumed that post-rendered work will be adjusted later, in a longer chain of film editing and postproduction software. Yet Unreal's default perspective viewport shows the final product. The press of a couple of buttons ensures that the scene's lighting is properly calculated; developer controls and other engine content are temporary hidden in the viewport. What the developer sees is what the player will see. The entire user interface, post-UE4, is the future game itself.

This dual transition in both visual and embodied navigation is worth dwelling on, I argue, as it reflects a broader historical and epistemic shift in game development software. As game engine developers shift toward multi-industry platformization, the engines themselves are shifting to produce more gamelike ludic action and interfaces. On its face this may seem counterintuitive; if game engines want to attract more industries into their platforms, why shift *away from*, rather than *toward*, those industry standards and practices? Yet the synthesis of ludic and production space ultimately represents a double win for Epic. Returning to Keogh's and Ash's analyses of the attunement of play and bodies in games,[28] this synthesis invites players into the design and development space by aligning software with their attuned, embodied expectations of interaction in virtual space and attunes non-gamers and new industries to a reorientation of their relationship with their labor.

Bruno Latour notes that the transformations of bodies and spaces into data and text serve as the foundations for epistemic alliances—the capacity to enroll them in contests of interpretation and validity.[29] Latour characterizes scientific and technological practice as agonistic, advancing not through linear progress and breakthroughs but through competition and contestation, the victors of which can enroll more favorable and reliable human and nonhuman allies. "My contention is that writing and imaging cannot by themselves explain the changes in our scientific societies," Latour writes, "except insofar as *they help to make this agonistic situation more favorable*."[30]

Unreal's ludic spatial navigation and orientation produces such allies who can be enrolled in reorienting disciplinary ways of understanding production and visualization processes. The goal for companies like Epic and Unity is not for non-game developers to ask, "How can this game engine do things my CAD software already does?" Rather, their goals are for them to ask, "How would incorporating gaming and play change my workflow? How might it allow me to imagine my product otherwise?"

Early uses of the engine in engineering and architecture leveraged Unreal as an aesthetic add-on. Architectural firms, for example, could present their clients with a game controller to do virtual walkthroughs of their designed spaces, which offered a sense of embodied place.[31] Within engineering, the automotive industry used Unreal similarly, to produce client visualizations and commercial hype generators. Audi, for example, worked extensively with Epic to use Unreal to produce a "virtual show-room," which resulted in kiosks at thousands of high-end car dealerships featuring gamelike environments for driving digital toy cars.[32]

These first uses, while flashy, didn't really push either Unreal Engine or non-game production into new ludic spaces. Rather, they remediated prior forms of play, with a goal to "keep the same production process but add a toy at the end for clients and customers."[33] However, as the incorporation of these toys into production continued, engineers and architects became used to them in their professional spaces. New experimental paradigms emerged that more fully engaged with ludic activity. Unreal's real-time rendering, for example, has allowed architects to rethink their client presentations. Rather than treating client meetings as sales pitches and report-outs, meetings could serve as miniature advanced-stage design charrettes. Clients and designers can now modify virtual spaces on the fly; rather than needing to reschedule meetings to show new renderings, firms can have client live sessions in which new colors, objects, and layouts are experimented with in real time. The automotive industry has gone even further, designing new software that directly interface between Unreal and their production pipeline to provide gamelike collaborative engineering environments. German car manufacturer Daimler AG's modeling and development wing, for example, has created UberEngine—an online VR conferencing plug-in for Unreal.[34] UberEngine allows Daimler engineers to import their CAD models into an Unreal scene and create a virtual mock-up of a car together. Their marketing team has labeled it a "Skype for 3D."[35]

None of this is to guarantee that Unreal—or any game engine, for that matter—will become the future of automotive manufacturing or architectural practice. What these software packages do show, though, is an increasing synthesis of play space and workspace, such as that facilitated by Unreal's interface design and mediated through Unreal's embodied configurations of play via the keyboard. Through WASD and its particular interface with 3D visualized space, Thresh's body too acts to shepherd disciplines outside of games comfortably into gaming software. This is no small feat; as the next section will show, different industries and workers have strongly visual and embodied understandings of space. This is particularly true in the case of engineering, a field that represents a huge potential source of revenue for game developers should their engines become integrated into engineering CAD workflows. Using gamelike structures to play with these spaces, as Unreal does, serves to reconfigure understandings of what those industry and disciplinary spaces can do, and how engineers and workers come to relate to their own spaces of labor.

Ending Spaces: Where Coordinates and Origins Go

Mark J. P. Wolf, in one of the only pieces of interpretive or historical scholarship found on the Z axis in games, notes that "the Z axis, which is perpendicular to the picture plane and traces the trajectory to and away from the viewer, is not physically present in a two-dimensional plane, so it differs from the x-axis and y-axis in that *it can only be implied in an image*."[36] Restoring depth to an image in a game engine is performed through the borrowing of ancient techniques of scale, shadow, movement, and distortion. The Z axis (here expressed as the eye-line, Z-out formation), unifies two-dimensional inscription and three-dimensional human aesthetic and spatial experience. Z thus actively plays different epistemic, aesthetic, and indexical roles across the game production pipeline. Removing Z allows an image to be rendered to a screen, whether that be the classical imagination of a monitor or stationary screen or, increasingly, the handheld and interactable screens of mobile phones and devices or the aligned stereoscopic lenses of virtual reality headsets. Implying Z, however, is necessary for that rendered image to connect the screen to human perception and experience. Learning how to "properly" use an engine thus involves continually centering and decentering different formations of space and perspective.

Wadstein's notion of orientating the user to Unreal via the performance of play is quite different from software that centers engineering production, despite their shared Z axis. Unreal's tutorials and interface ask that the user align their body within ludic space, both in terms of their WASD control scheme and their visual synthesis of production and play space. Engineering CAD programs, on the other hand, try to move the user *away* from the body as quickly as possible. Drawing from Gary Downey's ethnographic accounts of learning CAD instruction alongside engineering students in higher education,[37] CAD approaches reinforce engineering and computer science's abstracting the body away from the material and toward the mathematical.[38] In this extended quote, Downey notes that he and his engineering students, when first introduced to the software CADAM, experienced a profound sense of disorientation and confusion—until they were introduced to the X and Y coordinate grid at the bottom of the screen:

> After I entered START and then assigned a name to the drawing, CADAM sent back a reassuring picture of two arrows in the middle of the screen. Intersecting at right angles, or 90 degrees, the two arrows informed me that I was positioned. I had place. . . . This space was a world of mathematical agencies. Given the intensive experiences engineering students had with mathematics in their engineering science courses, I was not surprised that movement in CADAM would confront me with configurations of mathematical agencies and, accordingly, a sense of moving through different kinds of mathematical space. . . . The first, and possibly most important, mathematical practice built into the arrows was routine, and students barely noticed. Where I felt a sense of drama, they likely felt the comfort of control. The arrows had identified the famous X-axis and Y-axis of a two-dimensional coordinate system. Not only was I, as user, now in mathematical space, but I was also oriented. I had a right and a left, an up and a down. Any shapes I might build in this space would now occupy positions in relation to one another.[39]

Downey's ethnographic data was collected in the late 1990s, but a quick perusal of contemporary tutorials in engineering CAD software such as NX and AutoCAD demonstrate the same dimensional and abstractive approach. Current and legacy CAD software attune their users to engineering epistemologies. As we can see in Downey's writing, though this attunement and orientation move away from bodily space and toward mathematical space, it is not without affective and embodied dimensions. Downey's experiences with learning CADAM also reinforce the epistemic frame the quad-plane viewport interface implies. CADAM, like early versions of Unreal, treats its orthogonal projections as the most accurate and useful workspaces. Downey even suggests that students learn to see with "three eyes,"[40] each one representing the orthogonal viewpoints of front, side, and top. The software provides comfort through the presence of familiar mathematical concepts and orientations, such as the two-dimensional XY axis. Though users are mentally in a mathematical space, the axes still provide a sense of grounding. Axes offer a way of understanding how objects in this virtual world—including the user's eye and position in space—will come to relate to one another.

Similarly, although the body is abstracted out of view in CAD space, this does not mean that the body isn't otherwise present. Three-dimensional coordinate systems used in simulation and modeling software each express "handedness"—a way of relating the orientation and direction of the system to the body. In games and animation communities, handedness is usually treated as a quirky heuristic to use to quickly identify a software's spatial system. Software coordinates can be either "left-handed" or "right-handed." A right-handed system, generally regarded as more common, mimics the user holding their right hand ("finger gun" style) such that the index finger and thumb form a capital L shape. The middle finger then points inward, toward the body. Which way each finger points determines what direction each axis inherits. In the right-handed orientation, the vertical and horizontal axes are positive moving upward and to the right relative to the origin point, whereas the depth axis is positive along the middle finger, moving inward through the virtual eye/user body. If you make the same L shape with your left hand, the middle finger will extend outward, away from the screen and the user; similarly, the positive depth vector moves away from the screen. This is all further complicated by the Z-debate. A coordinate system has both handedness and either a Y-up or Z-up orientation (the only X-up orientation I have ever found has been for calculating relationships between Earth and outer space at NASA).[41] As documented by digital artist Freya Holmér (see figure 2.4) and scores of complaints on game development forums, the Unreal Engine is the only animation, CAD, or game development software that uses a left-handed and Z-up system, described by Tim Sweeney as an artifact of his being "young and this coordinate system stuff was confusing"[42] when he first wrote the original Unreal. Yet handedness matters.

From a rendering perspective, which directions are positive and negative becomes important for vector math and rendering equations. The "hidden surface problem," wherein a computer must determine what parts of an object are in-sight and out-of-sight of a viewer, became a central concern of computer graphics researchers like Ivan Sutherland throughout the 1960s and 1970s, as Jacob Gaboury traces.[43] One attempt at solving the hidden surface problem is through the Z buffer, which uses the Z axis as proxy for the viewer's eye, projected "outward" through the screen, to determine which polygonal surfaces to render and which to ignore. As Keogh describes the same phenomena, "to perceive a cube is to see some facets of it while others are hidden from view, yet those hidden faces are present in our perception of the cube *as* a cube."[44] The Z axis became the technical cut through this metaphysical Gordian knot; Z not only guided representation of sight, but also constituted the objects themselves as rendered in viewable space. In computer graphics, orientation and creation are inseparable.

2.4   Freya Holmér's (@FreyaHolmer) breakdown of the crossing of Y-up/Z-up and
handedness orientations in popular modeling, animation, development, and play
software. Unreal Engine is the only software to reflect a left-handed, Z-up coordinate
system (https://twitter.com/FreyaHolmer/status/1325557466529210369). Reprinted
with the permission of Freya Holmér. Copyright © Freya Holmér 2020.

From a modeling and game development perspective, the orientation of coordinate space impacts physics simulations, camera directions, and general gameplay scripting. Further, from a broader epistemic perspective, the figure of the hand in a coordinate system's handedness—quite literally how we imagine holding and shaping our hands when we use these heuristics—matter. For animators and game developers, what matters most is the orientation of the coordinate system to the screen, or "screen space." At the end of the day, whether a classical screen, a phone screen, or VR goggles, all of a game developer's work in Unreal's 3D editor, or "world space," must be translated onto screen space's two-dimensional grid of pixels. As such, the "finger gun plus middle finger" configuration of the hand—in addition to intimating a kind of juvenile humor the games industry is known for—helps developers identify one of the most important variables of transforming 3D coordinates into 2D ones: the direction and distance of the depth vector. As the depth vector is the core of the needed vector math, the orientation of Y-up or Z-up in world space doesn't really matter. Regardless, objects in a game's 3D space will always be transformed into a 2D, XY coordinate grid with a visually implied Z depth.

Engineering and physics don't have such flexibility, as they impose a mathematical and embodied rigidity. As Saumya Malviya shows in his own ethnographic work, while still articulating a right-handedness and left-handedness to their coordinate grids, engineers will articulate the hands themselves differently.[45] Here the hands are in a "thumbs-up" position, with the thumb pointed toward the sky (and almost always identified as the Z axis). Making an L shape with your index finger and middle finger can give you a quick sense of the directions of the ground plane, which are often depicted as lines of flight angled at 45 degrees and negative 45 degrees from the user's position, encapsulating them in space. The fingers on the hand, though, are often shown as curled, like a slightly loose thumbs-up, gripping an invisible Z axis. The curl and the thumb together represent the angular momentum of a particle spinning in the direction of the curled hands, which would fly off on the tangent of the thumb.

Like ludic space, WASD, and the playable body used to orient developers in Unreal, the body is also used to orient learners in mathematical software space. In examining how the coordinate system was explained in an engineering classroom, Malviya describes the

> dramatic sense [given] by the teacher by asking the students to consider the classroom itself as a three-dimensional coordinate system and place themselves as the origin of this system, where the origin was nothing but the right-hand corner of the classroom. It emerges

with this move that the orientation of the objects in space and the direction(s) in which they change depends on the presence of an observer. Putting it differently, the judgement of direction or orientation is literally mediated through the bodies of the learning subjects.[46]

Echoing Ahmed's theorization of the oriented body, game engine and CAD designers come to know the space they inhabit through its material and metaphorical relations to their own bodies and subject positions. The coordinate system handedness heuristics—again, quite literally rules of thumb—are not just a mnemonic device for remembering virtual space. They are also ways of entangling the user's body with the epistemological frameworks required for them to work in these coordinate spaces: understanding the screen as a camera with direction, understanding objects as needing to obey the laws of physics, understanding the differing spatial configurations of software interfaces as working spaces or aesthetic spaces.

In each orienting space—Wadstein's tutorials, and Downey's and Malviya's ethnographic data—we see the need to address how the user's body and bodies in the world each relate to and coconstitute one another. For Wadstein and Unreal, game objects represent bodies and fields of ludic activity, elements that can be played on and played with that need to be appropriately positioned to enable gameplay. For Downey's engineering students, objects are themselves end results of the modeling process, made up of shapes and line drawings that move an idea to manufacturing. For Malviya's math students, objects are abstracted entities with calculable properties that are also always entangled with one another. Objects in Unreal space and CAD space thus also serve as both bodily proxy and epistemological frames.

Aside from the aforementioned world space—the orienting mathematics that govern the field of possible placements of objects, events, and game interactions within the entire field of play—individual objects, too, have their own spaces and orientations, points of origin and manipulation. This "object space" also bears the legacies of broader infrastructural and institutional contexts. For example, in describing the spatial ontology of the 3D program Blender, Jara Rocha and Femke Snelting note that the relation of an object to its three-dimensional axis point—the mathematical "center point" of an object in object space—operates as

a constellation of x, y, z vectors that start from a mathematical point of origin, arbitrarily located in relation to a 3D object and automatically starting from x=o, y=o, z=o. Wherever this point is placed, all other planes, vertices and faces become relative to it and organize around it; the point performs as an "origin" for subsequent trans-formations.[47]

In other words, the XYZ gizmo that marks on object's center point is more than a control rig that allows the user to move, rotate, and scale that object in virtual space. The gizmo also reveals that the three vectors of X, Y, and Z describe and constitute objects in 3D spaces. Their abstracted datapoints in computational memory are made renderable and readable by the user only when they are given a central orientation point. The origin point literally serves as the central marker for enabling a data object to be visually rendered and made legible to a viewer. Other algorithms, too, will use this origin point as an object's center of gravity, to more efficiently render physical simulations that need to "look good" to the viewer but need not closely adhere to physical reality. By default, the object's visual and physical simulations will always treat the Z axis as the object's spine, and orient the object "upward" along Z.

In other programs the origin point plays more of a hybrid role. In CAD software, for example, while a single origin point partly determines an object's visual representation (as it does in Unreal), objects simultaneously have multiple origin points dispersed across their bodies. These other origin points determine the placement of machinery on the factory floor, including machine arms, mills, and 3D printers' spatial relationships.[48] Here again the point(s) of origin both describe and constitute the 3D object. In this case, the description translates an object's datapoints to a machine viewer, not a human one. The object is constituted through the wending of plastic and metal through machinic labor. Z is treated as the central bodily axis—the dimension that represents the pushing and pulling of a mechanical arm through infinitesimally narrow layers of an XY grid.

Unreal doesn't typically worry about 3D printers or manufacturing arms, but it is concerned with visual legibility and rendering speed—how objects in the field of view look and how quickly they can be rendered. One of Unreal's most powerful functions is its capacity to rapidly and smoothly mediate the translations between 3D object space, 3D world space, and 2D screen space. Not only do these translations require virtualizing the viewer eyeline to solve the hidden surface problem and imply depth, they also require writing the results of this translation to the screen—working alongside the system CPU and GPU to assemble images pixel-by-pixel on the viewer's screen.

Here again we have conflicting spatial orientations and metaphors, even though the screen is represented by an XY, 2D coordinate plane. Most computational rendering systems will orient the screen left-down, meaning that, as Unreal works with the GPU to write to the screen, it will do so by starting its first pixel, coordinate (0, 0), every frame in the origin point of the screen in the top-left corner. The left-down orientation is inherited from cathode ray tube (CRT) screens, which were designed to shoot rays of light at the screen. CRTs followed the Anglo-centric model of reading, beginning from the top left and moving right-then-down. However, when Unreal works with an OpenGL system—one of the most common graphics rendering pipelines for PCs in the early 2000s through late 2010s—the graphics system inverts the Y axis on its draw calls, assuming an origin point at the bottom-left corner of the screen. The metaphor here is graph paper. When working in math classes, the "natural" plane for work—which assumes positive values in both the X and Y directions—is in the upper-right quadrant. If we were to treat the upper-right quadrant as the "screen" and cut away the other three quadrants, the middle of the graph paper—the paper's own origin point—would be in the bottom left of that screen. Defenders of OpenGL's orientation will thus point to the system's privileging of Western mathematical vision over the Western literary eye as an epistemological strength—a theme this book will return to in its exploration of white photorealism.[49]

Ultimately, as most developers will tell you, aiming for *consistency* is key across orientations and epistemologies in game design and engineering. Developers advocate for picking a handedness and orientation and sticking with it. At this point in computation, the matrix math needed to translate among multiple software orientations in a single rendering or production pipeline is almost always negligible in terms of computing power or rendering speed. As such, what once began as different pragmatic approaches to digital space have now become subsumed into something more cultural—what spatial orientations you use says less about the computational system and more about your positionality within it, your embodied understanding of space, your discipline and background training, and your normative stance on the proper order of literate space. Graphics are a constant struggle between data architectures and visual representations, between their leaky ontological status as "both image and object."[50] Coordinates and interfaces in Unreal are always a kind of dance; pulling their users' bodies through multiple epistemic *and political* orientations. The contested Z axis underpins the larger production of space in the Unreal Engine. It is a constantly shifting and contested formation of bodies, data, disciplinary practices, and hardware. In such a way, the Z axis serves as an archaeological artifact, revealing the disciplinary, epistemic, and political tensions at work over the past sixty years of 3D graphics development and virtual production.

Conclusion

Unreal's spatial orientations act as bodily and disciplinary proxies—containers for and representations of the user's body and embodied interactions with gameworlds. Unreal enacts these embodiments across multiple axes: through the historical kinesthetics of 1990s first-person shooter gameplay, through industrial and labor metaphors of spatial visualization and the body, and through an ever-broadening educational apparatus that includes media, online tutorials and communities, and classrooms in higher education. Configuring users to naturalize orientations of digital space not only helps to lock them into certain software paradigms, it also produces a sense of identity and community. Users come to know themselves and one another through their capacities to operate within digital spaces. Whether you are an architect, engineer, or game developer is in part determined by what kind of software feels comfortable.

"Successfully" orienting in game development space, however, does not necessarily mean an uncritical acceptance of a single normative body. Akin to the queer theoretical frameworks drawn on by Ahmed in her phenomenological project, "failure" to orient, or rejecting normative orientations, can be leveraged in Unreal to creative and productive ends.[51] Queer media theorists and artists such as Legacy Russel, Jenny Sundén, and Arianna Gass, for example, have traced the long legacies of glitch art and other forms of computational "failure" in feminist and queer art practice.[52] Sundén explores historical examples of artists toying with audio skipping and failure in CD players to give voice to the nonhuman performers at play in computational systems—in her case, the literal lasers and spinners used to read and interpret the information encoded into CD-ROMs. Sundén links these performances to trans interventions in feminist theory, particularly through the trans theoretical refusal of political and aesthetic foreclosure. Gass further threads trans theoretical strands directly through experimental play with digital games and inside game engines. For Gass, the Z axis is especially important in queerly resistant forms of game art, giving examples of artists confusing the Z buffer to create aesthetics where polygons and colors seem to pucker through the surface of the screen, and hacking collision detection to force character models to interpenetrate one another, an act replete with both erotic play and subversive commentary on naturalized systems of game physics.

But an Unreal user does not need to be subversive to play across conflicting spatial orientations. In some ways, "mastering" Unreal requires the ability to exist in the unconformable interstices among disciplinary paradigms of space. Technical artists who can work across the rendering pipeline must be able to flow back and forth between Unreal's Z-up worldspace and OpenGL's Y-up screenspace. Unreal's source developers must be able to predict what mathematical transformations of datasets into visual objects will be most efficient for real-time rendering; 3D modelers must understand how the polygonal mesh of their characters will be algorithmically translated through Unreal's control rig. Even my students described at the beginning of the chapter would learn to shift spatial orientations between Rhino and Unreal. Their initial discomforts shifting between the two software packages eventually led to a deeper understanding of both, as the two orientations effectively denaturalize one another, revealing each other's disciplinary logics and embodied metaphors.

Learning when bodies and spaces can be effectively broken and disoriented can also provide visual storytelling tools for artists. Disney animator Tony Bonilla, for example, shows in a March 2023 Twitter thread the ways virtual bodies can be warped for the audience viewer.[53] In a Tweet showing a scene from Disney's *Encanto*, main character Mirabel stares intensely at glowing shards of broken glass, held in front of her face. The virtual camera is angled in a tight shot, visually close to her face, so that to the viewer, she appears to be holding the glass only inches in front of her eyes. As Bonilla shows in an in-engine view of the scene from the side, however, we can see Mirabel's body twisted and stretched wickedly out of proportion. The shards of glass remain in her eyeline, but at a relative distance of three or four feet away, held by eerily elongated arms. She sits in a kind of reverse squat, with her knees bent backward, with the bottom fringes of her dress interpenetrating with her legs and upper skirt.

Bonilla's *Encanto* scene works for the viewer because of their hybrid experience of worldspace and screenspace. The collapse of depth along the Z axis (here, as extended from the viewer's eye through the screen) caused by the virtual camera settings creates the appearance of the glowing glass directly in front of Mirabel's face. Her capacity to "break" her body to take advantage of the camera setting allows for the creation of a cinematic scene that is both fantastical and mundane—nearly impossible to film but appearing as natural as a photograph.

A "successful" orientation to graphical space is thus counterintuitively both an oriented and disoriented one, one that centers a particular normative attunement both to space and to bodies, but that also encourages a rule-breaking playfulness to those spaces and bodies. As chapter 3 traces, the playful approach to the body and to storytelling in Unreal space also demands new forms of literary interpretation, ones that account for the agential entanglements of character and space in gameworlds and engines.

I'm hurrying down a dark corridor of a maze, my rifle clenched high and tight against my chest. Around me float ambient sounds of the machinery and gears that keep the city floating 20,000 feet above the ground, punctuated by our leather boots smacking the rusted iron floor as we run. We had managed to ditch a group of armed men following us, but there's no telling how much time we have before more of them appear. We make a right turn down a hallway: steel double doors, locked.

"Booker," Elizabeth says to me, her blue eyes glancing to a small crack just beneath the door handle. "Here, let me." She extends her hand. I toss her one of the lock-picking sets that I had grabbed off a fallen foe earlier. She's better at picking locks than I am. She brushes a lock of auburn hair out of her face and bites her bottom lip as she sets to work. I turn my back to her and aim my rifle down the hallway, checking for any signs that we had been followed.

Seconds later, I hear giddy excitement in her voice. "Done!"

I take point, ready my rifle, and kick open the now-unlocked door. The darkness of the building is replaced by the blinding light of the sun, and the walls of the hallway give way to open sky. Wind blows around us as we make our way onto the platform. Now all we need to do is find the nearest Sky Line—the metal threads that connect the islands of this floating city, Columbia—and ride it to safety.

A bullet ricochets off the crate next to me. "There he is!" shouts a gruff voice, and four men stream onto the platform. Elizabeth and I split to find cover behind two concrete walls. I stand and return fire; a shot knocks a man off the platform, sending him hurtling toward the ground below. Two men take advantage of my temporary exposure; their bullets rip through my shield and lodge themselves in my left arm. I cringe and retreat behind the concrete.

"Booker, catch!" I hear Elizabeth yell. With a small flash of light, a healing potion appears in her hand. She tosses it to me across the battlefield, and the wounds in my arm disappear as I drain the bottle. I know that summoning items from across dimensions takes a lot out of her; I'll have to buy her a few moments of recovery time. I motion my now-healed arm at two of the men. Black feathers sprout throughout my limb and blow into the air, where they turn into crows. The birds descend to attack the men, pecking and clawing at their faces. While they're distracted, I fire.

I glance at Elizabeth, who has recovered. The remaining man has dug himself in deep behind a stack of crates. His eyes widen when he sees me break cover and expose myself in what appears to be a suicide charge. He leans out with his rifle and prepares to fire.

As he pulls the trigger, blue energy flashes in front of me. A turret falls out of midair and hits the platform with a loud crash. His bullets bounce off the turret back at him. Threat eliminated, I scan behind me for Elizabeth. She stumbles from behind her cover, clearly exhausted. Pulling a turret through space and time is a bit more complex than giving me a health potion. She recovers quickly and smiles at me. We dash to the edge of the platform and locate the Sky Line. We leap and hook onto the silvery thread before disappearing into the clouds.

The story of BioShock Infinite, developed by Irrational Games and programmed on a customized version of Unreal Engine 3, centers on the interactions of Booker DeWitt—a gun- and magic-wielding mercenary— and Elizabeth, a mysterious woman locked in a tower. She possesses the ability to use tears: powerful science-sorcery that can bridge the gaps between dimensions and alternative timelines. Booker and Elizabeth each have unique powers and abilities, each of which must be utilized together to successfully navigate the game levels and story.

However, whereas Booker is a playable character, Elizabeth isn't (at least, not until a later expansion pack). The player controls Booker's actions—his combat advancement, his adventuring, and his storyline choices—whereas Elizabeth operates as an autonomous figure, a "companion" artificial intelligence agent.[1] Players can prompt Elizabeth to take certain actions, such as asking her to pick locks or summon cover for Booker in combat. However, she is experienced by players as an independent contributor to the game experience. Elizabeth will heal or attempt to restore the player's magical abilities without prompting and will also point out gameplay elements, such as the presence of pickable locks or hidden treasure. Elizabeth's AI goes beyond simple triggered events. She also explores the gameworld alongside and yet independent of the player; while Booker may be looking to buy weapons or ammunition from a street vendor, Elizabeth may be smelling flowers growing next to the vendor's cart, or dancing to street music being played nearby.

These events are not simple-scripted. Elizabeth won't repeat the same behavior every time a player visits the same area, or even on subsequent playthroughs. Instead, she has a wide variety of possible logics that she may apply to any given situation. The logics she chooses are determined by her previous experiences in the gameworld, Booker's interactions, and a dash of computational randomness. The substantial parts of the game in which Elizabeth and the player are co-present can be read as though they play the game together. They each influence each other's decision-making as gameplay progresses, and learn about the gameworld in unique ways. Moreover, *BioShock Infinite*'s narrative arc—the evolving relationship among Booker, Elizabeth, and the floating city of Columbia—draws its affective impact from small, mundane, and surprising moments of semi-scripted play. The gameplay and narrative experience of *BioShock Infinite* is co-enacted between the player and Elizabeth.

This chapter focuses on questions of being and agency. As we engage in rewriting and reenacting the boundaries of the Unreal Engine, and in game engines in general, our literary and methodological toolsets or evaluating narratives much also change. Who and what is Elizabeth? How does she come to be enacted as an "agent" with and through the player, *Infinite*'s development team, and the Unreal Engine? Agency, as Stephanie Jennings has traced, has a long and complicated history within games studies, replete with competing definitions and theories drawn across literary studies, sociology, and the cognitive and computational sciences.[2] The most common deployment of gamic agency derives from Janet Murray's foundational agency-as-aesthetics approach from the mid-1990s. To Murray, agency represents the feeling of control that a player has over a game's narrative, systems, or both.[3] Her hybrid humanistic-design approach sees in digital literature the unique capacity of a reader-player to influence both story and system, to be "both the dancer and the caller of the dance."[4] More textualist approaches, such as TreaAndrea Russworm's, approach the relationship between player narrative agency and character agency in terms of how much space is allowed for individual characters to exert personal or systemic influence over a game's story or outcomes.[5] Further, scholars like Russworm and Jennings argue that the interaction between player and non-player characters and story structures contain both narratological and political elements. That is, the relative agencies that character and story produce can mimic, enhance, or subvert broader raced, gendered, and ideological systems within and outside of the text.[6]

Actor-network approaches that account for both human and nonhuman (often, computational) agency, Jennings argues, are less common in games studies.[7] Drawing from the early works of Bruno Latour and Michel Callon, D. Fox Harrell and Jichen Zhu argue that agency is coproduced among social and computational elements of games. Their concept of "systems agency" highlights how procedural systems in interactive media (such as on-the-fly narrative generators) can dynamically create new story events and characters. Because they don't require input from a designer or writer, digital systems take on an authorial and dramatic agency typically reserved for human actors.[8] Harrell and Zhu's ideas echo those of humanistic and art historical research. Humanists situate computer and game engines as having "co-creative" agency in the development process, either through procedural content or "agency-as-resistance"—such as the material and political consequences designers and developers face working with and against the "grain" of software.[9]

Though the disciplinary traditions from which agency in game studies descends each have their own ontological and narratological concerns, agency-as-authorship—the ability for an actant to modify and control their gameworlds—remains an undercurrent. In more literary accounts, agency becomes the authorial relationship between a player as a reader-constructor of a text—less in terms of reader response/interpretation and more about a player's ludic ability.[10] In computational or cognitive accounts, agency references the ability for a computational system to make choices or decisions that mimic or replace a human author.[11]

Given the undercurrent of authorship calling into question the exclusivity of human authorship, it is surprising that studies of agency have only recently turned toward examining game developers themselves and their role in the game production process. Studio ethnographies and game production studies—like those written by Casey O'Donnell,[12] John Banks,[13] and Jen Whitson[14]—explore the everyday practices of game developers as they negotiate deadlines, corporate directives, and technological hurdles. Scholars of labor and empire like Nick Dyer-Witheford and Greig de Peuter, and Aleena Chia have explored how developers are swept up in broader issues of international labor rights and automation.[15] More recently, Brendan Keogh argues through his extensive ethnographic study of Australian independent game developers that the interrelations between game developers, players, technology, and computational *craft* are more dynamic than game studies has typically been capable of addressing.[16] As such, Keogh argues for a breaking open of game studies' conception of agency as "closed circuit of videogame-and-player" to include game developers and their technological practices. Further, Keogh argues that his call is goes beyond unpacking the "black box" of game development, but has methodological and analytic implications for literary branches of game studies:

> The insights from [platform studies and studio studies] could be fruitfully combined with the detailed textual, narrative, and mechanical analyses of game studies to reveal new sites and articulations of how, and in what contexts, the player-and-videogame generates cultural meaning. Any sense of player agency emergent from or mediated by the videogame could itself be contextualised as mediated and co-constituted by the craft of the videogame producer as they negotiate with their existing skills, the tools of their trade, and the social expectations of their field.[17]

In taking up Keogh's call, this chapter examines the case of Elizabeth, from *BioShock Infinite* and its DLC (downloadable content) expansions *Burial at Sea*, to examine the relationships among players, developers at Irrational Games, and the Unreal Engine, which together constituted the player experience of Elizabeth. However, this chapter also pushes Keogh's argument further. In addition to bringing more critical platform studies insights into gamic understanding of agency, it adds feminist and queer literary framings to read the deeply affective entanglements of reader, system, character. I argue that Elizabeth doesn't just act as a character in a text but becomes herself enacted as a representation of multiple interconnected threads of agency. Elizabeth in my reading emerges not as a discrete object with agential properties, but as a "vibration" of the entanglements of human and nonhuman worlds that occur in the making and playing of digital games. Elizabeth is perhaps not an agent, but agency itself.

Reading Elizabeth(s)

The games that make up the *BioShock* trilogy—*BioShock*, *BioShock 2*, and *BioShock Infinite*—constitute a "prestige text" for game audiences and game scholars alike.[18] Though these games have varying degrees of interlocking narratives—*BioShock 2* serves as a direct sequel to *BioShock*, whereas *BioShock Infinite* is only tangentially linked—the series is heavily linked by narrative themes of transhumanism and objectivism, as it questions free will. The original *BioShock*'s narrative—in which player character Jack discovers that his major choices in the game thus far had been directed by two opposing villainous forces in the game's underwater city, Rapture—serves as a metacommentary on videogames themselves.[19] *BioShock* calls into question players' experiences of ludic and narrative: How many of their decisions and how much in-game play have been their own making? Is the player merely following explicit or implicit calls-to-play from a game's design team? This metanarrative challenges early theories of electronic literature that argued that user-driven narrative differentiated digital texts from analog ones.[20] As such, as Stephanie Jennings notes, the *BioShock* series serves as a foundation in studies of gaming agency.[21]

BioShock Infinite departs from the art-deco-styled Rapture and objectivist plot points. Instead it places the player in the floating city of Columbia, with architecture inspired by the Neoclassical themes of the 1893 World's Columbian Exposition (the Chicago world's fair) and politics representing a Reconstruction-era version of American Christo-fascism and white nationalism. The game's scientific curiosities also shift, moving from genetic manipulation and human modification to quantum physics and space-time. Elizabeth has the ability to open "tears" in the fabric of space-time, allowing her to transverse parallel "quantum" realities and timelines. As the story proceeds, Elizabeth's explorations of these tears afford her near-omnipotence; she becomes able to see possible futures that may occur, given actions taken by other characters. Ultimately, she exposes the mysterious origins of *Infinite*'s antagonist—Columbia's fascist leader and "prophet" Comstock—by reexperiencing past events and viewing alternative forks in time.

Elizabeth thus navigates the gameworld in a manner radically different from the game's gun-toting playable character, Booker DeWitt. While Booker shoots his way through the game narrative, Elizabeth phases through time and space, confounding enemies by revealing multiple configurations of parallel worlds and unraveling the mysteries of the game's plot by exploring alternative world histories and events. Though the player's initial encounter with Elizabeth frames her as a "damsel in distress"—a trope that she never quite fully escapes (the player *rescues her from a tower*, after all)—the narrative of *BioShock Infinite* quickly recasts Elizabeth as a wielder of mystical power.

While *Infinite* tends to narrow how Elizabeth folds quantum worlds together in her combat roles, the game's narrative arc allows her more freedom. Unlike most companion AI characters in first-person shooter (FPS) games, Elizabeth is substantially more powerful than the player character. Her supernatural abilities are not just background flavor, they impact the player's experience of the game. During a short sequence in which Elizabeth is running away from Booker, she summons freight trains, marching bands, and parade balloons from other quantum worlds to slow him down. Eventually she slips into another dimension herself. In real-time combat, Elizabeth assists the player by summoning weapons, ammunition, health items, and cover. She is ultimately cast as the hero of the game when, after joining with alternative versions of herself from forking timelines, she discovers that Booker and Comstock are the same person from different branches in time—and Elizabeth's father too. Booker and Comstock meet because of a quantum-powered conspiracy, which sets in motion the rise of Columbia that inadvertently led to Elizabeth's birth and gave her quantum powers.

Infinite's culminating narrative event features multiple versions of Elizabeth across multiple realities converging to drown Booker—thus saving herself and an oppressed underclass of Columbia from fascist rule (see figure 3.1). Once again, the metanarrative commentary common across *BioShock* titles emerges: the removal of the player from the game-world allows for a fuller realization of agency for non-player characters. *Infinite* attempts to subvert the FPS trope of the companion character as player adjunct or escort mission; instead we come to learn that Booker (and thus the player who controls him) were instead always already in service of Elizabeth's emerging character agency.

3.1 Screenshot of the culminating scene of *BioShock Infinite*: multiple realities of Elizabeth about to drown the player. An earlier version of the Liz model can be seen on the far-left side (https://www.youtube.com/watch?v=YPmzA_cRMgM).

Given the prominence of the *BioShock* text in games' cultural memory, there is no shortage of popular writing and scholarship on Liz. Particularly compelling are those pieces that apply feminist and critical race theories to Liz's character and agency, challenging to what extent *BioShock Infinite* actually succeeds in granting narrative or mechanic agency to Elizabeth.[22] After all, Elizabeth's story cannot progress without the input from and permission of the player. It can be argued that throughout most of the game Elizabeth serves not as a companion character, but rather as a player mechanics extension—essentially the player's lockpick and health/magic/ ammunition storage closet.[23] There are also moments when Elizabeth exhibits interpersonal glitches; Elizabeth's scripting rarely crashes the game, but can cause her to behave in socially inappropriate or "creepy" ways. Most commonly, Elizabeth occasionally disregards personal space. She will wander uncomfortably close to the player character, stand still, and stare directly at them until the player continues moving. Dismissing these moments as only technical glitches—rather than as an important part of the Elizabeth character, the player's ludo experience of Elizabeth, and the work of *Infinite*'s development staff—would only widen the divide between technical and narrative approaches to agency.

How might threading through platform studies and intersectional feminist technoscience lenses improve the ways games studies can understand the Elizabeth character? What methodological and analytic techniques can we adopt to perform this analysis? Centering Elizabeth's interpersonal glitches and *Infinite*'s final scene may be fruitful. As Booker grapples with the realization that he is both the protagonist and antagonist of the gameworld, multiple Elizabeths begin walking into view. Each Liz represents a different quantum reality and exhibits minor differences in clothing, haircuts, and life events (one Liz even walks into frame covered in blood). Of these different background Elizabeths, one especially stands out. She enters from the left side of the screen with hair more bowl-shaped and flatter than on her other selves, complete with pasted-on looking bangs. Her outfit is also a much tighter fit, with a waist-to-bust ratio that borders on the comedic, suggesting that rather than just being a different texture or cloth simulation, the 3D geometry that makes up her base body model is markedly different from that of the other Elizabeths. In fact, it is.

Bowl-cut Elizabeth is a beta version of the Elizabeth character model that was featured in non-playable gameplay demos and mid-development promotional materials for *BioShock Infinite*. The beta demo featured an early 3D model of Liz that participated more in combat, allowing the player to summon defensive, offensive, or supportive terrain and weapons from across interdimensional realities. Her powers are also notably more environmentally destructive, with each combat phase leaving permanent scars on Columbia's surface.

The multiple worlds of *BioShock Infinite* are heterogeneous and situated. They represent different potential choices made by the characters and represent different design and technology choices made by the Irrational Games team members themselves. The drowning scene intersects with different narrative futures and as different potential futures of *BioShock Infinite*. To be able to interpret that scene as such, the reader-player must also be either one of the designers of the game or one of the game's long-term fans. The games fans commonly read paratextual documents such as hype videos, developer interviews, and prerelease development footage. The bowl-cut Liz serves as an Easter egg for both developers and superfans, as well as an archaeological invitation. Just as Elizabeth must delve through her narrative past to understand Columbia's founding and the circumstances that gave her quantum abilities, players are invited to dive into Elizabeth's development past. They are invited to understand the narrative, ludic, and technological reasons Elizabeth's gameplay now functions the way it does.

Further, we can read an affective dimension to this scene, not only for the players and the Booker character, but for the development team. They brought one of the many changed and discarded versions of Elizabeth—their labor—into the game. Irrational Games creative director Ken Levine, the lead designer behind the *BioShock* series, is notoriously fickle, known for demanding wholesale changes to his games, even late in development. *Infinite*'s release was delayed several times, and stories about the chaos and toxicity of the work environment still continue to emerge nearly ten years later. Elizabeth herself went through a vast array of development and aesthetic changes close to *BioShock*'s release date. The cosplayer who would be hired to serve as the official "press face" for the Elizabeth character complained about how often she had to remake her outfit.[24] Given the attachment the development team exhibited to the Elizabeth character, one can imagine a certain catharsis in narratively incorporating those stalled labors into the game.

Reading Elizabeth as a character—including her character as represented in the text of *Infinite*—requires a synthesis of literary and platform criticism. Such an approach shouldn't treat the narrative of the game as a surface effect, nor the Unreal Engine and development team as behind-the-scenes trivia. Instead, a synthesized approach would examine how Elizabeth—as an emerging series of narrative, technical, and social relationships—simultaneously represents the entanglement of human, narrative, and technology.

This is, of course, not the first instance of a hybridized approach to literary and material criticism in games and new media studies, which hosts multiple of such traditions. Ian Bogost's "unit operations" and "procedural rhetoric" frameworks, for example, each highlights how underlying technical systems express themselves through a game's narrative, or communicate cultural and political value.[25] Similarly, Katherine Hayles has called for a "media-specific" analysis of literature that can attend to the "deepness" of code made evident through digital narrative, even likening code to a machinic unconscious.[26] However, these hybridized approaches re-entrench the surface/depth divide between code and narrative, even as they acknowledge their interaction. A fuller understanding of Elizabeth's agency must grapple with the uncertain and ever-situated seams among the technical and the narratological.[27] It demands something more feminist, more queer. Aubrey Anable's work on the queer affect of games offers such an analytical groundwork.

Anable too is concerned with the "atomization"[28] of games studies among literary approaches and proceduralist ones, which impacts our capacities to engage with the gendered and political dimensions of gameplay. The positioning of code and procedural systems as underpinning the "surface effects" of narrative and representation, which Anable labels as "proceduralist,"[29] not only undermines literary approaches to game texts—especially literary approaches from feminist and queer traditions—but also boxes game analysis into an untenable ontological position. This "bottom-up" framework ignores how meaning is also shaped phenomenologically and interpersonally. Meaning is not hidden content waiting to be unearthed by the reader-player—it resides within communities and across bodies, and is shaped as much by elements "outside" a text as within it.

Importing feminist and queer literary lenses into platform studies can provide us with analytic language to capture affective and agential qualities of computational media without falling back on a false (representationalist/proceduralist) surface/depth split. A concern with affect also highlights how the language of game studies is already bound up with intersubjective relations. The multiple uses of agency described at the beginning of this chapter each entangle in their definitions player experience of the system. For Janet Murray, for example, the agential quality of digital games is not reducible to the technical capacity for a player to actually modify or author game content. Rather, agency is aesthetic and affective—the player must *feel* as though their actions are relevant to the game's narrative and systems. This feeling is only partly related to a game's computational openness to player modification and change. Radically open-ended authorship in a game can even inhibit player sense of agency, as too many options can overwhelm a player with choice, leading to paralysis. Perceptions of agency are also rooted in one's subject position, social identities, and locations within regimes of power and knowledge. A given software's openness to modification does not mean that software is universally accessible.[30] Literacy in or prior experience with programming or other game systems improves the capacity of a player to engage with material dimensions of editing and authorship of a digital text, as does a player's acceptance into the raced and gendered knowledge communities crucial to expanding literacy.

Designers also express affective agential relations with their objects of production. A designer's affective relationship can be an interpersonal one with players, mediated through computation. A well-known rule of thumb in game design is that player agency is perceptual, not actual. That is, the job of the designer is not to allow the player to do whatever they want in a gameworld. Rather, their job is to make the player feel that the actions they are directed to take are actually their own.[31] Like the meta-narrative of the first *BioShock*, it is an illusion of choice that makes the player empowered in a highly constrained world, which serves as a kind of walled garden. Queerly affective relations can also manifest with the tools of production themselves; designers describe affectionate or combative interpersonal dynamics with their game engines and other development environments.[32] As we will see, these affectionate and combative relationships are used to describe the agency of the products of game design, too. The *BioShock Infinite* development team's relationship with Elizabeth is fraught with feelings typically reserved for a frustrating office mate, as well as infused with parental pride and tenderness at her growing ability to navigate the gameworld.

Anable posits queer theories of affect—particularly the cybernetically informed theories of psychologist Silvan Tomkins and the "structures of feeling" posited by cultural theorist Raymond Williams—as frames for helping game studies better grapple with messy entanglements of human and nonhuman perception and relation. Anable describes theories of affect represented in queer and feminist traditions as "the aspects of emotions, feelings, and bodily engagement that circulate through people and things, . . . a deeply relational force that attaches itself to and is expressed through all kinds of cultural texts."[33] Unlike Deleuzian models of affect, however, in which affective forces are defined as separate from individual subjects,[34] Anable's deployment of Tomkins locates affect as a relational act among bodies, subjects, texts, and technologies. Relating to one another, to nonhumans, to technologies, and to cultural texts is more than a series of cognitive acts. Acts of relating are acts of folding—gut feelings about how to navigate, make sense of, and represent ourselves and one another. Affect, in other words, is a fundamental quality of both interaction and representation. As such, it serves as a bridge between proceduralist and narrative accounts of games. In showing how the "structures of feeling" of interactive media themselves represent "emergent shared feelings that are not yet present in language, but in which we might sense the rhythms and tones of new ways of being in the world,"[35] Anable reveals how games are part of the way we collectively feel out our living within a computational world. Because we may not have language to capture affect, our thinking-through of the nonhuman agency of computational systems and characters are part of this collective sensemaking.

Reading Anable through feminist technoscience studies provides us with a hermeneutic for understanding gamic agency. Such a hermeneutic of agency entangles the materialist analyses of platform studies with the intersubjective, affective forms of sensemaking of interpretive textual scholarship. When we imagine affect as a fundamental quality of relation, we move away from a humanist framing of affect as something held or owned by an individual person and toward something more connective and posthuman. Affect as a quality of relation mirrors definitions of agency from feminist technoscience studies scholars, particularly philosopher-physicist Karen Barad's theory of "agential realism." Inspired by quantum physics, Barad argues for a relational understanding of agency that replaces the idea of an individual agent with the ability to exert force, with reading agency as an emergent quality of an apparatus. Agency then becomes the conditions of possibility that an apparatus produces.[36] Key for Barad is moving from interactive imaginings of agency—the kind of billiard-ball model of discrete, individual objects that act on one another and the world—to an *intra-active* model. Intra-active models of agency assume no preexisting agents or actants. Rather, all capacities to act emerge through human-nonhuman apparatuses. The "apparatuses" Barad gives as examples are often technoscientific, such as research labs, experiments, and scientific practices of knowledge-sharing like conferences and journals. These apparatuses are not just the setting of science, but they condition the possibilities of science itself. As classical quantum physics has shown, changing the experimental apparatus changes the results of the experiment; measuring reality changes reality. In the case of games, apparatuses may include game production processes, development environments like game engines, play sessions, critical readings of game texts, and broader flows of capital and power that games are produced through. Each of these apparatuses changes the conditions of possibility for how we play, how we read, and how we create. We ourselves are shaped by and through—we are—these apparatuses.

The intra-active model of agency for Barad has material and political implications. Reconfiguring understanding of creative processes as intra-active rather than interactive reframes the role of conflict in games studies and platform studies. Note how so many understandings of agency and authorship above can be read with an implicit sense of agonism, assuming contestation as the root of agency. Developers must work with and also overcome the grain of a game engine.[37] Code and platforms resist their users and set the preconditions for the narratives that occur in a game.[38] Players have agency when they are able to push back and change the computational system that they play in.[39] Characters have agency when they are able to resist or otherwise move beyond the player.[40] Given that *agōn*—the Greek root of "competition"—has been used to demarcate formalized and masculinized definitions of "games" from broader and more fluid notions of "play,"[41] we as analysts should take care whenever centering competition or zero-sum relations in our own theories and critical readings of games.

Feminist technoscience studies and queer theories of affect open readings of game characters and engines that are more multiplicatively relational, and can analyze agency as political, discursive, and intersubjective. While Anable has framed her own work as moving past structuralist/linguistic dominance in games studies, the reconfiguration of depth and surface, procedure and representation also refreshes our prior tools and methods. Our tools for understanding games, their systems, and their characters—including structuralist and materialist accounts of gamic agency—can be remixed and reapplied. The narrative becomes a site for investigating the material; conversely, system explores story. Narratively, Elizabeth is driven by quantum mechanics; ontologically, she is constituted as part of a larger authorial apparatus that includes players, designers, and the Unreal Engine.

The remainder of this chapter traces Elizabeth through two threads in the *BioShock Infinite* apparatus. My analysis will show how a queering of our readings and methods allows us to forge new understandings of character and gamic agency that are centered on relation and care, rather than on competition. The first traces Elizabeth's development story though "Liz Squad"—the internal team at Irrational Games responsible for creating Liz's "lifelike" behavior—and the Unreal Engine, particularly UE3's Kismet AI and scripting system. Through queer and poststructuralist lenses, we can read Elizabeth's development as a distributed body of semes and "word clusters" that enact Elizabeth by creating relations of affection and care with her designers and the computer. The second thread traces Elizabeth's narrative disempowerment in *Infinite*'s DLC sequels, *Burial at Sea 1* and *2*, through the Unreal Engine. In this analysis I highlight how interactive versus intra-active conceptions of agency lead to radically different political readings of the role of Unreal in *Burial at Sea*. An interactive reading can show Elizabeth is an example of the "Ms. Male" trope—a woman character who reads and plays as a weaker copy of a male character. An intra-active reading, on the other hand, situates Elizabeth's narrative as representing her becoming more entangled with the Unreal apparatus and the player, becoming an affective glitch that queers the computational system.

Weaving Kismet

How might agency emerge from intra-actions of designer, system, player, and character? Feminist literary critics have been asking this kind of question—though often of noncomputational media—for decades. In examining the relationships among author, text, and reader, Suzanne Keen notes an ontological disconnect between the material/textual makeup of a literary character and that character's affective connections to the reader:

> Characters, says the formalist or poststructuralist theorist, are non-human word-masses, existents, actants, narrative-men, Nobodies, or the products of semes traversing proper names. Yet readers persist in regarding characters as more human than "substantial hypothetical beings," more like friends or neighbors.[42]

Keen notes that answering "where" and "how" a literary character exists—or how they might exert agency within and through a text—is complicated. On the one hand, borrowing from formalist analyses, a character can be understood as collections of words or units of meaning that span pages of a text. When linearly processed through reading, these words or meanings form a character. We could imagine a similar definition for digital characters posited by code formalists; lines of code, art assets, sound files, and animation rigs stitched together by the act of play form the narrative experience of a singular character. On the other hand, characters are irreducible to their formal existences within a text, as they also exist within the mind of the reader. For Keen, what makes a character successful or agential is partly an affective relation—how effectively a reader is able to forge an empathetic or caring relationship with them. Again, we can extend this analysis to alleviate the tensions within games studies as well. Espen Aarseth's now-infamous ludological statement that when a player plays *Tomb Raider* they ignore and "see through" Lara Croft[43] is not just a phenomenological argument about the act of play. Aarseth's is an affective argument that players don't really care about or for Lara during play; her characterizations, backstory, and even her in-game avatar are merely set dressing on deeper ludic elements.

Keen posits that literary characters exist across a continuum of text and minds united through the affective ways readers relate to a text. However, she also argues against universalizing the reader.[44] Characters come to be through their interrelations with the reader, and those interrelations are always situated and subjective. As such, characters are always individually constituted and therefore ontologically multiple. Importantly, though, Keen is not advocating for a radically relativist account of character—that there is no shared connection that can ground an analysis of literary figures. Rather, Keen argues that skilled authors use textual techniques and technologies to produce affective and empathetic sensations in their readers. Similar to Keogh's call to broaden the ways designers participate in player-game agency, Keen calls for closer inspections of the techniques authors use to evoke empathy for characters, and turns to cognitive studies and neuroscience to account for how readers' receptions vary.

While I don't share Keen's turn toward the cognitive, analyses of Elizabeth's development are flush with talk of how to produce affective and empathetic relationships between Liz and the player. The members of Liz Squad—Irrational Games' interdisciplinary development team of artists, writers, and programmers—understood their task as twofold. First, Liz had to work as a literary character; for the narrative of *BioShock Infinite* to hold together until its dramatic conclusion, the player needed to form a meaningful connection with Liz. This connection could partially be formed through more classical literary and cinematic techniques like dialogue and cutscenes. Yet the team also believed the player-Liz dynamic would be more robust if it were also built over smaller, quieter, more ambient moments during the game. Liz was envisioned as part and parcel of *Infinite*'s broader environmental storytelling; she would comment on events occurring in the game, while wandering and engaging with the gameworld semi-independent of the player. As such, the team imagined Liz as an interactor with the game environment and part of that environment, helping to ground herself, the player, and their relationship within Columbia's universe.

Building such a strong affective dynamic is difficult, leading to Liz Squad's second task—to materially support Liz's narrative function and her relationship with the player within the gameworld. Elizabeth and Columbia's affective roles for the player further complicated this task. Above all else, the Liz Squad didn't want Elizabeth to annoy the player; common complaints about companion characters in games include them "getting in the way" of a player trying to navigate the gameworld. Being vulnerable or slow demand outsized player attention, while repeating animations or lines of dialogue annoy players. Liz's environmental interactions thus had to be evident to the player without interrupting the player, limiting the dev team's ability to use common storytelling techniques, like forcing the player camera to look at a character when an animation event is triggered. Further, the design of Columbia itself introduced storytelling challenges. Columbia's brightly lit, sprawling vistas were a stark departure from *BioShock 1* and *2*'s Rapture—an underwater city experienced through long dark tunnels and hallways. For Levine, Columbia represented both a narrative and technical break from the first *BioShock* games; *Infinite* was supposed to be a statement of Irrational Games'—and Levine's—mastery of the medium:

> [In] *BioShock 1*, you're a single guy in a corridor, fighting a monster or two, with views that don't go out very far. . . . [Using] the Unreal Engine, that's exactly what you wanna make. And we still pushed it at the time, we thought to its limits, when we made that game. It wasn't like we [said] "Oh, this is easy!" We worked really hard. We had to optimize and make all these decisions. . . . And then we go on to make [*BioShock Infinite*] which has these huge vistas and floating buildings and tons of characters around you.[45]

Given that one of Unreal's core differentiators in the 1990s was its capacity to render both indoor and outdoor scenes, Levine's quote reflects a bit of public relations hype. Still, Irrational's development practices were heavily shaped by their experiences with *BioShock 1* and *2*, each of which was developed through a bespoke version of Unreal Engine 2 (the base version of UE2 was partially shaped through collaborations with the US Army—see chapter 1). Each game reflected the genre and material conventions of their day: long dark hallways, a small number of enemy combatants, and a limited number of interactable characters onscreen at once. Unreal Engine 3 was made available to developers in 2005 and was essentially scaffolded on the same codebase that Unreal had been developing since the late 1990s. This engine featured new shader protocols that made for more customizable—and thus more efficiently renderable—lighting models. A more thorough integration of object-oriented programming (OOP) architectures through Epic's in-house UnrealScript programming language was also implemented. OOP further aligned Unreal with growing standard of coding practices throughout software engineering and game development in the 2000s.[46]

Unreal's growing rendering efficiency and object-orientation paved the way for the development of the foundational software module Kismet (see figure 3.2). It featured a visual programming language that allowed developers to combine prebuilt or custom UnrealScript modules—snippets of executable code—with triggers that read and report input from the player, the gameworld, or the operating system. Kismet in UE3 would be leveraged by Liz Squad to create Liz's literary and material agencies. Assets such as 3D models, animations, sounds, and data tables are connected to a game level through Kismet; a Kismet call or UnrealScript function spawns an asset in the level once triggered by an event. These trigger events could be functions like timers, changes to a player character's health (indicating damage taken), or responses to system calls (such as a level being loaded into or deleted from memory). Each UnrealScript module appears as a graphical node in a broader field of potential programmable actions and is woven together with other nodes to form more complex behaviors and events.

In a manner of speaking, Kismet is how assets in UE3 become meaningful. Before their deployment through Kismet (or their calling through text-based UnrealScript), assets connected to Unreal are essentially addresses, merely pointers within a data table to locations on a hard drive or network. As Ranjodh Singh Dhaliwal has argued, addressability—the capacity for units of meaning to be stored, indexed, identified, and located—serves as the fundamental quality of contemporary computation.[47] Kismet acts as the organizational thread that transforms an address into a concrete *reference*. When an asset is called by Kismet, an instance

3.2   Screenshot of UE3's Kismet (https://www.youtube.com/watch?v=1AjI7C-G4hM).

of it is created and contextualized within the game level. In addition to spatial coordinates, the asset is connected to behavioral trees (i.e., artificial intelligence), given a dedicated space in memory, and created as a discrete object within the gameworld that can be interacted with by the player and the game system. Following Dhaliwal's invocation of Althusser, we can say that Kismet's referential logics *interpellate* into ludic being the abstract objects addressed in memory.[48] The frame of interpellation highlights the dual ontological and political roles Kismet's threads play. Not only does it instantiate objects into material being, it gives them a purpose and a role in the interconnected hierarchy of the level. They are made into a subject in the gameworld.

Kismet also interpellates Unreal's users. It redefines the subject position of "game programmer," and changes when users with different skill sets can be made relevant at certain points in the design process. In other words, it redefines who gets to *be* a game developer. Kismet was originally designed in a "non-programmer-friendly" style of programming. Its later, more robust, implementation "Blueprints" in UE4 and UE5 was part of a larger push by Epic and Tim Sweeney to make the Unreal Engine more accessible to entry-level developer skill sets (see figure 3.3). As such, Kismet served as a boundary object[49] within Liz Squad and the Unreal Engine itself. It connected programmers, level designers, and narrative designers, each passing Kismet modules back and forth to one another. Each exchange slowly built an intra-team consensus on the dynamics of Elizabeth's

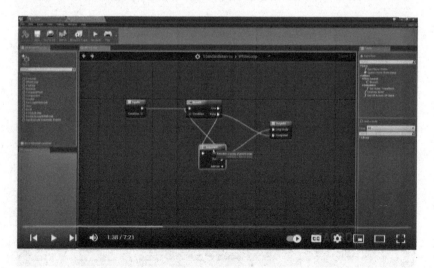

3.3 Screenshot of Blueprints in an official Unreal tutorial video (https://www.youtube.com/watch?v=Mxw391exhVg&list=PLZlv_No_O1ga2b_ZaJoaR5dLHOFw4-MMl&index=14).

interactions with the player and the gameworld. Kismet became such a fundamental part of the practice of building *Infinite* that Levine would claim that "without that [Kismet and Unreal authoring tools], there is no *BioShock*."[50]

Though Levine refers to it as a tool, I prefer the term "language" to describe Kismet. One could argue that Kismet is merely a container for UnrealScript—a visualization and simplification of deeper structures of code that Kismet's users are unable to directly access. From this perspective, Kismet would be merely an interface or visual editor. Anable has argued that interfaces are deeply meaningful, as they operate as sites of affective connections between code and human.[51] An interface framing of Kismet, though, obscures two major elements of Kismet's entanglement with Unreal, one material and one enacted. On the material end, Kismet networks are functionally irreducible to the UnrealScript containers that they call and arrange. The topology of the interconnected map of nodes and behaviors becomes fundamental to that map's functionality. Such irreducibility is most evident with Kismet's later Blueprints iteration in UE4/5. While serving essentially the same function as its older cousin, Blueprints reflects Unreal's major late-2000s overhaul. This revision converted the entire engine from Epic's proprietary UnrealScript language to the more commonly used C++. Blueprints and C++ thus share a relationship akin to Kismet and UnrealScript. UE4 allows developers to convert their Blueprints visual files into C++ textual files, a function that was commonly requested of Kismet by UE3 developers. The conversion "works," in that Unreal produces C++ code that is sometimes compileable. However, the generated code is rarely human-readable—even when it functions—and it's rarely possible to convert the code back from text into a Blueprint map.

There is, in other words, something more to the weaving together of the Kismet and Blueprints maps than simply deploying and connecting packets of code. The trails, knots, and threads worked on by Kismet developers are *semantically meaningful*; they provide functionality irreducible to textual code and become a key part of the web of meaning used by game authors to write the game's text. This semantic significance is, for computer scientist Margaret Burnett, what differentiates a visual programming language from a textual one:

> Although traditional textual programming languages often incorporate two-dimensional syntax devices in a limited way—an x-dimension to convey a legal linear string in the language, and a y-dimension allowing the optional line spacing as documentation device or for limited semantics (such as "continued from previous line")—only one of these

dimensions conveys semantics, and the second dimension has been limited to a teletype notion of spatial relationships so as to be expressible in a one-dimensional string grammar. Thus, multidimensionality is the essential difference between VPLs [visual programming languages] and strictly textual languages.[52]

This semantic-spatial multidimensionality leads us to regard Kismet's enacted impacts as a language or semantic map. That is, Kismet changes the ways game developers speak within and beyond Unreal. It becomes part of the fundamental discursive techniques game developers use to produce agency through a game's characters and create affective relationships with a game's players. In Kismet's tangles we can see parallels with the kinds of structural-semantic theories of writing of Roland Barthes and Algirdas Julien Greimas.[53] Base *semes* of computation discourse (numeric variables and digital assets) become categorized and contextualized (akin to Greimas' *classeme*) through the Kismet functions they are wrapped within. Semes are given meaning and discursive impact through their repeated computational utterances (Greimas's *anaphora*)— Kismet's threads and spatial tangles. Elizabeth discursively comes to be through Kismet's linguistic techniques and qualities, as developers learn to speak to one another—and to Unreal—through Kismet.

What might this structuralist analogue bring to games studies? Like a literary or cinematic character, we tend to associate Elizabeth with her 3D model and voice in each game level. However, Kismet's semantic structure reveals that Liz can also be read as representative of a distributed material and discursive network. Writing on the relationship between hypertext and poststructuralism, George Landow and Paul Delany once said that the two were "almost embarrassingly literal embodiment(s)" of one another; with hypertext's nonlinearity and enrollment of the reader as coauthor mirroring the literary play of Barthes and Derrida.[54] The same could be said for Unreal, game engines in general, and actor-network theory (ANT).[55]

The act of interpellating an addressed asset into a level through Kismet literally produces that asset as an "actor," drawn from the metaphor of actors onstage in a play. The actors in this play, however, are ontologically heterogeneous. Everything instantiated in an Unreal scene—character models, physics objects, cameras, lighting models, and player characters—are all actors. Upon being placed into a scene, each actor is connected to others and to Unreal's level through a multidimensional relational network. Some of this network topology is flat, in that heterogeneous actors like character models and event triggers are placed into a horizontal, nonhierarchical relationship. Other sections of this network are hierarchical, in that heterogeneous datatypes can be placed into a top-down relationship. Each "child" inherits spatial location, artificial intelligence, and other ludic properties from its "parent" in the network. This bumpy network topology is also fractal; as a developer double-clicks on each actor within a scene, they "zoom" into the internal networks of actors and assets that make up each actor. Designing and debugging games through Kismet requires that game developers learn to navigate and trace heterogeneous networks at multiple levels of scale—exactly the analytic interventions Latour claims of ANT.[56]

The semantic similarities between Kismet and ANT allow us to read how Elizabeth's agency and being emerge out of a distributed, heterogeneous network connected by affect. ANT enrolls the analyst—as well as the developer and the player—into the production of actors throughout the network. As I've written elsewhere,

> An object or a text comes to be through relations of actor, network, and analyst. Text and context are not fixed. Rather, they are more like an autostereogram—a "magic eye" puzzle—where background and foreground have as much to do with where we fix our eye as with the printed image itself. As we move our eyes, our heads, our hands, as we reorient our relationship to the page, new shapes, contours, and figures emerge—they reach out to us. The image only becomes fixed when we hold our gazes and bodies stable.[57]

Echoing Keen and Anable, our affective relationships with a character are part of that character's constitutive whole—as much as any code or animation asset weaves throughout a Kismet network. We interpellate Elizabeth through the context of gamespace and through our interactions with her Kismet networks.

To return to *BioShock*, as noted above, Liz Squad's goal was not just to make Liz programmatically functional, it was to make her affectively functional. She had to engage the player in dynamic, non-annoying ways. Eliciting a sense of care for her in the player was at the emotional and narrative heart of *Infinite*. According to *Infinite*'s animation director, Shawn Robertson, Elizabeth needed to generate the "illusion of life."[58] Initial designs, according to Levine, produced less-than-desirable effects:

> [There] are days that I wouldn't want wake up and go to work because there were things that were so hard to figure out . . . times that Elizabeth would be walking into walls. Literally, for months and months and months she was just . . . "Where's Elizabeth? She disappeared.

She fell through the ground. She walked through a wall. She's coming up to you and staring at you creepily. She's missing her marks. She's interacting with the wrong thing." Remember the shark in *Jaws*? All those classic stories. She was our shark in *Jaws*.[59]

Liz Squad was confronted with two major related design problems. First, Liz had to interact in a natural and lifelike way with each level without appearing overly scripted. Part of Elizabeth's navigation of the level depended on the player. A core part of *Infinite*'s design was open vistas that allowed the player to wander and explore; there was no set path in a given environment that the player had to follow, like the linear hallways of the earlier *BioShock* series games. A high level of player unpredictability meant that Liz couldn't be programmed to follow a set path through a level—she had to pay attention to the player.

Normally, paying attention to a player has a simple programming solution—the companion character uses a pathfinding script to follow the player character. However, the second design problem complicated this solution. While Liz was to serve as the player's connection and guide to Columbia, fostering a sense of her independence from the player was key to her narrative arc. In combat, Liz could predict enemy movements and alert the player to obstacles and resources the player hadn't yet noticed. During level exploration, Liz's childlike demeanor led her to run in front of the player to interact with something interesting. In these cases, she served a double role identifying landmarks and narrative touchstones to the player, while also allowing Booker to experience Columbia through Elizabeth's eyes, affectively foreshadowing their parent-child relationship. Having Elizabeth simply tag behind the player would create a sense of dissonance, undermine the emotional impact of the game, and present Liz as merely an extension of the player rather than as an agential force.

Perhaps presaging Liz's own distributed presence across *BioShock*'s multiverse, Liz Squad's solution to these problems was to use Kismet to distribute Liz's body and agency across the gameworld and the Unreal editor. Rather than imagining Liz's AI as a mirror of the player—a single digital body piloted by a "brain" of player input or algorithmic decision trees—Liz was reimagined as a part of the level itself. She was constituted from components that could break game rules and the laws of (game) physics to produce the desired narrative and emotional responses in the player. Similar to Latour's ANT, content and context could be collapsed; Elizabeth would serve as both figure and ground for the player.

BioShock Infinite's debugging mode, WTFLiz ("What The Fuck, Liz?") serves as a window into Liz's hybridity and distribution. WTFLiz is a custom developer tool that overlays a heads-up display (HUD) on *Infinite*'s gameplay within the Unreal Engine. A text readout on the left side of the screen brings important background computational processes into the foreground, illuminating information such as the average number of executable Kismet and Blueprints commands Liz's distributed self is executing per tic, and spatial tracks Liz's and the player's bodies in the game level. WTFLiz also comes equipped with HUD overlays that visualize separate elements of Liz's decision-making matrix. These overlays allow developers to see which parts of Liz are being interpellated by the level and the player at any given moment. They also show how Liz is interpreting or thinking through the gameworld and the game engine. In other words, WTFLiz translates between Liz's bodymind and the player.

One of WTFLiz's overlays shows a long green line extending from the player's origin point behind the camera, which bends and meanders toward a point in the distance of the level (see figure 3.4). Another green line connects it to one of Liz's 3D avatars. As players move through the level, reorient themselves, or change their camera position, the green line between them and the distant point shifts and distorts, and Liz and her line follow. Liz is not completely tethered by this line, however; she will at times run to other parts of the level in front of the player, extending and tugging at her own connection to the green thread. However, when the player sprints in front of Liz, pushing her out of camera view, her

3.4 Screenshot of Irrational Games' GDC 2014 talk, showing Elizabeth's relationship with the Golden Path, visualized through WTFLiz as an interconnected line among Booker, Liz, and the narrative goal of the level (https://www.youtube.com/watch?v=wusK-mciCVc).

connected thread begins rapidly popping and shorting, rather smoothly shifting, as it did when Liz was in front of the player's camera. If the player remains stationary, Liz's line motion becomes smooth again, and she quickly runs back into player view.

This line was dubbed by Liz Squad as the "Golden Path." It represents a relatively simple trigonometric function that determines the most efficient path between the player's current position in the gameworld and their goalpoint—whatever the next spatial trigger point is that the player needs to cross to progress the narrative of the game. As the player moves throughout the level, the function continually updates the player's Golden Path, providing Liz with a constant stream of information about the most likely path a player will take. Liz's avatar then runs to intercept the player. Rather than just making a beeline for the player avatar, however, Liz's movements are controlled to doubly "block" the player. First, in terms of stage blocking, Liz attempts to frame her avatar within the player camera's view by following cinematic rules—visually balancing the shot and aligning herself to one of the thirds of the screen. Her triggered "economy of animations,"[60] featuring edited motion capture by actress Heather Gordon, mimics the exaggerated bodyplay of stage acting, designed to further draw the player's eye to Elizabeth. Second, Liz Squad instituted the golden rule of "goal side blocking" to the Golden Path.[61] In soccer strategy, goal side blocking means that defenders always remain "goal side" of an attacking player with the ball. There should never be a direct path from an attacker to the goal without a defensive player (aside from the goalie) between them and the goal. When chasing down an attacking player, defenders should always attempt to take an angle that would allow them to intersect their trajectory between the attacker and the goal, rather than running straight toward the attacker. Above all else, Liz's Kismet network positions her avatar goal side—always trying to remain between the player and the targeted narrative goal at the end of the Golden Path.

Echoing her narrative "tear" abilities, Elizabeth can break the rules of the gameworld in order to maintain her avatar's position to the player. The reason her Golden Path line will occasionally pop or tear in space is because Liz despawns and respawns her avatar actor (loading a new version) to catch up to the player. Importantly, Liz will use her editor tear powers only when she is out of camera view of the player. Getting in front of Elizabeth and then running backward toward the level goal while keeping Liz in sight will prevent her from despawning and respawning. Here again we find parallels between Liz's quantum narrative and her Kismet agency; Liz has near-limitless capacity to modify herself and move throughout the level—until her uncertain status encounters player observation.

While the relationship between Liz and the player is narratively and ontologically important, it is not the only one Liz's Kismet network cares about. Elizabeth's desire, in fact, is quite literally materialized and distributed throughout the Unreal level. As I've argued earlier, Liz's interactions with the gameworld were fundamental for her character arc and served as a vehicle for Booker—and the player—to learn more about Columbia and its history. Typically, when companion or non-player character (NPC) attention to a game level is important, developers will either have that character "bark"—play an audio file for the player signaling content, often not accompanied by a triggered animation—or forcibly pause the player and pivot their camera to look at the NPC, creating a mini-cutscene. As Liz Squad wanted Elizabeth and the player's relationship to be dynamic and non-agonistic—they shouldn't be competing for camera or world control—neither of these common solutions were ideal.

Liz Squad's solution was to combine her blocking behaviors with custom Kismet triggers that would represent Elizabeth's desire to explore part of the level. These desire points, which appeared as grayscale two-dimensional eyeballs in the Unreal editor, attract Liz's avatar to nearby points of interest, away from the player's Golden Path. Notably, the desire points are not guaranteed triggers. Just because a desire point exists does not necessarily mean that Liz will move her avatar toward it, as Liz Squad introduced randomness to whether Liz will care enough to attend to a desire point. Irrational Games' developers and narrative designers could thus deploy an amount of artistry in their level crafting; the more important they felt it was for Liz to interact with a level actor, the more desire points they would place on and around that actor. Figure 3.5, for example, shows a painting of Lady Comstock—the antagonist's wife and Elizabeth's adoptive mother—copies of which are hung throughout Columbia. One of the largest paintings of her, encountered while exploring with Liz, is shown in the editor covered in desire points and coupled with a look target and Kismet audio trigger. This amount of materially embedded yearning is highly likely to entice Liz to stop and stare at the painting, triggering the look target to pivot her avatar's head toward the painting, playing while Booker explores other parts of the memorial.

In addition to her assets being materially interpellated through Kismet, Liz is affectively interpellated as well. Liz's affectual interpellation depends on a combination of player movement and position, her relative yearning for an in-game actor, and random chance. Her avatar is hailed by other parts of her across the gameworld to produce narrative cues and emotional responses in the player. These narrative and affective interpellations are materially expensive, however.

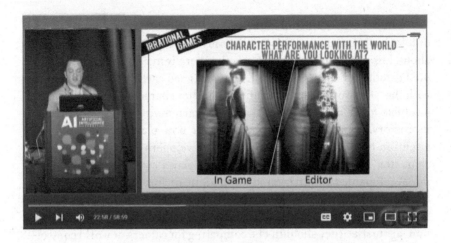

3.5 Screenshot of Irrational Games' John Abercrombie, describing how Elizabeth "sees" in the Unreal Engine. The eyemarks signal moments of desire for Liz, causing her to pause and contemplate the painting (https://www.youtube.com/watch?v=wusK -mciCVc).

The constant predictive pathfinding enmeshed in the Golden Path requires many operations per tick, as do triggering and storing Liz's history of chance encounters with her desire points. Further still, Liz's blocking techniques and need to consistently position her avatar in front of the player camera has a dual impact on *Infinite*'s graphical processing. Not only does the consistent rendering of another character add to memory cost, but the choice to use theater-like blocking and stage techniques means that Liz's character avatars needed to be more detailed. She required more points in her body and facial rig, and a denser polygonal mesh or "polycount" (the number of polygonal faces that make up her avatar model) to overcome the impression of being stiff or doll-like.

To compensate for computationally intensive graphics, Irrational's team decreased the polycount and the behavioral capacity of *Infinite*'s "chumps"—Irrational's internal name for the NPCs that populate Columbia, which serve as set dressing or objects to be shot at. In addition to their lower detailed models, chumps materially differ from both Elizabeth and more prominent NPCs present in the game. Chump actors are agents spawned by a Kismet crowd simulation node, and move based on randomized variations on one set of simple commands. Notably, this means that chumps are a different order of actor than Elizabeth or Booker. Both Liz and Booker's avatar actors are Pawns—subtypes of actors marked by Unreal as having the capacity to be controlled by an intelligence; Booker is controlled by the player, and Liz by Kismet networks that tie together the varying threads of her presence throughout the level. Though chumps can be said to have some level of behavior (in that they will hunt for and shoot at Booker), neither Unreal nor Irrational Games' dev team considers them to have artificial intelligence. Elizabeth's transformations of chumps into non-Pawns impacts the potential complexity of their behavior, making them little more than bullet sponges. Her reducing their polycount pushes them farther to the background, where increased distance from the player camera hides their lower resolution models.

As WTFLiz and Kismet reveal, Liz's presence in the level—both in terms of her material/textual realities, and in her agency to shape the gameworld and game narrative—cannot be reduced to a single character model or AI script. Rather, Liz's presence and agency are intra-active, emerging through a combination of interpellated assets, Kismet threads, rendering tricks, and the player's ludo-narrative experience. Liz's presence quite literally reshapes the entire *BioShock Infinite* apparatus. Irrational created a new kind of interdisciplinary team to design her, which modified the Unreal Engine to represent her desires. They shaped game levels to incorporate her body, breaking physics to allow her to warp through gamespace and time. Enemies were shrunk to give her space in computational memory, and the player was enrolled as an active coparticipant in her actions throughout the game.

The Liz Squad and their acts of care had an authorial role in Elizabeth's agency—not only in shaping the game to provoke senses of care in the player, but also in their care for Elizabeth. The narrative needs that Liz exhibited were demanding, but using simpler logics such as having her follow behind the player or signal environmental interest using only barks would have been narratively insufficient. That Elizabeth is still analyzed by games scholars nearly a decade after *Infinite*'s release speaks to the craft and effort exhibited by Liz Squad, and their success at using Unreal to shape Liz's agency and emotional impact by blending narrative and design techniques.

Liz's affective impact on the design team was evident as well. Throughout *BioShock*'s development and in postmortem interviews, Liz is spoken of as a fellow team member. Developers express frustration,[62] concern,[63] and even pride[64] in her. Following Anable, we can read Liz as affectively emerging to become the interface among code and text, and among human collaborators in her design. Following Keen, her emergence was experienced by both her readers and her writers as interpersonal, moving beyond the semes and word clusters that her Kismet and actor networks comprised. Finally, following Barad's quantum lens, Liz's shaping of the entirety of the *Infinite* apparatus reaches backward through time as well. She was shaping her own authorship even before she was fully written.

Conclusion: Relating Otherwise in *Burial at Sea*

BioShock Infinite was a critical and commercial success, firmly establishing the *BioShock* series as a popular prestige text. The game's technical and narrative achievements cemented Levine's status as an auteur figure with the gaming press (despite his relative lack of contribution to Elizabeth, the most technically and narratively challenging part of *Infinite*'s development). Levine would later leverage his growing reputation to secure the financing needed to shut down Irrational Games and rebrand as a smaller "indie" studio, laying off all but fifteen members of Irrational's staff. In 2014, Levine announced the two-year winding down and eventual closure of Irrational, but committed to fans that the remaining content in development for *Infinite*, which was designed to unite all three *BioShock* games (and hastily correct some plot holes in *Infinite* itself), would still be completed. The two narratively driven DLC minisequels—collectively titled *Burial at Sea*—would feature two major elements of fan service: players would return to Columbia, the underwater setting of the first two *BioShock* games and, in *BaS: Episode 2*, would be able to play as Elizabeth, marking the end of her narrative arc and the series. This playable Elizabeth would be an older, more jaded, figure than the one encountered in *Infinite*, with an avatar and personality resembling a noir femme fatale archetype.

The *BaS* miniseries, produced under the whispers of layoffs and Irrational Games' closure, highlights the material-narrative challenges involved in shifting Liz to a playable character, as well as the exhaustion and ennui that *BioShock* developers must have felt working under the impending closure of their studio. The series was released to only mildly positive reviews and was criticized for relying on overly stereotypical narrative tropes and lacking polish and completeness.

Central to these critiques was Elizabeth, whose femme fatale character in *Episode 1* felt disconnected from the Liz that players had gotten to know and care for in *Infinite* and who, in *Episode 2*, exhibited substantially different interactions with the gameworld than before. During prerelease interviews with *Burial at Sea*'s development staff, designers emphasized their desire for players controlling Elizabeth to have a gameplay experience that was authentic to her character, rather than playing as "Booker in a dress." *BaS* level designer Amanda Jeffrey makes clear that the game mechanics of the DLC should change to be faithful to Elizabeth's character and distributed agency:

We're still trying to work out exactly how extensive Liz's tear abilities will be in the playable Liz sequence. . . . She has an understanding of this universe and the various universes that she can visit, and she knows, once again, constants and variables. . . . If we were to just put Booker in a dress, then that would be the most awful betrayal of what we're doing for Liz.[65]

Booker's use of "vigors"—a form of chemical techno-magic in *Infinite*—compliment his use of guns and other projectile weaponry, as almost all of Booker's abilities are heavily combat oriented. Elizabeth's tear abilities, in contrast, are generally noncombative. Elizabeth's strength is her ability to explore, not to kill. Jeffrey notes during prerelease interviews that the team's goal was to design a gameplay experience that reflected Elizabeth's orientation to the world:

There's all of these different kinds of ways of being more thoughtful, and—I hesitate to say it—almost more feminine way of approaching a problem, where there's all of these people and, to be very brutally honest about it, they have the advantage in strength. But Elizabeth has the advantage in smarts.[66]

Despite the admittedly clumsy and gendered rhetoric, there did seem to be a sincere drive by the *BaS* development staff to avoid recreating what Anita Sarkeesian has identified as the "Ms. Male" trope. This trope involves a playable woman character whose major characteristics are derived from an already-well-established male character. For example, Ms. Pac Man is literally a "Ms. Male."[67] A well-designed Elizabeth player character would create a gameplay experience that allows players to experience gameplay styles that offer alternative, more "feminine" play than is often afforded in mainstream titles. During development time, there was a sense that *BaS* may have been a much-needed advance in industry gameplay design, inspired by critical discourse.

Unfortunately, the reality of *Burial at Sea: Episode 2* did not live up to the hopeful promises of development interviews. Instead of featuring gameplay mechanics that took advantage of Elizabeth's tear abilities, the development team took shortcuts. They instead installed a hastily scripted narrative workaround, and removed Elizabeth's powers at the start of the game. In *Burial at Sea*, Elizabeth travels back in time to save Sally, a new character retconned into being one of the Little Sisters of the original *Bio-Shock* games—young girls who have been mutated with vigors and can be harvested for their magical power. In the original *BioShock*, the player has a choice of either harvesting Little Sisters—killing them but granting the player new combat powers—or saving them, leading to a weaker player but a kinder narrative ending. Elizabeth's *Burial at Sea* arc mimics the choice players can make in *BioShock 1* and *2*. By traveling to the past, Liz loses some of her memories and breaks her ability to use interdimensional tears—and, ultimately, gives her life for Sally's.

Elizabeth, instead of being a character with knowledge of infinite possible branching timelines, was cast as a semi-amnesiac surrounded by enemies that could easily kill her. Elizabeth uses guns, vigors, and crossbows to kill or knock out unsuspecting enemies from behind, but has access to little enough ammunition, making hiding and running away generally better tactics. The gameplay in *Burial at Sea*, then, represents not a radical shift in problem-solving or exploratory game design from *BioShock Infinite*, but rather a minor shift between two subcategories of the FPS genre: action-adventure to survival horror. Rather than being a mystically powered woman, Elizabeth plays as a weakened Booker.

When I first wrote about Elizabeth several years ago,[68] I characterized this narrative, material, and agential depowering as a surrender to the constraints of AAA development schedules—DLC releases are allocated less funding and time than the main titles they extend—and to the Unreal Engine itself, whose base code samples simplified Newtonian physics. The resulting game deprivileged the free-form physical and reality-bending play that would have been expected of Liz. With the architecture of Unreal applied to *BioShock Infinite* as a constraint, I argued that playable Elizabeth's differences from Booker manifested as her *inability* to apply violence as effectively as Booker, while still being required to navigate the violent gameworld. The removal of Elizabeth's tear abilities and introduction of stealth mechanics reduced Liz to a weaker, sneakier Booker. Elizabeth became another in a long list of woman game characters forced to ineffectively navigate game systems designed for violent characters and masculine problem-solving strategies.

Jeffrey notes that existing computational and economic constraints would shape Liz's reality:

> Some things for the playable Liz will have to be the same. We don't have enough time to make an entirely new game. We're building on an existing set of systems and all the rest of it. . . . However, I will say that, more than anything, we are trying to focus on making sure that the feel of playing as Elizabeth and just moving through the environment is a very different experience, both in the way that the player

interacts with their control pad or the mouse and keyboard, and in the way that the player's thinking about the environment.[69]

While Irrational Games developers certainly didn't lose their care for Liz and her material-narrative interactions with the player, their business realities left little room for the craft devoted to Liz's agency in *Infinite*.

However, I also believe that the feminist and queer theories of affect and agency at play in this chapter—and the intra-active readings of Liz's emerging agency through Unreal and Kismet—leave room for another, perhaps more sympathetic interpretation of Liz's final official agential manifestation.

In moving toward intra-active readings of agency, queer and feminist scholars strive to reject agonistic framings of agency—the idea that agency is held by an individual who exerts the capacity to overcome other agents or free themselves from constraints and entanglements.[70] Rather, as both agency and being are brought into being by our interrelations, there is no such thing as "breaking away" from entanglement or attaining a radical individual freedom. Instead of the capacity to break relations, agency becomes redefined as the act of materially and affectively *relating otherwise* to bring about a more desirable apparatus.

I now think that in *Burial at Sea*, Elizabeth and Liz Squad were not overcome by the Unreal Engine or by the crushing realities of AAA development. Rather, they together chose to rearrange and relate to these systems differently to complete Liz's and Irrational Games' narrative arcs. Liz Squad and Elizabeth gave way to Liz's narrative and material agencies in *Infinite* by working through Kismet, deeply entangling her with the gameworld and Unreal. By dispersing her body, desires, and intelligence throughout each level, Liz leverages her Pawn actor type to achieve an agency unavailable to the player. Where the player, as Booker, remains entangled in a relationship to the game that requires linear story and narrative progression, Liz can functionally glitch both the narrative and materiality of each level, disobeying the laws of Unreal's physics as she does those of Columbia. While throughout most of the game Liz commits few violent acts, her relationship with Unreal multiply helps Booker in combat. Not only can she point out enemies and toss the player the occasional ammo box or health kit—her sapping of system resources makes the enemy AI slower, simpler, and farther away. Her ultimate act of *Infinite*—the summoning of multiple avatars to a single space to drown and kill the player—is enabled by her body not being narratively or computationally tied to any one single instant in time or instance in space.

Burial at Sea Liz makes the opposite choice, which requires relating to Unreal and the gameworld differently. In her final act to save Sally, Liz is forced to give up her tear abilities—this means narratively disentangling with the multiple universes of *BioShock*. Like the player characters of each game, she becomes bound to just one—Rapture. Her decision also requires entangling herself with an entirely different set of Kismet threads. Liz saves Sally by becoming one with the player—both through gameplay and by inhabiting and modifying the Kismet networks designed for Booker in *Infinite*. For Liz Squad, having the player inhabit a Booker-ified Elizabeth centers her character in the narrative—fulfilling their *Infinite* goal of having Elizabeth and the player be deeply and meaningfully interconnected—while deleting everything material that exhibited their own care for Liz, like her complex level design and Kismet network. In other words, their final act for Irrational Games was to erase the work that made *BioShock Infinite* such a success by narratively and computationally de-interpellating Elizabeth.

White Photorealism

[Arc II]

In the fall of 2014, NVIDIA proved the moon landing.

Coupling their company's graphics processing unit (GPU) hardware and global illumination (GI) software with Unreal Engine 4, NVIDIA researchers and artists developed a simulation of the July 1969 US moon landing. The team digitally rebuilt the Mare Tranquillitatis—the "Sea of Tranquility" that served as the landing site for the three NASA astronauts on the Apollo 11 mission—as well as the lunar excursion module (LEM)— the bi-sectioned, spiderlike vehicle that would ferry the Apollo team to and from the surface (see figure 4.1). These reconstructions required geometry—the topological digital information that makes up what we could colloquially call the "actors" and "set" of the scene—as well as envi- ronmental information. The lighting conditions, visual atmospheric qualities, and camera effects made the scene feel physically grounded and visually real. The graphical rendering of the scene is "photorealis- tic" in multiple senses of the word. It is photoreal in the colloquial way the term is employed as a stand-in for visual mimesis and also, in more literal terms, as a reproduction of the quirks of a particular photographic apparatus: the combination of the unique lighting conditions on the Moon with Buzz Aldrin's Hasselblad 500 EL camera.

NVIDIA's target was the moon landing conspiracy theory, a long- standing fable that the moon landing was faked by the US government. The landing, conspiracists argue, served as propaganda, highlighting US sci- entific dominance over the Soviet Union and diverting attention from the Vietnam War. The theory, like many successful conspiracy campaigns,[1] is a

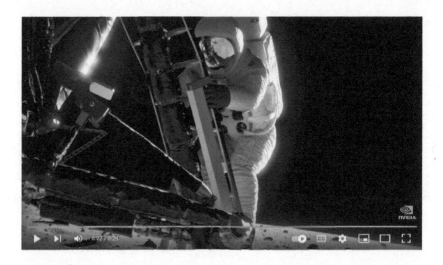

4.1 Screenshot from NVIDIA's moon landing demo (https://www.youtube.com/watch?v=QIap1jL14WU).

multifaceted, interlocking, and sometimes contradictory series of stories and narrators, filled with half-truths, uncharitable interpretations, dog whistles, and outright lies, circulated on message boards and social media and mainstreamed by right-wing outlets like Fox News.[2] Some of these narratives focus on technical and scientific themes—doubting the capacity to produce the amount of energy needed to get to the moon, claiming the Apollo team would have succumbed to radiation poisoning from the Van Allen belt, theorizing that lunar daytime heat would have melted camera equipment. However, the most well-trafficked claims are visual. They suggest that the United States government collaborated with Hollywood (particularly Stanley Kubrick) to fake the moon landing film and television broadcast.

The ocular-centric evidence levied against Kubrick and the moon landing are wide and varied, and include a fluttering flag in a windless atmosphere and the lack of star visibility in a black lunar sky. NVIDIA's demo, however, was focused on the theory's concern with light—its sources, reflections, ambient quality, and direction. No other single element of the moon landing has been more treated by conspiracists as a stand-in for truth than light, which serves as a useful vehicle to clad antisemitic narratives of joint Hollywood-government conspiracies in the cloth of scientific objectivity. Some of these stories question the naturalness of the light on the lunar surface—how specular glints bounce off of lunar dust, and the length and sharpness of the shadows cast by the LEM and by the Apollo team. Other stories highlight the entanglement of light and technology. They suggest that hot spots of bright areas on the lunar surface are studio lighting equipment, and question the availability of camera technology that allowed a rapid fifty frames per second of film to be captured in an extraterrestrial environment.

NVIDIA's moon landing demo is a fascinating case of transmedia[3] storytelling. Viewers experience NVIDIA's re-creation though a multitude of media formats including press releases, conference keynotes, and video documentaries, alongside simulation footage interspersed with developer interviews. In 2019, a downloadable version of the interactive visualization tool kit was released to the public, which presented users with a real-time rendering of Armstrong, Aldrin, the LEM, and the lunar surface. When the program is first launched, a slow and sweeping camera pans the viewer's eye artfully over the landing site, as lo-fi audio recordings of conversations between the Apollo team and mission control play in the background. The pans are Kubrick-like in their speed and motion, perhaps in a wink to the theory's attacks on the famous director. As the camera moves, the figures of Aldrin and Armstrong are frozen in time, lending an ethereal, diorama-like quality to the scene.

Simultaneously, users are presented with gamelike tools through which they are able to visually manipulate aspects of the scene, such as the camera angle and the lunar time of day. Some of these manipulations directly counter conspiracy claims; they allow users to change camera angles, experiment with the position of the sun in the sky above the landing site to see its effect on shadows, and adjust camera exposure in order to see stars (while also blowing out and making unseeable the lunar surface). Player-viewers can toggle Armstrong's presence on the lunar surface on and off. His bright white spacesuit provides bounced light that brightens Aldrin's descent from the LEM and creates an illusion of a studio fill light on the moon. These interactive systems are packaged with a text-based README file describing how each visualization option directly refutes a conspiracy narrative. Put together, they provide a compelling illustration of how the apparatus of Moon-camera-astronaut produced the unique visual effects seen in the actual photography of the moon landing.

Other tools, however, are designed to highlight the computational work NVIDIA's software is doing behind the scenes. Players are able to view wireframes—skeletal frameworks of the polygonal meshes that make up 3D models—of the scene and turn on and off the material displacement mapping that adds the illusion of depth to flat surfaces. Players can also view the scene in its boxy "voxel mode," which renders the scene as abstracted cubes of color that serve as the backbone for NVIDIA's global

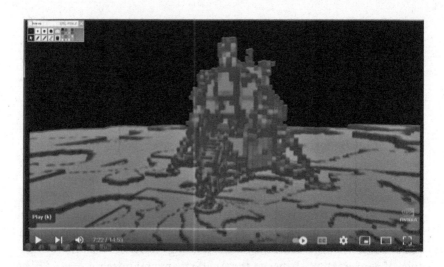

4.2 Screenshot of the moon landing demo's "voxel" mode, which shows the different boxes of light that serve as base calculation units for rendering the scene. (https://www.youtube.com/watch?v=QIap1jL14WU)

illumination lighting and shading algorithms (see figure 4.2). This may initially feel odd, as these options essentially show how even "photorealistic" computer graphics are elaborate smokescreens. The real-time computationally rendered image is a collage of shortcuts, hacks, and visual tricks, all creatively duct-taped together to allow for an image to be redrawn on the screen thirty to sixty times per second. The bounces, color shifts, and refractions of light are particularly complicated to render. The most achievable goal of real-time rendering is not to accurately model the world, but to reproduce in its viewer a feeling of being in a lit world. Exposing the illusion to the user, as NVIDIA does, would seem to undermine a demo ostensibly designed to prove the scientific validity of the moon landing.

It's easy to be cynical about these graphical options. This demo is more about selling NVIDIA graphics cards and Unreal software than about contributing to public scientific discourse. The moon landing demo and the press releases surrounding it highlighted NVIDIA's Maxwell graphics card architecture, as well as Unreal Engine 4's newest implementation of NVIDIA raytracing models. Press releases aside, NVIDIA did not actually "prove" the moon landing, beyond the ways the conspiracy theory has been debunked many times through a variety of media, technologies, and documentation over the past decades. Nor, as this chapter highlights, is Unreal's rendering system a completely physically accurate reproduction of light. But to focus solely on NVIDIA and Epic's marketing goals would

gloss over a core aspect of the demo: the visualization tools act as an epistemic and affective tool within the NVIDIA demo, allowing the viewer to
peel back layers of light and shape. As the user strips and relayers these
visualization tools, bumps in the LEM emerge and subside. Light morphs
from rays into blocks and back again, stars brighten and recede in the
black sky. The moon landing is presented to the user not only as a visualization of data, but also as a triumph of technological progress over the
ignorance of the conspiracy theory. The demo traffics in the affective as
much as it does in truth.

NVIDIA's Unreal moon landing demo thus allows for users to play
with multiple "ways of seeing,"[4] alternatively seeing as though they were
Aldrin's camera; as an imagined highly flexible contemporary camera
capturing the 1969 scene; as a cinematic and aesthetic moment replete
with camera pans and audio swells; and as Unreal itself, understanding
the scene as voxels of simulated light and color. These ways of seeing are
each entanglements of truth claims and affect—the wrapping together of
scientific validity and technical progress, of the accuracy of the lighting
model with American twentieth-century nostalgia. Dominic Kao and D.
Fox Harrell have argued that these multiple ways of seeing have always
been present and coproductive in games practice.[5] They work together to
make each other—in game design parlance—"juicy":[6] the combination of
rhetorical and ludic elements used as a rough rule of thumb in game design
for whether or not a particular gameplay or visual feature looks and feels
"good." They also work together to provide aesthetic and interpretive heuristics: though Epic and NIVIDA ask us to understand the moon landing
demo through the lens of truth and visual mimesis, Kao and Harrell note
that the kind of scientific viewpoint encouraged here is only one form of
visual heuristic that we might think the scene through:

> Many visual methodologies exist, and any one of them is valid: compo-
> sitional interpretation, cultural analysis, discourse analysis, semiology,
> etc. How harmonious are the colors? What is the spatial organization?
> Where is the viewer's eye drawn to? How will interpretation differ
> across people? How is power being constructed and reproduced? [7]

These visual methodologies are themselves entangled. Critical media
theorist André Brock identifies the blending of fact and affect as a core
component of all speech, including scientific speech: "logic (logos)
depends on a particular style of presentation (objectivism), a particular
set of values and beliefs (rationality and positivism), and specific techniques of argumentation (e.g., the scientific method and syllogism) in

order to be effective, rendering 'science' as a set of emotional appeals to a specific audience."[8] Light, truth, science, affect, and technology are entangled in the NVIDIA demo.

This entanglement is what makes the demo persuasive. Its attendant README files and video interviews with NVIDIA developers on the promotional website for the demo provide an affective sense of "doing science."[9] Mathematical models and simulation graphics grace computer screens in the background of promotional videos. A host of talking heads of white men present their painstaking processes of discovery and "eureka" moments as they rebuild the landing site. The demo's slow camera pans, highly detailed models, rendering processes, interactive visualization tools, and ambient radio dialogue all contribute to feelings of excitement, wonder, and isolation. Through the demo, the Apollo team, NVIDIA team, and demo audience become linked by a shared immersion in the technical sublime.[10] The technological sublime—the ability for the technological to transcend human embodied limitations and express something greater and more real—is an essential quality of digital media, information technologies, and scientific discourse.

The acknowledgment of affective and discursive systems within technical discourse demands a closer examination of the historical and political legacies of those systems. As Brock argues through Joel Dinerstein, that same affective quality is historically linked with discourses of whiteness-as-technical, whiteness-as-rational, whiteness-as-universal:

> But if one accepts Dinerstein's figuration of whiteness as seminal to the American technocultural mythos, then the characteristics of whiteness—organization, embodiment, disembodiment, and enterprise—can be understood as jouissance, or desires, of new media and information technologies as well. Dinerstein also references "religion"—in this case, Carey's technological sublime—to highlight how relating information technologies to the domain of "the spirit" locates new media and information desire in transcendence. That is, removing the limitations of embodiment from travelling through space and time—or even he identification of a disembodied, ephemeral textual practice—defaults to whiteness.[11]

Race, in other words, is always a part of scientific practice and discourse. Whiteness becomes ontologically and epistemologically enacted with-and-through digital technologies in the NVIDIA demo.

This chapter and the next are concerned with what I label "white photorealism," the coproduction of graphical realism, scientific authority, labor, race, and bodies in computer graphics. Ontologically, how the world is produced in digital spaces is wrapped up in white logics of sublime transcendence. NVIDIA's "god trick" of the positionless, generic viewer unbound by human time and space is intended to make the demo feel *more* representative of the truth of the moon landing, not less. Epistemologically, the organizational structures of knowledge at play—including the mathematical rhetorical style employed by descriptions of global illumination and physically based rendering, as well as the interactive visualization tool kits that layer light and geometric detail on the scene—imply that the "realist" style in the NVIDIA demo is not a style or a rhetoric at all, but rather a clear-eyed reading of universal truth. That the demo is entangled with a pivotal moment in white American history only adds to its perceived epistemic value. Through intersectional feminist critiques of science, I argue that Unreal too participates in the enactment of the broader visual and epistemic construction of race, particularly that of pure objectivity as a component of whiteness, and that of the Black body as a derivation from the white body.

This argument is made in two steps. This chapter takes the first: I examine the history and practices of the pursuit of "good graphics" in Unreal, generally defined as photorealism, and as enacted through Unreal's turn toward physically based rendering (PBR) models and its "materials editor," through which artists access those models. PBR, I argue, succeeds because its aesthetic claims are grounded in cinematic and scientific logics of whiteness—an odd mix of the presumed objective (white) eye of scientific inquiry over that of human experience with the stylistics of (white) cinema. Chapter 5 takes the second step: that the cinematic apparatus, from which Unreal's PBR derives, inherits cinema's material depriviledging of Black persons and introduces new forms of capturing and warping Black bodies against standards of whiteness. PBR is successful in part because of its alliance with whiteness—it clads itself in (white men) physics scholars' epistemic authority, as mediated through Unreal and the broader games industry, and through that "*effective, productive, profitable, exploitable*"[12] authority contributes to the mechanization of racialized labor and the devaluing of Black perspectives and bodies.

Physically based rendering is an older technique in computer graphics that attempts to photo-accurately replicate the laws of optical physics in order to produce visual representations of the world. While initially promising, the technique was rarely used in the 1980s and 1990s, as its reliance on light-bounce calculations, raytracing, and physical simulation of multiple properties of a model's surface made the practice too computationally intensive for real-time rendering. Recent developments in

PBR, however, leverage new software models that allow currently available graphical processing units (GPUs) to render scenes more efficiently using parallel processing, increasing render power without requiring more hardware power. Coupled with more efficient raytracing methods, high-quality PBR render times can be as low as 1/80 of a second, making them ideal for use as live-action, in-camera effects for television and film, as seen in Disney's use of Unreal for set design in *The Mandalorian*. Beyond PBR's technical efficiency, however, the technique is celebrated for its supposed connection to physics—that it represents a move away from subjective judgements of light and color and toward a standardized adherence to "the real." Evangelists for the technique will often frame PBR less as a rendering practice and more like a scientific breakthrough. PBR's narrative of simulating reality, however, is a fantasy. It emerges from what physicist Chanda Prescod-Weinstein calls "white empiricism," or the presumption that the white man researcher has an epistemic privilege on objective, universal reality, whereas other identities—particularly those of Black women—are "produced as an ontological other."[13] Echoing Brock, the draw and relative legitimacy of these physical models are as much affective—and raced—as they are mathematical.

Standardizing Unreal Materials

Of all the work a game engine does, its capacity for rendering graphical output on the screen is by far the most evident to players. Despite the arguments by scholars and designers for more deeply interrogating multiple sensory experiences at play when interacting with a digital game,[14] game culture and game development software remain stubbornly ocular-centric,[15] with new game and game engine releases often accompanied by PR campaigns highlighting new visual technologies at play.

There is a material and cultural tension at play when examining game engine graphics. On the one hand, game engines certainly do have different material properties and practices that produce their visual outputs. These properties are recognized by game developers and players, to the point where game engines become characterized as having particular visual quirks. Casey O'Donnell, for example, has noted the broad perception of the Unreal Engine as having a "shiny" look to its games, due to the particular way Unreal handles lighting and specularity.[16] On the other hand, game style as produced with various engines comes in part from the practices and techniques entangled with those software packages. For example, in an interview with *BioShock Infinite* creative director Ken Levine, both he and *Unreal Tournament* and *Gears of War* developer Cliff

Bleszinski express frustration with the general perception that a game engine determines a game's aesthetics:

Bleszinski: When people [say] "Oh I don't like the way games in the Unreal Engine look . . ." and you're like, what happened was that *Gears* largely defined a visual style for games in this generation because, to be fair it had really good art direction, right? It kind of had an intentionally desaturated look to it, and a grainy, you know concretes and metal showing up.

Levine: And the engine does not.

Bleszinski: It's just pixels!

Levine: It's just pixels. The engine has almost nothing to say about its art direction.

Bleszinski: But what happens is that in certain studios people license the [Unreal] Engine and they'd see the way we build the assets, and they'd use similar specular values or use similar [polygon] counts instead of making their own path for it and so you wind up with stuff you can somehow spot and tell [is made in the same Engine].[17]

While we should be a little cautious with this quote—Bleszinski and Levine after all have a vested interest in making known that their aesthetic and design decisions are not totally driven by the technologies they are using—it does provide a valuable counterpoint to the popular conflation of engine and design. As Bleszinski notes, technique and labor, as much as engine power, are central to the look and feel of a game. Generational aesthetics of games are just as determined by the shared resources and practices of game developers as they are by the software being used.

The discussion of agential tension between engine properties and artist technique doesn't necessarily sell engine licenses, however. Epic Games has certainly worked hard to have the public perceive the Unreal Engine itself as powering the pinnacle of graphical fidelity in games. In 1997, a year before *Unreal*'s release, gaming magazine *NEXT Generation* published a cover story featuring a blocky, polygonal, sword-wielding alien from *Unreal*, provocatively titled "UNREAL! (Yes, this is an actual PC game screenshot)." Though rudimentary by today's standards, *Unreal*'s graphical leap forward from contemporary competitors like *Quake* not only helped sell the game. Such visuals in popular magazines also convinced a generation of first-person shooter developers to license the at-the-time-unnamed Unreal Engine as the graphical backbone of their own games.[18] *Unreal* marketing director Mark Rein made sure in press interviews to hype the toolset as much as he hyped the game: "All you have to do is look at [*Unreal*], how much better the textures look in 16- and 24-bit color and the way it blends, look at the water, and how much better the transparency is."[19] The gaming press was all too happy to oblige Epic's salesmanship. *NEXT* described *Unreal* as "built around one of the fastest, most flexible and sophisticated 3D engines ever designed, running at high resolution 16-bit color. It boasts real-time, multi-colored, and extremely dynamic light sourcing and sports a huge number of the most highly detailed texture maps *NEXT Generation* has yet seen in a game."[20]

Twenty-five years later, Unreal Engine's lighting and graphical rendering packages are themselves promoted as stand-alone products with distinct, marketable names and recognizable promotional campaigns. Much of the press coverage of Unreal Engine 5 (UE5), for example, has focused on the geometry rendering package Nanite and lighting package Lumen. Further demonstrating Epic's "build and they will come" strategy that unifies co-marketing and development, stripped-down beta releases of UE5 were made available prior to its full release that allowed developers to play with—and subsequently upload to YouTube—the Lumen and Nanite packages. The returns were a pseudo-guerilla marketing campaign in which Unreal fans generated photorealistic forests, landscapes, and golden retrievers. Their videos were often accompanied by gushing reviews of the engine, or fans marveling at the impressive technical tricks used by Epic's programmers to keep the engine running and performing well.

Photorealism is the coin of the realm in graphics engine hype. Stephanie Boluk, Patrick Lemieux, and Eric Freedman have argued that the focus on realistic graphics in games engines has changed how players and designers approach their work.[21] Traditional games and computational media workflows give center-stage objects a proportionally large share of the polygon count in a scene. By contrast, hyperrealist game expectations have led to a "visual economy" in which all assets are treated equally, and even the most banal subjects require "graphical overkill."[22] While that claim may sound hyperbolic, UE5 press releases celebrating the geometry and shadows of pebbles next to a character's feet demonstrate Epic's continued investment in highlighting Unreal's graphical capacities down to the smallest polygon. As evidenced by Bleszinski and Levine's conversation above, this dedication can at times lead to consumer misunderstanding of the Unreal Engine as *only* capable of producing graphically complex games, when in fact the Engine is licensed by companies with a wide array of visual styles.

Games' photorealistic rendering is often situated in opposition to "expressive" or "stylized" rendering; this distinction obscures important historical and technical markers. To begin, we should understand photorealism itself as a style, a mix of affective and aesthetic choices to create visual and narrative mood. Game's photorealistic style is in part inherited from cinema. As cinema studies scholar Julie Turnock demonstrates, realism and photorealism have become naturalized over time, made to be understood as the pure pursuit to visually reflect nature; however, "realism" has had multiple definitions within cinematic history, "emphasiz[ing] different aspects [of reality] at different times."[23] Cinematic realism, Turnock notes, has included aesthetic and political elements varying from appropriate location scouting, actor choice, editing selections, narrative and script selections, and stylistic documentarian methods such as those found in cinéma verité.[24] Only in the late twentieth century, beginning with the visual and commercial success of 2001: A Space Odyssey and as refined through the major studio effects house Industrial Light and Magic (ILM), did "realism" come to be largely associated with computer graphics and special effects. This new association also popularly redefined the qualities of realism away from aesthetic decisions of filmmakers and instead toward pseudo-scientific narratives of a "natural or inevitable"[25] march toward "better" graphics.

This naturalized definition of computer graphics would also result in the making-invisible of photorealism's aesthetic and embodied qualities. Turnock argues, for example, that photorealism today is best understood as ILM photorealism: that of Industrial Light and Magic's house style. This style is doubly marked, visually by Star Wars director George Lucas's desire to synthesize the "credible and totally fantastic at the same time,"[26] and practically in Oscar-winning visual effects producer Dennis Muren's "eyeball test," or "proving the effect's realism because it looks right."[27] ILM graphics became the standard by which all photorealistic styles and practices were judged. While Lucas's combination of the "credible and the fantastic" recall the combination of truth claims and affective style embodied by the moon landing demo, Muren's, perhaps unintentionally, brings positionality into the photorealistic picture as well. What "looks right" to the eye, what is understood to be "credible," depends on the person watching. That both Lucas and Muren were well-connected white men is not lost on computer graphics researcher Ted Kim, who demonstrates how Lucas, Muren, and ILM effectively leveraged white narratives of "the scrappy startup" now common in Silicon Valley to write a history wherein their raced and classed positions had no impact on their cinematic and monetary success.[28]

ILM has an enduring impact on photorealist graphics from a material standpoint, as well. Turnock notes that, post 1980s, computer graphics tools have been shaped to "bend to the ILM aesthetic rather than the other way around."[29] In addition to demonstrating ILM's continued stylistic dominance, ILM's material gravity further blurs the artificial boundaries between photoreal and "expressive" rendering: in Unreal Engine, the processes for deploying the styles of photorealism and expressivism, as well as the shading algorithms that drive their calculations of light and color, heavily overlap. From a game developer's point of view, the vast majority of 3D rendering processes result from an entanglement of four elements in a given scene: the geometry, the position and direction of light, the shaders assigned to each object, and the position and properties of the virtual camera, which acts as a stand-in for the position of the player's body. Shaders are algorithmic processes instanced to each geometric element in the scene. They can be thought of as a layer of magical paint that coats a 3D model. I say "magical" because, in addition to determining the hue and reflectance of an object, shaders are used to create transparency, animations, subsurface lighting effects, glowing effects, and a host of other visual phenomena. Further, through the use of displacement algorithms and height maps, shaders can radically alter the shape of the underlying geometry of the model they are applied to. This shading technique is regularly leveraged in the games graphics pipeline to add geometric detail to simplified 3D models, which allows developers to keep visual detail high while keeping polygon counts (and therefore, computational memory usage) low. Each object in a 3D scene, then, is not just computational clay with a slick coat of digital paint. Each is an assemblage that emerges from the intra-actions of polygonal data and shading processes.

Since Unreal Engine 3 (UE3), game developers have worked on photoreal and stylized shader processes through Unreal's Materials Editor,[30] a node-based graph editor that allows developers to visually build shaders by connecting various datasets and algorithmic processes together (see figure 4.3). When in the editor, mathematical equations, texture maps, time, and space are treated equally, a logic of ontological-flattening-for-interoperability that is present throughout many of Unreal's packages and operational logics.[31] Hybrid interoperability is one of the first major epistemic hurdles new digital artists have to overcome when learning shading in Unreal. Artists must quickly become acclimated to workflows that involve subtracting images from one another, multiplying color by time, and using two-dimensional grayscale maps to generate three-dimensional geometry. There is a palpable feeling of wizardry that comes from successfully creating new visual phenomena that feel irreducible to the textures and equations that constitute them; there is even an entire genre of Twitter clout-play by skilled shader artists posting the cool visual effects they are able to produce through

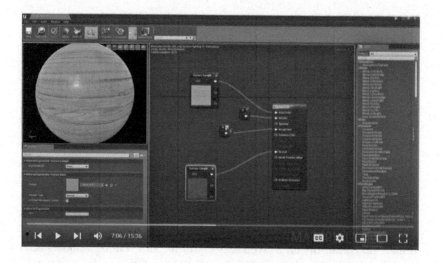

4.3 Screenshot showing how to use UE4's Materials Editor from an official Unreal tutorial (https://www.youtube.com/watch?v=sIMmDVLqh1s&list=PLZlv_No _O1gbQjgYonDwZNYe_N8IcYWS-&index=3).

unconventionally combining a hybridity of node types. Game shaders, quite literally, are more than the sum of their parts.

Each element in the Material Editor is presented to the user as a material expression: color-coded blocks have input channels and output channels, which are connected with digital thread in an ever-expanding tapestry. The term "expression" doubles as a mathematical and aesthetic term; each node simultaneously represents a single statement of at least two values connected by a mathematical operator and also acts as a step that contributes to the visual and aesthetic values expressed to the user. Unlike Deleuzian imaginations of the ever-emergent, rhizomatic structure of networks,[32] however, Unreal's material expression networks are strictly directional: no matter how complicated the network gets, all connections are eventually plugged into a single unique final expression node. Its output is visibly expressed on simple geometry—usually a sphere or cube—in a separate panel in the editor. Much of the work of the final stages of setting up a material network is figuring out the appropriate expression nodes needed to successfully reduce material expressions into the limited input slots of the master output node, with even many of the most complicated expression networks resulting in only four to five "final" output channels.

The "reduce-down-the-pipeline" model in the expression network workflow reinforces game development's operational logic of interoperability while also providing a new illusion of a standardized shading and rendering process. From the early 1990s through the mid-2000s, the shading process in graphics software (including UE and UE2) made explicit the need to select between different shading models for each piece of geometry in the scene. These different shading models used different algorithmic processes—including different inputs and outputs—to perform their visual work. Often, diverse models were used as rules of thumb to reproduce different physical phenomena and to create distinct visual effects. "Lambert" models—the brightly colored highlight on the surface of an object that gives a glossy or shiny look—for example, have no specular component to them. This makes them ideal for visualizing dull surfaces or for creating flat, cartoon-like coloring. Other times, multiple shader models are more visually consistent but have background processes that impact their viability for a given scene. "Blinn" and "Phong" models each contain specular highlights and are used to re-create metallic or plastic-like surfaces. Phong models, however, have a more complex specular calculation, which gives artists more control over the look of their objects while also requiring more computing power. A developer will make a decision whether to use Blinn or Phong for an individual object based on weighing multiple aesthetic, material, and relational judgements. They consider the visual importance of the object in the scene, the acceptable range of hardware required to render the game, the position of the camera and viewer's angle in relation to the object, and the presence (and computational expense) of other objects in the scene.

In Unreal, game artists are no longer presented with an array of shading models, but instead with the totalizing visual logic of the Materials Editor. Notably, artists *do* choose from multiple shaders, but in a subtler way. Nested across several editor submenus are options like "blend mode," "material domain," and "shading model"; these are different shaders cast as customizable options for a material. Depending on options selected in these submenus, input channels in the final material output node flicker on and off, and the visual qualities of the resulting material radically shift. Though visually understated, the continued presence of these models is important; there are many visual phenomena in the world that can be captured by standard shading models, and then there are "weird" phenomena that complicate the process. These weird phenomena are enacted due to both aesthetic and technical concerns. Some phenomena, like cartoon shading, can't be described using typical photographic mathematical expressions, and thus require custom shading models. Again, these phenomena tend to be clumped together as "expressive" visual rendering. Others, like how light is refracted and warped in a solid translucent object, *can* be described using basic physics, but require so much calculative work that re-creating the phenomena isn't yet feasible in real-time graphics, thus requiring a custom shader to "fake" the effect.

The layout of the Materials Editor does important epistemic work. It encourages the majority of game developers and artists to imagine materials creation as a standardized process with occasional offshoots. This imagination dovetails with increasing pushes toward overall pipeline standardization in game development.[33] This is not an accident: standardization and graphical fidelity go hand-in-hand: as industry-hyped consumer expectations for graphics increase, game developers face pressure to ensure their products consistently look "good" on a range of hardware. Players on desktop computers, multiple generations of home consoles, VR devices, and mobile platforms have been primed to expect hyperrealistic graphics, and as the market for multi-device play continues to expand, inter-device translational demands are skyrocketing. Game engines are beginning to reflect this increased need through standardization. Developers now expect engines to handle device translatability mostly in the background; any advantage an engine can give that eliminates the need to prepare multiple versions of assets or spend time mucking around in the code to boost framerates for individual devices is a massive financial incentive for AAA studios. The financial demands of AAA developers are further recast, often speciously, as being in the best interests of the independent dev community as well. Unreal and its chief competitor, Unity, have each characterized the hardware interoperability their software provides as a "democratizing" force for game development, allowing small and independent studios access to the same cross-development tools as AAA studios.[34] The current state of photorealistic game rendering pipelines, then, is an entanglement of the push for graphical fidelity, hardware variability, the shifting economic realities of the games market, and top-down, industry driven rhetoric of democratizing technical progress, all of which are contributing to technical and conceptual graphics standardization practices.

Physically Based Rendering

Standardization practices always assume some form of universality, either in input (i.e., that the world is made knowable through some repeatable process) or output (i.e., that the standardization of process produces a predictable or stable outcome), or both. From a user interface orientation, Unreal seems to privilege output; the main goal of the engine is preserving a universal play experience no matter the player's hardware paradigm.[35] Probing further into Unreal's rendering mechanics highlights how ontological universality—an assumed universalness to how the world works—also undergirds Unreal's graphical project. Unreal's physically based rendering processes explode the tension between the ontological and the phenomenological, placing the game developer at the center of a material and political fold.

While the Materials Editor is the primary interface for editing shaders in Unreal, much of the look of the shaders themselves is determined by algorithmic processes outside of the artist's control. Because of Unreal's shared source license, many AAA developers take advantage of the technical ability to alter and replace fundamental light and physics calculations at play in the Materials Editor. But for most users, Unreal's physically based materials system exerts tremendous influence over how a given scene will look, and how the artist needs to conceptualize the graphics pipeline.

Unreal's physically based materials are part of a larger push toward physically based rendering (PBR) in the games and animation industries—PBR models are quickly becoming the standardized approach to rendering across the majority of software packages. Despite this push, it was difficult in interviews with computer graphics developers to pin down a single, concrete definition or approach to PBR. What is consistent is the same turn toward naturalization of photorealism evidenced in cinema through the mass adoption of ILM house style. Despite PBR's rendering algorithms historically and aesthetically influenced by ILM, developers described PBR to me as "thinking about the world scientifically, instead of artistically," "modeling how light actually works, instead of how light looks," "a focus on the real world over fake ones," and "a graphical movement towards realism over expressivity." Discussions and research documents belied a fervor for the technique just beneath the surface; not only was PBR considered "more real" and "better looking," but there was a palpable desire for developers to "evangelize PBR to game teams" and artists.[36] The vast majority of developers and research documents I encountered consistently framed PBR as a more empirical, universal, and truthful representation of the world than non-physically based (NPB) approaches. This rhetoric would also reappear in NVIDIA's moon landing demo, which leveraged Unreal's physically based materials to claim that the fidelity of the simulation was a ground truth.

In this, both ILM and PBR's production of photorealism as both scientific and affective reflect the broader aesthetic and epistemic traditions of whiteness as chronicled by Richard Dyer. Dyer, in tracing the etymological use of "white" as connoting both the presence of all colors (as in the optical form of white light) and also the pure and unmarked (as in the blankness of the white canvas), argues that whiteness's duality allows it to operate as both a universal element and something "above" the stains of the world. "The slippage between white as a color and white as colorlessness," Dyer argues, "forms part of a system of thought and affect whereby white people are both particular and nothing in particular, both something and non-existent."[37]

We can characterize physically based rendering as a broad set of techniques that both produce computer graphics and also reproduce whiteness. PBR is an approach to computer graphics that attempts to reverse-engineer the physical properties of light and color to develop a standardized, systematized approach to rendering. Much of this reverse-engineering focuses on simulated physical properties of objects as represented by shader algorithms, such as whether or not an object is metal, how rough its surface is, whether it absorbs or refracts light. PBR derives its name from this simulated physicality. This mathematical standardization is enacted alongside evangelism that preaches the scientific and artistic superiority of universalized models of color and light. PBR is both a hailed scientific achievement and also the mundane representation of everyday life.

While PBR is often hyped as the bleeding edge of computer graphics, the technique is fairly old in computer graphics research; foundational papers on the subject were published between 1980 and 1982.[38] The technique had originally relied on raytracing, a process that tracks individual beams of light in a scene, enabling the artist to calculate soft bounced light, render photorealistic reflections, and change the accumulated color of an individual ray as it bounces off different colored surfaces. Tracing rays is computationally intensive, though, which has traditionally made the process (and therefore PBR) useful only for pre-rendered footage and still imagery. Recently, however, advances in both computer hardware and software have made PBR possible for real-time graphics engines. GPU hardware packs more computing power and forms of data architecture that allow for greater parallel processing, increasing their efficiency. Software-side, some PBR techniques have replaced raytracing methods with the same probabilistic random sampling method now widely employed across economic and political sentiment analysis[39] to determine the direction and color of light. While new methods produce less accurate results, they require substantially less computing time and can be fine-tuned by the artist to look "real enough," making them an ideal calculation method for real-time PBR.[40]

Color in PBR is made up of a combination of the temperature and intensity of light sources in the scene and the shader, which is applied to the objects in the scene. While non-physically based (NPB) shaders like Phong, Lambert, and Blinn are designed to create particular visual effects, PBR materials mimic the way light physically interacts with the physical structure of a surface. The color of a given pixel on a viewer's screen is determined by the shader, as applied to the geometry cast to that pixel. A PBR shader determines color by leveraging the object's base color, assigned physical properties, cast and reflected light, and other nearby objects. Think of this process as taking different approaches to graphically representing an apple. A PBR approach would be to determine the waxiness of the skin, the amount of porousness of the apple, if there are any chemical traces on the fruit's surface, the color of nearby objects, and the surface roughness of the apple. Then it would model an equation that measures how light will refract off and move through the apple given those properties. Conversely, an NPB approach would be to simply pick a red paint that matches the apple's color and gloss.

Despite the push toward universalization, there is no standard PBR formula or implementation across software packages. Unreal's models are based on PBR models developed at Disney for the 2012 film *Wreck-It Ralph*, though decomplexified so as to be viable for real-time rendering.[41] However, most PBR models (including Unreal's) center two core physical models of how light and surface interact: microfacet theory and the conservation of energy.

Microfacet theory abstracts the interaction of a ray of light with the surface and subsurface of an object. Light is modeled as a carrier of information. Human vision interprets the color of light via the angle the light takes to the eye, as well as the qualities of the surface the light has bounced off of. In the classic example, white light—made up of an equal distribution of all human-visible wavelengths of the color spectrum—hits a surface, say, again, an apple. The properties of the surface of the apple absorb many of the white light's wavelengths but reflect some back—in our case, those in the red part of the spectrum. The reflected light travels to the viewer's eye, where the spectral information is interpreted as the color of the surface: the red skin of an apple.

The direction and uniformity of light plays a role in vision as well. Microfacet theory posits that when rays of light hit a surface, their resulting directions are determined (1) by how light penetrates the surface membrane, bounces around inside the object, and exits the object, a process alternately called "subsurface scattering" or "diffusion," and (2) by microfacets, microscopic ridges, deformations, and divots in the surface of an object that deflect light rays. Diffusion contributes to an object's perceived color, while microfacets in the surface alter an object's reflectivity; the "rougher" the surface of an object is, the more it disrupts the uniform informational patterns of light, and the less image information is observed. The smoother an object's surface, the more reflective the object.

Microfacet theory is represented in graphical interface through a new, PBR-specific material channel called "roughness." A grayscale image map becomes mathematically interpreted (a black pixel = 0, a white pixel = 1, a middle gray pixel = 0.5) to drive how broken or uniform a surface is, and thus how reflective it is. A pixel in a roughness map that is closer to black is closer to 0, and thus smoother and more reflective. These images themselves need not be uniform, a quality taken advantage of by artists to introduce "real world grit" into a material. For example, a dark gray roughness map with random streaks of light gray, if applied to a smooth chrome sphere, will make it appear as though the sphere has rough scratches across its surface.

A universal roughness channel replaces the need for different calculations of specular values that marked the NPB era of Blinn and Phong shaders. This is where the conservation of energy enters the PBR equation. Since light is either diffused by a surface or reflected by it, diffused color and reflectivity are mutually exclusive.[42] A reflective surface bounces light almost immediately, limiting the ability of light to scatter inside the object and provide a diffused color. Coupled with the conversation of energy, in which the amount of light that leaves an object can never exceed the amount that was cast on that object, reflective objects' colors appear more black than an artist might expect. Conversely, the more diffuse color an object represents, the less reflection is possible, and the more the color trends toward white.

Finally, PBR's conservation of energy model splits the material world into a binary of conductive versus insulating materials. Conductive materials, almost universally metal, have high reflective values and tend to not scatter light, thus offering no diffuse color. Insulators, like most non-metals, will generally scatter some light, contributing to a brighter diffuse color. Reflectivity also changes depending on conductivity, with metals sometimes tinting the color of their reflections. In PBR, this binary is translated into a "metalness" channel for shaders. The value that PBR artists assign—metal or non-metal— fundamentally changes the physics calculations in the material.[43]

PBR's universalized, physics-based approach to photorealistic rendering has pragmatic and epistemic implications. Pragmatically, the movement toward a standardized shader equation limits the artist's need to manage multiple shader types with varying inputs and outputs (such as the Blinn, Phong, and Lambert models described above). Standardization also makes it easier for developers to move between different game and graphics engines without needing to learn completely new rendering workflows. Further, a physically based, universalized lighting and shading model allows for shaders to appear logically consistent, no matter their lighting conditions. In NPB rendering workflows, it was commonly required for graphics artists to develop separate shaders for the same object for different scenes. For example, an NPB shader for a character's leather jacket might look correct under ambient blue light approximating daylight but appear too dark or too specular under angled orange light in a later sunset scene. This difference in appearance would require artists to swap between "daytime" and "dusk" shaders depending on scene context. The microfacet and energy conservation principles in physically based models, in theory, circumvent this problem, as the leather jacket should appear in any simulated lighting conditions similar to how it would to the human eye in the physical world.

While the PBR artist is responsible for creating visually pleasing images and setting a visual mood appropriate to the game narrative, their render techniques now center a model of a universalized material world. Technical artist Joe Wilson argues that even "fantastical" stories and visions should be understood through the lens of physical reality:

> If your goal is to create a fantastical, stylized world, having accurate material definition is still very important. Even if you're creating a unicorn that farts rainbows, you still generally want that unicorn to obey the physics of light and matter.[44]

In PBR, even fantasy must subordinate to the laws of light and computer graphics' "quest for realism."[45] While this pragmatist approach to rendering may save the artist time, its true strength is saving production and management time. PBR increases studios' profits by both making the individual artist more efficient and creating a systemic practice of production that makes all artist output interoperable.[46] Assets produced by any artist will look the same in any scene, and thus a game's art style depends more on the systemization and managerial directing of an artist workforce, rather than on techniques and tastes of any individual artist. We shouldn't overstate PBR's labor impact, as game production has been increasingly systematized and managed over the past twenty years, even in NBP workflows. Still, PBR provides managers another tool in their toolbox to Taylorize even the most qualitative forms of labor.

Epistemically, PBR further encourages a shift in digital graphics toward physical simulation and systematized production, and away from what Heinrich Wölfflin calls a "painterly" way of knowing—an affective, phenomenological attention to the shape and quality of individual human experiences of color.[47] NPB lighting workflows, for example, often selectively apply multiple competing models of color to achieve different visual and affective reactions in the viewer. An artist may choose to follow complementary color shading, in which the specular highlights and cast shadows from an object are tinted in complement to the object's diffuse color, thus making the object appear more vibrant. A red apple, for example, may have a slight green tint to its highlight and shadow. Complementary color shading creates hot spots of shape and movement that appear both natural and ethereal, drawing in and immersing the viewer into new ways of experiencing color.

While this technique has been used by painters and watercolorists for hundreds of years, and is *phenomenologically* correct—in that complementary shading impacts human perception of color—it is *physically* incorrect from a universalized, mathematics-based model of color. Simultaneously, individual objects obeying unique rules for specular and shadow color introduce variation and unpredictability into the production pipeline, increasing development time and cost. As such, painterly elements like shadow color and specular color are wrested from the artist's control in PBR and are handled by algorithmic processes modifiable only by developers who have source-level engine access.

Diffracting PBR

I have thus far described how photorealism is not grounded in an objective understanding of visual reality, but instead in the cinematic styles and aesthetics of the film industry. These styles have been made natural in part because of the epistemic authority established by white men at the heights of the film industry, as well as in service of the game industry's desire to automate labor. The resulting naturalized industry narrative of PBR is that, as computer hardware becomes more capable, physics simulations get faster and more accurate, leading to better looking—and more truthful—representations of the world. This narrative produces media like the moon landing demo, which leverages the story to enact real-time graphics-as-truth. In the demo, light and physics are universally consistent, as PBR accurately models them, and thus a real-time visualization of the lunar surface can stand in for empirical and historical reality. Realtime PBR is hyped as its own scientific breakthrough. Yet, its mass adoption by computer graphics artists, influenced by PBR evangelists and management-benefiting time and labor reduction, reinforces the game industry's own techno-libertarian leanings. PBR represents an exciting triumph of technology, whose physical accuracy and industry adoption are entangled. PBR proves that graphics technology marches on toward perfectly simulating reality. The moon landing demo's exposing of the toolset behind the simulation thus, for viewers, *reinforces* the truth of the lunar diorama, as achieved through the triumph of technology, rather than undermines it.

It matters, though, that so much of the hype around PBR is grounded in narratives about the technique's grounding in physics. Not only does the rhetorical synthesis of physics and aesthetics mirror the broader interconnectedness of truth claims and affect traced in this chapter, but also the white masculinity of the field of physics itself lends cultural and epistemic validity to the naturalized and neoliberal claims of PBR advocates.

In her foundational work *Meeting the Universe Halfway*, physicist and feminist theorist Karen Barad argues for the adoption of "diffractive" reading and thinking practices in the sciences and humanities. Diffraction is a model in classical physics that characterizes the ripple patterns formed when waves encounter objects, passages, or other waves. Experiments with light in the nineteenth century showed that light exhibited both diffractive properties of waves and ray-like properties of particles. In the twentieth century, diffraction became famously associated with quantum experimentation that demonstrated how matter too follows wave-like behavior. Such diffractive patterns tend to overlap onto themselves to create ever more intricate patterns. Like ripples in a pond, they bounce off each other, the edges of the pond, and objects in the water. The water, the boundaries of the pond, the objects within it, and the objects that pass through it all make up what Barad calls "the apparatus" of the pond. To remove any of them would fundamentally change the apparatus, and thereby change the pond. Barad takes up the term diffraction as a call for "reading patterns of differences that make a difference."[48] Barad continues:

> The shift towards diffraction, towards differences that matter, is really a matter of what physicists call physical optics as compared to geometrical optics. Geometrical optics does not pay any attention to the nature of light. Actually, it is an approximation that gets used to study the optics of different lenses, or mirrors. And you just treat light as if it were a ray (an abstract notion). In other words, it is completely agnostic about whether light is a particle or a wave or anything else. It is just an approximation scheme for studying various apparatuses. By

contrast, diffraction allows you to study both the nature of the apparatus and also the object. That is, both the nature of light and also the nature of the apparatus itself.[49]

Barad's definition of diffraction is doubly useful for us. First, she suggests that scientific, technological, and visual phenomena are co-constitutive. The scientific apparatus does not unveil an external reality, but is instead an active participant in producing that reality. Studying light, in Barad's example, sometimes tells us more about the mechanisms used to study light than it does about the nature of light itself. This brings us to how Barad's diffractive analysis underscores the rhetorical work that the term "based" does in "physically based rendering." Raytracing literally traces rays of light, thereby, applying Barad, simulating an apparatus of lenses and mirrors more than it grapples with the nature of light and matter. Despite evangelists' claims to simulate physical reality, PBR is not based on a universal physical reality, but rather on a specific arrangement of photoreality. The apparatus of PBR is thus as entangled with histories and epistemologies of the camera as it is with physics.

I have in this chapter already touched on some of the constitutive parts of the PBR apparatus: market forces and managerial logics that reflect intuitional scientific reasoning, producing PBR as a symbol of scientific and technological progress. The PBR model itself is a historically, materially, and politically specific apparatus, rather than the universal translator of light that it is advertised as in the NVIDIA demo. "A model is a work of fiction," philosopher of science Nancy Cartwright argues.[50] "Some properties ascribed in the model will be genuine properties of the objects modeled, but others will be merely properties of convenience."[51] Cartwright notes that while some properties of convenience are idealizations or abstractions of phenomena that make calculations easier—such as approximating light as a ray—others will be "pure fictions." They will contain elements not based in physical reality that make the model function better in conjunction with other laws of physics and mathematics.[52]

PBR is replete with these kinds of properties of convenience. The Disney PBR shading model, on which a vast majority of PBR models—including Unreal's—are derived, is labeled and designed as a "principled BRDF" model. BRDF stands for the bidirectional reflectance distribution function, a function for measuring the interaction of light and an opaque surface that, "describes how a surface reflects light for any illumination direction, any viewing direction, and any wavelength."[53] The BRDF serves as the backbone for almost all models of three-dimensional simulated light and color, including PBR and NPB shading techniques. The principles in the "principled shader" refer not to physical principles and properties, but instead to use case. Its variables, parameters, and value ranges were designed to be familiar to artists, even if that meant sometimes violating or tweaking physical laws. According to Disney programmer Brent Burley, development of PBR shading models was always biased toward the following five principles:

1. Intuitive rather than physical.
2. As few parameters as possible.
3. Parameters are zero to one over their plausible range.
4. Parameters are allowed to be pushed beyond their plausible range where it makes sense.
5. All combinations of parameters should be as robust and plausible as possible.[54]

The apparatus of the PBR BRDF, then, is already a hybrid of the intuitions of physicists and programmers. Physicists have epistemically produced light as a phenomenon to be modeled, and programmers have approached artists (and their "intuitions") as a subject to be modeled *for*. Some of the artist conveniences in the Disney model include the parametrization of values from zero to one (zero being "off," one being "on"), as we have seen implemented in the unique PBR roughness and metalness values. Another convenience is the ability to exceed physical reality "where it makes sense," which should be read as "when the mood of the narrative or visual impact requires it." The PBR apparatus is also biased toward the technical demands of the system it is constitutive of. Part of this bias toward technical demands is certainly reasonable. The principle that parameter combinations must be "plausible and robust" translates to "no combination of variables should break the visual acuity of the shader, nor cause fatal mathematical errors in the software." It would certainly impact artists' quality of life if the shading model they centrally relied on was capable of crashing their software.

But the conveniences of PBR also serve as a lens to illustrate the foundation of white empiricism on which contemporary PBR practices are built. As the principled model aims to ask artists for as few parameters as possible, the limited parameters fed into a PBR model have a large impact on the final look of the shader, making getting those parameters "right" a key concern to game artists. As a result, an entire paratextual[55] industry around Unreal's PBR models has emerged. Artists, engineers, and PBR enthusiasts share parameter data for various real-world materials. Their shared texts range from message boards where artists give advice on one another's shaders, engine and game "postmortem" documentation that details the construction of major game shaders, and infographics that show photographic imagery of real-world materials and the numerical translations needed to create them in Unreal's PBR.

One of the most popular PBR infographics comes from self-described PBR "evangelist" Sébastien Lagarde and his colleagues Sophie Van de Velde and Laurent Harduin at DONTNOD Entertainment.[56] The chart walks new PBR artists through various combinations of diffuse color, roughness, and metalness, and illustrates how successful integrations of these values can produce radically different, yet still physically real, material qualities. Though the chart was first developed in 2012, various iterations and links to Lagarde's blog posts about it still circulate on Unreal development forums today.

In one of these forums, Unreal developer James Baxter asks the most important question for PBR evangelists: "That looks good, I'm wondering though, are those [color] values based off of real-world examples or just what the artist thought looked good?"[57] This question serves as another example of a consistent PBR social phenomena we explore in chapter 5: the epistemic value of an objective, separate "real world" over a subjective visual that "just" looks good to the human eye. In PBR communities and rhetoric, PBR represents a triumph of empirical, objective measurement and simulation. A "real-world example," in this case, is not an artist's interpretation of an image of a material, but rather a measurement of a material's BRDF, as generated by a gonioreflectometer, a complex arrangement of lights, cameras, rotating mechanical arms, and rapid data processing units. The gonioreflectometer is designed to produce Haraway's "god trick," the simultaneous "view from everywhere" and "view from nowhere." By rotating around an object and measuring how specular reflections and shadows move and shift, dependent on the position of the camera, the gonioreflectometer can materially engineer an empirically impossible calculation—how does light bounce off an object when there is no observer to see it?—through the probabilistic stitching together of myriad image datasets.

As Barad's illustration of diffractive light shows us, however, measurements of light are produced by the apparatuses designed to measure them. They reveal to us as much about the material and social arrangements of scientific practice as they do about universal properties of light. Gonioreflectometers can produce findings only for a limited subset of physical materials; if light reflects off an object's surface too uniformly (i.e., the object is too glossy or mirrorlike), it becomes difficult, if not impossible, for cameras to capture the high dynamic range of that object's brightness and darkness.[58] Thus the objects chosen for goniore-flectometry tend to be beneath a certain gloss range, therefore limiting what of the "real world" can be measured and simulated by PBR. Alternatively, they are slightly roughened or deglossed before image capture, producing an inaccurate, but "good enough," BRDF capture. You wouldn't know this from perusing various PBR forums, however; there, decontextualized graphs and tables from scientific papers, and charts measuring BRDFs and other indices of light, are presented as universal truths to be replicated. BRDF indices used in PBR, then, are enacted as representative of a universal material reality through the denial of the material conditions that allowed those indices to come into being.

The "god trick" is not just an ontological claim about the legitimacy of empirical data, or of the philosophical limits of posing an objective world beyond the self. It is also an epistemic and political claim about what kinds of knowledge are made knowable and who counts as a legitimate knower in social and technical regimes. The impacts of what is knowable and who is a knower shapes our social and technical worlds; what counts as a "real" or "true" representation of the real world in a given system depends in part on whose voice in knowledge regimes is recognized as being able to speak to the real, or whose voice is an "appropriate" presence in a discussion of the real. The consternation over whether a PBR guide is based on BRDF measurements or eye is just one example of the contestation of knowledge: in this instance, who is a more appropriate knower, a mechanical apparatus or an artist? While artist knowledge and practice are clearly valued in the PBR development community (hence the artist-first principled BRDF), they are also framed as not an appropriate voice for determining the "true" parameters of a physically based shader.

The construction of "truth" in PBR as based on disciplinary prestige, rather than on other embodied or epistemic positions, mirrors a similar phenomenon in the practice of physics itself. Drawing from Joseph Martin's concept of prestige asymmetry,[59] Prescod-Weinstein argues that physics subfields like high energy physics that have more white men are constructed as more intellectually expansive than other subfields, while also being held to lower standards of empirical proof. String theory, for example, one of the most influential and—thanks to public-facing scientists like Stephen Hawking—popular models of the universe, has no observational or experimental evidence supporting it. Its popularity is instead fueled by a combination of compelling mathematical models, charismatic promises to unify multiple models of quantum gravity and space-time physics, and the celebrity status of its (white men) proponents. This does not necessarily mean that string theory is *wrong*, Prescod-Weinstein argues. Rather, what is recognized as "prestigious" physics has less to do with the empirical processes of the scientific method and more to do with who is understood as having the capacity to speak representatively about the order of the physical world. This enactment is culturally and affectively powerful. "If you ever want to see physicists get emotional," Prescod-Weinstein quips, "stick proponents of different quantum gravity models in a room and tell them to discuss the relative merits of their models."[60]

Helen Longino and Sandra Harding have, respectively, advocated for understanding scientific knowledge as a form of social knowledge and for a "strong" objectivity that acknowledges how the position of the researcher shapes the outcome of research.[61] Further, Prescod-Weinstein builds on critical social theorist Patricia Hill Collins, who argues that Black women's thought is epistemically suppressed by the actions and cultures of scientific practice. In scientific practice, white men are constructed as more important figures, leading to a citational divide between men and everyone else.[62] It is also useful to read the concept of physics' white empiricism through feminist philosopher Luce Irigaray, who argues that physics' mencenteredness has not only dominated its cultures and practices, but also fundamentally permeated the methods and laws of physics themselves. In her essay "Is the Subject of Science Sexed?" Irigaray argues that not only are the conductors and observers of scientific practice sexed—their claims to rationality and objectivity are enabled by their maleness—but that also the processes and outcomes of science are imbued with Western masculine ideology, which emerges in practice through what Irigaray labels the scientist's "intuition."[63] She provides examples of scientific intuition: "proving the model's *universality*" and "posing *one* world before oneself, constituting a world *in front of* oneself, and of proving that the discovery is *effective, productive, profitable, exploitable*. And this signifies *progress*.[64]"

For Irigaray, the subject of science is doubly sexed: both the practicing subjects and the subjects practiced are sexed as male. To draw from Prescod-Weinstein's lens of white empiricism, we can argue that the subjects of physics, and in PBR, the subjects of light, are also doubly raced: the practicing subjects and the subjects practiced enact white epistemological and ontological frames.

The cultures, epistemologies, and ontologies of physics trickle down into cultures of PBR. Much of PBR's cultural cache among computer graphics researchers descends from its supposed adherence to prestigious models of light and matter from physics. Whereas NPB models merely "look good," PBR is ostensibly "real" (while also, importantly, "looking good"). Because PBR is "universal," its destiny is to eventually be the standard shading model for all graphical scenes, even "fantastical" ones.

Conclusion

Physically based rendering traffics in multiple kinds of white vision and authority: that of Dennis Muren's "eyeball" positionality, George Lucas's blending of the mundane and the fantastic, and the discipline of physics' white empirical epistemic authority. Ironically, PBR's god trick and triumph of science over artist are, paradoxically, both a sign of success and a marked reversal from the pursuit of photorealistic style in cinema from which Unreal's renderer derives. On the one hand, Lucas and Muren's style and models of production were so culturally successful that they became ahistoricized and naturalized. Their photorealistic styles worked, the story now goes, because Lucas and Muren were able to capture something about reality through technology. Simultaneously, the prowess of their well-trained cinematic eyes put them in the best positions to make judgments about how well their films reflected reality, and to build cinematic-technical-computational apparatuses that would come to be at both the technical and economic forefront of visual effects.

However, this naturalized mythos, cinematic and ludic photorealism as natural and inevitable, also sets the stage for the de-skilling of the visual artists who would follow in Lucas and Muren's steps. If what ILM did was discover a hidden, objective truth about the optical world, why can't a formula or algorithm be developed to discover those truths automatically? And while the cinematic eye brought to computer graphics and photorealism through the eyeball test was useful at the time, wouldn't the godlike, computerized eye be even more accurate, particularly if it was trained to follow the objective laws of physics? Who needs artist eyes and labor when the most successful an artist can be is to accurately render the real world—something a proper automated graphics system could do more quickly and more cheaply?

In chapter 5, I explore the ripple effects of the naturalization of photorealism and PBR on raced labor and bodies. As Aleena Chia has argued, the standardization of the game graphics pipeline made possible by shifts brought about by PBR and its translation in 3D image capturing produces a racialized automation of game art assets.[65] The "non-hero" and other background assets and environments most commonly automated through PBR are assets that, over the past decade, have been increasingly produced by gendered, racialized, outsourced labor.[66] Simultaneously, within "hero" characters themselves, the rendering of human skin inherits aesthetic and technical decisions that mark the white body as preferable and the human standard, decisions which, like that of photorealism more broadly, have been rendered natural through technical and cultural processes.

As chapter 5 argues, PBR practices in Unreal reproduce longer histories of race across painting, photography, and cinema, where white skin and the ideal white body are centered as the ideal human form. However, PBR's inheritance of the epistemic privilege of the field of physics allows for a further depriviliging of nonwhite bodies. Unflattering skin tones and representations can be framed not as an aesthetic choice of the author, but rather as the "ground truth" of the physically real lighting scenario—any problems, in other words, become placed on the bodies represented, not in the act of representation. Woven throughout naturalized histories of PBR and their impacts on graphics and labor practices are the whispers of whiteness: who gets to claim best reference to the natural world, whose stances and positions become understood as most objective, whose methods and practices are most naturally aligned with "the real"; whose labor and bodies are necessary—and whose are not.

The future of digital humans, Epic would tell you, is the MetaHuman Creator project. This UE5 plug-in promises easy integration of pre-rigged, lifelike humans into any Unreal-developed project. When first download-ing and running the project's "Meet the MetaHumans" demo, users are presented with a T-posed Black woman, who, for reasons made clear later in the chapter, we will call 001. Upon running the simulation, the in-game camera shifts to a closeup of the woman's face (see figure 5.1). She smiles and introduces herself with a soft British accent: "I am a MetaHuman." The skin around her cheeks puffs and swells as she speaks, and her fore-head wrinkles and softens as she raises and lowers her eyebrows. As 001 narrates the strengths of the MetaHuman project, she proudly declares that she "is fully rigged." With a stiff hand motion, blue and purple boxes and lines of light wrap themselves around her arms and shoulders, and golden rings clasp around her neck and head. A 2D box with yellow points of light that map onto quantized parts of her lips appears next to her face.

This is her "control rig"—manipulatable jigs, rotational values, and sliders used in character animation to streamline the animation process. As she continues talking, she begins to visually observe her own body. Arrows on her hand flare with her hand movements, and the dot-matrix next to her face traces out the contours of her lips. Though it looks like 001 is driving the rig, the rig is, of course, driving her—the arrows, dots, clasps, and lines make the animation data that generates her movements visible to humans. She smiles again, and puts her hand down; the rig disappears, and her body appears, for the moment, to once again be her own. She

5.1 Screenshot of MetaHuman 001 with a visualization of her control rig from Epic's "Meet the MetaHumans" trailer (https://www.youtube.com/watch?v=HuAAdsZPLlE).

continues: "With everything running live on Unreal Engine, my motion works seamlessly—"; she suddenly disappears, replaced by an East Asian man, 004, who finishes the sentence: "—on other characters" (figure 5.2).

The transition is somewhat jarring. This is intentional, of course—the ebbs and flows of the control rig, the closeup camera angles, and the sudden character swap are all manicured to provoke that same sense of affective, technological wonder as the seen in chapter 4's moon landing demo. But there's another reason the switch is disconcerting; the second Asian character stands out more in the video than the first, a Black woman. At first glance, the sharpness of the transition can be explained by simple color choice: the background of the MetaHuman is a deep gray, and the paler skin tones of 004 contrast and "pop" against that backdrop more than those of the Black character. But as you look closer, you can see that "pop" has less to do with the background and more to do with the skin itself. While both characters are underlit, the Asian character's skin is more vibrant.

Highlights help define the features of the 004's face. His midtones and fleshtones are never pushed too far toward white, and his lowlights and shadows don't dissolve into flattened gray or black tones. The diffusion of light just under the surface of his skin gives a slight pinkish undertone, preventing the skin material from looking too flat or painted on. On the other hand, 001 features blown-out highlights on her skin, and what highlights are there appear softened and muddled. Her brown midtones are flat, and her lowlights fade to a gray-black, causing her face

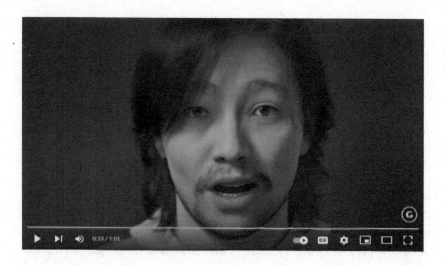

5.2 Screenshot of 004 in Unreal's "Meet the MetaHumans" trailer (https://www .youtube.com/watch?v=HuAAdsZPLlE).

to lose definition and fade into the background. She has a similar reddish undertone as 004, but her skin looks claylike, as though it were pancaked on to the facial rig. She looks flat. She doesn't shine.

This chapter is the second part of my examination of Unreal's participation in the production of what I call "white photorealism." White photorealism is the production of graphical realism, scientific authority, labor, race, and bodies in computer graphics that centers white bodies and ways of knowing as objective and authoritative, and all others as derivative or deviant. Chapter 4 introduced Unreal's physically based rendering (PBR) system, a new implementation of an older computer graphics technique that attempts to model photoreality. PBR's greatest contribution to real-time gaming is its introduction of standardized rendering models. Rather than needing to build custom lighting and shading models for all objects in the scene, PBR produces a standardized shader model that can handle most in-game assets, including those made from a host of physical materials ranging from metal to plastic to flesh. PBR thus works aesthetically by attempting to reverse-engineer physically accurate models of the interaction of light and surface, and it works institutionally to standardize and automate labor across the game art pipeline.[1]

PBR, I previously argued, is a successful graphics technology because of its alignment with whiteness. First, from an aesthetic perspective, the shading technique's modeling of photoreality is not necessarily aligned with physical reality, but rather with that of white Hollywood cinematic photorealism, as defined and institutionalized by the graphics production house Industrial Light and Magic (ILM) in the 1980s through the 2000s.[2] As Julie Turnock has documented, ILM's photoreal "house style" was a synthesis of George Lucas's desire to blend mundane lighting and camera effects with fantastical elements with Dennis Muren's "eyeball test": that cinematic realism was best achieved through the eye of the director, who could judge whether or not a shot would "look right" to an audience.[3] ILM's cinematic success and commercial popularity would influence the industry writ large, leading toward effects houses aiming to replicate ILM's style and computer graphics technologies developed in directions that technically and artistically aligned themselves with ILM.[4] Thus, not only did ILM's particular photorealistic style become broadly naturalized—assumed by industry and general audiences to be the result of a natural progression of technology and cinematic technique—so too did the practices of ILM's art directors: the presumption that the well-trained directorial eye had the capacity to objectively evaluate the "realness" of a scene. As Ted Kim has argued, that ILM was helmed by and connected to rich white men lent credence to the company's claims of capturing the universal aesthetic of fantastical realness.[5]

Second, from a labor perspective, PBR aligns itself with what Chanda Prescod-Weinstein has called the "white empiricism" of scientific practice, or the combination of assumed objectivity and field prestige that occurs in whitened spaces in the scientific community. PBR's aesthetic validity is derived from its rhetorical closeness to physics—that, because PBR accurately simulates physical phenomena, its judgement on how an object appears can be valued alongside, even above, that of the artist's eye, which is polluted by subjectivity. PBR's alignment with physics also grants it the cultural and political prestige of that field—that of being "effective, productive, profitable, exploitable."[6] Due to its quick and effective reproduction of optical physics—or, rather, of the naturalized photoreality of ILM as rendered through physics—PBR is seen as a method of replacing artists with computational systems or, at the very least, of automating away the "boring" parts of game art.[7]

Assumptions, intuitions, cinema, scientific publications, and affect all diffract within the apparatus of Unreal's PBR, enacting white ways of knowing and seeing. Though Unreal's PBR is a part of a larger production of whiteness, it is also important to note, following Patrick Wolfe, how whiteness, like all productions of race, is not an essential quality of a thing, but rather an ongoing historical practice, one of which we must be continually reminded, and one that involves multiple, sometimes incompatible and incommensurable qualities.[8] Wendy Chun reminds us to understand race both in and as technology, as something that can be found in and through our technical practices, but also as something that allows us to "do" things in the world.[9]

I have thus far traced only some of the ways that PBR acts to produce whiteness. The white eye is produced as both a situated and affective—though ultimately correct—judgement (through Lucas and Muren), as well as a universal, rational whole (through the practice of physics). Similarly, computer graphics are posited as a particular stylistic choice that can be made only by some of the most highly trained digital artists around (ILM), as well as a natural and inevitable discovery of fundamental truths about the material and optical world. The artist is both central to the production of computer graphics and also eminently replaceable. Of course, as Aleena Chia notes, those artists who have found their jobs made replaceable by PBR have tended to be those in environment and "non-hero" art assets, which are often produced by laborers of color in the economic periphery, while jobs held by (often white, male) hero artists and game directors remain safe.[10]

This chapter traces another production of whiteness through Unreal: Unreal's physically based renderer and its reverberations throughout the MetaHuman Creator project is entangled with the raced histories of physics, computational vision, light, and skin. Unreal thus participates in a "mattering" of race[11]—both in terms of how racialized logics *come to matter* in real-time computer graphics and also in terms of how digital light, skin, and "the real" interact to produce raced "truths," enacting a way of computational seeing.

Unreal's MetaHuman project and its synthesis of PBR techniques with body-capturing technologies mark the white body as standard and others as deviant. At the same time, Unreal's MetaHuman assumes a universality to the body, as an object whose embodied conditions can be easily modified and replaced. Just as with the incommensurable whiteness of the director's eye and the physicists' eye, then, the MetaHuman body and its graphical apparatus are bound together by overlapping yet incommensurable aspects of whiteness—that of uniqueness and that of universality.

To make this argument, I trace the MetaHuman capturing and rendering of human skin, particularly that of its rendering of white skin as both an aesthetic and ontological universal, which is made more evident when MetaHuman's PBR shaders are used to render Black skin. This enactment of race—particularly whiteness and Blackness—includes the digital phenotypical dimensions of identity representation that have been explored by scholars like Amanda Phillips,[12] Evan Narcisse,[13] and Theodore Kim.[14] However, whiteness and Blackness in Unreal are both entangled with and transcend these representations of the body. Light and color in game engines are enacted through an entanglement of prebuilt code and rendering packages, "best practices" of knowing and understanding light, and both contemporary and legacy hardware formats that determine what can be calculated and what can be displayed.

Embodied race is multiply rendered by Unreal. It is rendered at the time of display, such as through the lighting and shading models deployed in real time on 001's and 004's skins during the "Meet the MetaHumans" demo. It is rendered historically and materially through the reproduction of cinematic and artistic techniques, techniques that have both mimetically centered the representation of white bodies over those of others while also producing darker bodies as deviant or less-than. It is rendered ontologically, where the dualistic logics of PBR will align melanated skin as more akin to an object than to a human. It is rendered at time of capture, particularly through the use of photogrammetric technologies in attempting to capture the "ground truth" of an actor's skin.[15] And race becomes rendered as invisible when attempts to question its effects within computer graphics are made.

This multiple rendering of race in/through Unreal, and particularly of the centrality of whiteness, aligns with prior investigations into computer graphics and representations of race, including recent writing on the MetaHuman Creator. Alison Reed and Amanda Phillips have argued that the pipeline of computer graphics generally, and motion and body capture specifically, create an additive production of race:

> Technologies preoccupied with "realism" inscribe race in a moment obsessed with the myth of post-raciality. The link between the tradition of minstrelsy and the multicultural celebration of difference as additive, rather than embodied, exposes how whiteness must animate itself against a fictitious "Other" imagined as embodying culture. At the same time, discourses of colorblindness assume that race no longer constitutes a significant category of analysis—a move that negates the daily lived realities and material manifestations of power operating on bodies in order to foreclose conversations about ongoing racial injustice.[16]

Reed and Phillips find in their study of motion capture performance and "digital Blackface" similar tensions at play as we see through PBR: the simultaneous rendering of whiteness as universal and postracial while also producing an affective tension to assert itself against a defined "Other," thus revealing the fantasy of contemporary postracialism. This affective tension dovetails with André Brock's illustration of technology's entangling of whiteness with the need to disavow and dispose of the other.[17] Drawing on the work of Jean-François Lyotard, Frank Wilderson, and Jared Sexton, Brock traces moments where racialization manifests when the universality of the white cinematic apparatus meets the destruction of Black persons. As an example, Brock points to activism generated by video documentation and dash-cam footage of police shootings of Black people in the United States. The video recordings and the gutting, viscerally emotional moments they capture stimulated public outrage that would turn these police shootings from statistical mundanity into sustained political action. "The recording itself is invested with a libidinal energy," Brock argues, "we often take the regard of the camera as a 'truth' to be trusted even as we understand that the perception of the truth varies with each individual, institution, or system."[18] The dash-cam footage entangles the rational and the emotional to produce a truth that cannot be understood by statistical data alone.

In an interview with Brock, J. Khadijah Abdurahman summarizes this use of "libidinal" as emphasizing "that emotional intensities, such as desire or antiblackness, drive 'rational self-interest' or political-economic modes of thinking."[19] For Brock, through Wilderson and Fred Moten, the use of the libidinal gives purchase to analyze the racialized ways in which seemingly "rational" or "objective" videographic vision and light work. Though the camera has been critiqued as acting in service of the "god trick"—an observer-less, objective, and universalized point of view[20]—Brock notes that the camera is always used to produce affective and embodied interactions. The libidinal dimensions of camerawork and vision, Brock argues, can be thought of in terms of *pathos*, which Brock associates with "style"—the familiarity with and appeal to an "audience's value and belief systems, preferred presentation styles, and techniques of argumentation."[21] We see traces here of the incommensurable naturalization of white reality through the camera lens, similar to the incommensurable naturalization of white photoreality through computer graphics. The dash camera represents both the apparatus of objective white sight as well as aesthetic antiblackness.

Reed and Phillips specifically contrast the kinds of racialized forms of "universalism" seen in the performances of motion capture actors in *Mass Effect* with those of Dr. Aki Ross in the film *Final Fantasy: The Spirits Within*. *Mass Effect*'s standardized set of motion-captured dialogue animations, applied to characters of highly varying cultures, identities, species, and bodies, flattens the embodied cultural motions of these racialized characters, intimating that nonverbal communication is a universal collection of motions and gesticulations. *Final Fantasy*'s Ross, on the other hand, represents racialization as a muddled composite of the Other, which Reed and Phillips read as "fetishi[zing] racial ambiguity":[22]

> Aki Ross is a composite of multiple human actors, faces, bodies and voices—some of whom are credited and some of whom are not. Ross's physical gestures were animated in large part by actor Tori Eldridge, whose own mixed ethnic descent—Hawaiian, Chinese and Norwegian—seems to have motivated the appearance of Ross herself, while her voice was acted by Chinese American actress Ming-Na Wen. The performance capture was largely bodily, as Ross's facial expressions were compiled by Roy Sato, according to Jessica Aldred, "after a combination of Ming-Na's expressions during her videotaped vocal recording, and his own facial expressions, as examined in a mirror he kept next to his computer." . . . This merging and severing of reality and fantasy pinpoints the core aim of performance capture technologies: to produce the lifelike with a variety of human actors whose amalgamated efforts create a super-human who is at once believable and fantastical, a whitewashed figure who is in actuality a repository of difference—various genders, gestures, ethnicities, voices, technologies and performances.[23]

Aki Ross thus represents both the whole and the Other; an amalgamation of the bodies and labor of actors and artists of color, fused together and varnished with whiteness. Like the house style of ILM, her realism is to be found in her fantastical elements; that she both can and cannot exist is what makes her photoreal. Similarly, the figures in the MetaHuman project, 001 and 004 included, emerge through the muddled synthesis of captured bodies. In his own look at the MetaHuman Creator, Eric Freedman explains that MetaHumans are produced through the blending of thousands of body scans, resulting in a set of default-rigged characters that "represent the generalized contours of racial, ethnic, and gender diversity."[24] Following Epic's advertising claim that Unreal's MetaHumans are awaiting players to give them "a story,"[25] Freedman argues that the MetaHuman generator is "not a narrative engine," but rather reflects the gaming marketplace's demand for "efficient plug-and-play build, edit, and design systems"[26] that treat white and nonwhite bodies as interchangeable variables in asset production. Freedman continues:

> The MetaHuman Creator has mastered cosmetic human diversity alongside the organic and inorganic diversity of the material world, and the quick fabrication of multiculturalism seems to suggest

technology can be color blind and embrace a certain in-betweenness by offering up a high degree of consumer-driven customization.[27]

Freedman notes that, despite Epic's parroting of industry claims that more realistically rendered characters can vaguely "increase empathy,"[28] the MetaHuman Creator cannot capture the kinds of lived experiences and struggles of the diverse bodies it captures and crunches together. However, I think both of Freedman's points—that MetaHuman Creator is not a narrative engine, nor can it capture lived experience—can be pushed on, as 001 and 004 demonstrate. Certainly, MetaHuman is not a narrative engine in the sense of procedurally generating level designs or dialogue, but the distinction between 001's and 004's lighting and shading do tell a story. That story is not a full capturing of the struggles of nonwhite and marginalized persons, but it does reflect some small aspects of it— literally, as this chapter will demonstrate, in the shines and reflections both present and absent on 001's skin.

The abuse of nonwhite bodies, particularly of skin and hair, through digital photorealism is a known phenomenon among nonwhite and indigenous artists and game developers; to the point where some choose to critically reject the photorealistic apparatus. As Joshua Miner has illustrated, "low res"[29] modeling and graphical practices have been leveraged by indigenous game designers as a style of refusal, rejecting the objectivist, universalized settler-colonial rendering of light and space, and instead highlighting culturally situated aesthetics.[30] Other writers, such as Evan Narcisse, find resistant moments of play that emerge from racialized rendering and narrative. Narcisse simultaneously criticizes the kinds of retrograde aesthetic politics exhibited by games' poor rendering of Black hair—particularly that of the afro—while also poignantly celebrating the kinds of gameplay made possible when designers thread racialized history through their graphical systems.[31] In exploring the eighteenth-century biracial heroine Aveline de Granpre from *Assassin's Creed Liberation*, Narcisse highlights how Aveline's heritage and light skin are mechanized in the game through clothing swaps that grant her access to different social environments and actions: "As a high-society Lady, she can bribe officials for access to closed-off areas. She can cause riots while wearing the tattered rags of the Slave."[32] Aveline's agency emerges through the intraactive productions of her carefully crafted narrative design and the rendering systems that treat her biracial skin more kindly than that of other Black characters in the game.[33]

White photorealism as enacted through Unreal and MetaHuman is thus more than just a graphical issue. It in part produces what kinds of bodies belong in game spaces, and what those bodies are capable of. It draws from a longer cinematic history that has privileged the white eye and subjectivity, and it reproduces those privileges in computational systems. As such, white photorealism is part of a larger arc of the production of racialization and of whiteness, which Sara Ahmed articulates phenomenologically as "an ongoing and unfinished history, which orientates bodies in specific directions, affecting how they 'take up' space, and what they 'can do.'"[34]

This chapter examines two entangled aspects of Unreal's white photorealism as produced with PBR and the MetaHuman Creator—first in the act of capture, and second in the act of display.

First, skin has been understood by the white eye through the vivisection of its layers, peeling each one of them back as though they were mineral strata. This layered ontology, where the surface of white skin is treated as pristine while Black skin is seen as containing a foreign Other, is historically threaded throughout Western cinematic and art practices, particularly when it comes to the interaction of light and specularity with the skin, politically entangling relative "shininess" of white skin compared to nonwhite, and especially Black, skin. This surface/depth vivisection is racially replicated in MetaHumans and PBR: both through the attempted slicing and layering of photogrammetrically captured nonwhite bodies. Capturing skin for use in MetaHumans involves vivisecting both the skin and its light, flattening shine and specularity in order to make nonwhite skin interoperable with white skin.

Second, after the MetaHuman body has been reassembled, whiteness is reproduced during the act of rendering, in the mathematical calculations of light and its bounces that become translated to the viewer's screen. Black skin becomes produced as flat and gray. I argue that this flatness is a result of the historical depriviliging of nonwhite skin that is coded into the ontology of shading models within Unreal, a depriviliging that is met by Denis Muren's eyeball test. The ontological rendering of the "subsurface," or the translucency and reflectance of the skin below its outermost membrane aligns of Blackness and melanin with minerality in the logics of PBR, producing Black skin as both a resource to be exploited and also as something less human. These renderings are allowed to circulate because they have passed the eyeball test—implicitly the test of the white eye. Skin and shine are as political and aesthetic as they are biological—it matters who renders, who judges what "looks right."

This analysis is inherently fraught. Ahmed, citing Fine, Weiss, Powell, and Wong, notes the problem of studying whiteness and white ways of knowing as concrete objects of study.[35] In so doing, we may produce a "reified whiteness as a fixed category of experience; allow[ing] it to be treated as a monolith, in the singular, as an 'essential something.'"[36] Similarly, studying whiteness as a point of reference for Blackness, or for the rendering of Black skin, risks both reinstantiating Blackness as a point of derivation from whiteness and essentializing Blackness too. To say that PBR is poor at "rendering Black skin" is to imply a political or embodied universality to Blackness and to Black persons. Conversely, to say only that PBR is poor at "rendering melanin" or "melanated skin," feels both incorrect (as all skin has melanin) and mealymouthed: melanated skin is poorly rendered because of its historical entanglements with Blackness and the dominance of white ways of seeing, not because of any objective material properties of the chemical. For clarity of writing and for acknowledgment of the historical and material realities of white supremacy, I use "Black" and "melanated" where each feels analytically appropriate, while simultaneously acknowledging here the risks of essentialism and the racialized constructions inherent within my own eye. My hope is to leave this chapter having contributed, in some small way, to the longer histories of opening up spaces previously "rendered technical"[37] to critique grounded in an analysis of race, and not having contributed to those forces who seek ever race's interpretive closure.

The Raced Politics of Surface, Shine, and Light

As discussed in chapter 4, the algorithmic productions of physically based rendering (PBR) are influenced by and expressed through Unreal's Materials Editor, the interface that allows game artists to visually program shaders. The Materials Editor features a node-based, directional network through which artists participate in a kind of heterogeneous engineering. Images are plugged into mathematical equations, operations that "listen" to the world change the position of individual dots of color on an object, JPEGs are sliced into multiple chroma layers and are added, multiplied, and divided among each other.

The Materials Editor is multidimensional; it allows us to "dive down" into each of these heterogeneous components as well, to see the images and variables that make them up. Moving back and forth between threading objects through the editor's node-based network and plumbing the computational depths of those objects is a key part of making shaders work in Unreal.

The "Meet the MetaHumans" video includes an option to download the Unreal Engine 4 scene (through MetaHuman is part of the Unreal Engine 5 marketing push, the demo itself was developed in a later version of UE4).

If you download and dive into the project files for the MetaHuman demo, you can find parts of the apparatus that make up our two characters: BP_metahuman_001 (hence 001, our Black actress) and BP_metahuman_004 (004, our East Asian actor). Like most Unreal actors, 001 and 004 comprise multiple meshes, materials, textures, and animation data; we can pull them apart, component by component, to perform an archeological analysis of how their digital bodies are produced. Isolating 001's face and head in the editor produces a drastically different 001 than the one in the video (figure 5.3): under the harsh, universal lighting of the materials visualizer, 001's skin appears pinkish, and not all that dissimilar from 004's. Upon delving further, we can view the texture map that defines the diffuse color information for 001's face (figure 5.4). This texture map, which features a human face "unwrapped" into a flat square pattern, reveals a skin tone with some semblance of depth, produced by the AI system combining scanned assets from the MetaHuman library: 001's highlights, midtones, and lowlights detailed, and relative melanin concentration—especially around her hands and feet—have been at least somewhat taken into account. We thus have at least three different color productions of 001 present in the Meta-Human project: a flat, gray 001 in the demo animation, a reddish 001 in the materials visualizer, and a vivisected texture map in her diffuse channel.

I want to spend time on two elements of the 001 deep dive: the function of the layering of skin and that layering's intersection with light and shine. Each represent an interrelated moment in the attempt to make

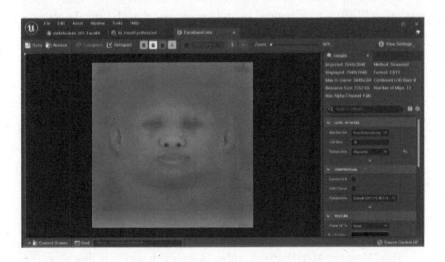

5.3 Screenshot by the author of Epic's MetaHuman demo, in the Unreal Engine texture editor with 001's Facial Texture Map.

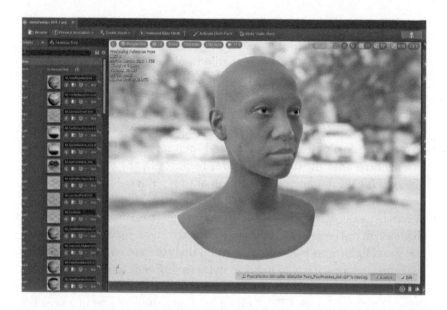

5.4 Screenshot by the author of Epic's MetaHuman demo, featuring 001's Head Model in the Materials Editor Preview Window.

skin universalizable (and therefore digitally reproduceable), while also centering white skin. The MetaHuman textures recall Richard Dyer's analysis of whiteness in art as simultaneously containing both every color in existence and also representing the pure and unmarked: "The slippage between white as a color and white as colorlessness forms part of a system of thought and affect whereby white people are both particular and nothing in particular, both something and non-existent." White skin in MetaHumans acts as both an interchangeable collection of all skin tones and also as the painterly surface (in this case, the algorithm as applied to the screen) on which nonwhite skin tones are marked.

Seeing the kind of eldritch horror of the flayed and stretched face for the first time is always a little shocking to new game artists. The technique of the flattened, flayed, square skin map wrapped around a 3D model of a human head has existed for as long as human representation in 3D games has existed—even if it has not always been well-implemented. Rare's celebrated James Bond game for the Nintendo 64, *Goldeneye 007*, for example, is widely ridiculed—even by its legion of fans—for the visual results of its use of actor photographs layered onto flat 3D faces.

Aside from the jump in polygonal count for character models made available over the past twenty years, contemporary game artists also think differently about the interactions of material texture and light than artists in the 1990s did. Lighting engines of the 1990s and 2000s were useful mostly for creating broad ambient lighting and basic shadows—essentially, lighting was used to enable to player to see what was going on in the scene, with changes in color or light intensity used to create senses of mood or space. To produce extra lighting details in the scene that would be too expensive to calculate in real time, digital artists would use the practice of "baking" light, or precomputing the way light would fall on an individual object in a scene, and then layering that precomputed shadow map onto the object's texture. Technically, the term "baking" is reserved for the automated conversion of pre-rendered light to a model, but in a broader sense, digital artists "bake" manually, as well, painting by hand streaks of light and shine on their object's textures. The light and shadows on the faces of the *Goldeneye 007* characters, for example, feature as neutral lighting as possible baked onto their texture maps, so as to look appropriate for a variety of lighting styles in different levels of the game.

Baking pre-rendered light is still an important part of developing real-time 3D games, though UE5's Lumen lighting system is part of a broader industry push toward real-time lighting even for the smallest geometric detail in a scene. Hero models, though—those featured prominently in view and often interactable and moveable by the player—increasingly demand to be as dynamically lit as possible in real time. This is particularly true of human faces, where imperfections in lighting and shadow can create "Uncanny Valley"-esque, puppet-like characters, or otherwise make a character feel disconnected from the visual scene.

The increasing use of real-time lighting and shadowing has impact on how texture maps are colored. Traces of light and shadow present on the texture will remain during runtime, leading to immobile, predrawn shadows interacting with the dynamic ones crisscrossing a character's body and face as they move about the scene. As such, materials artists working on characters must produce texture maps that feature only the "base" color of the character's skin, called the "diffuse" lighting or the "albedo,"[38] without any specular highlights or shadows. This type of texture design is doubly important for systems that mix and match premade or precaptured maps, like MetaHumans, as imperfections in light rendered on the texture map will be carried through—baked—into the calculated model.[39]

The MetaHuman Creator allows for its users to blend and synthesize over thirty prebuilt models—themselves the results of AI generated and synthesized imagery—to create and rig new characters. During a livestream introduction to the MetaHuman Creator, Epic art director Alexsandar Popov walks the audience through synthesizing three template MetaHumans, to create a new MetaHuman model (figure 5.5). Popov combines these

5.5 Screenshot during a livestream introduction to the MetaHuman Creator, Epic art director Alexsandar Popov walks the audience through synthesizing three template MetaHumans—each differently racialized—to create a new MetaHuman model (https://www.youtube.com/watch?v=ys3JivS-iXU).

templates—featuring one virtual actor who presents as white, one as East Asian, and one as Black—to produce a tripartite "middle ground" among them: a racially indistinct woman. The livestream here lines up with Freedman's observation that these kinds of character-creation tools are often used to mimic shallowly progressive "race blending" imagery, as seen in the 1993 "New Face of America" cover image of *TIME* magazine.[40] Amanda Phillips has further traced the ways that race emerges in metricized character creators: players are often presented with multiple racialized "templates" that they can choose from and modify, and these templates tend to bake in stereotypical assumptions about raced bodies.[41] MetaHuman Creator multiply produces this kind of racialization—one at the same level that Phillips finds in their study of *Fallout 3*'s character avatar generator, and one at the level of the photometric apparatus: the combination of texture map and image capturing techniques used to create the MetaHuman templates in the first place.

The texture maps synthesized to create MetaHumans introduce an additional difficulty for real-time graphics artists. While hand-painted textures can be created in a way that creates the effect of an object lit evenly from all directions and angles, scanned and photogrammetric objects must always be produced from a particular location in space and light—that of the camera lens. The use of a gonioreflectometer system, as discussed in chapter 4, can be used to create an approximation of impossible, universal light for physical objects. MetaHuman's "Live Link Face" app, which connects to iOS devices like the iPhone, allows for a user to simulate a gonioreflectometer by taking a series of images encircling a user's body, and then using AI to create a rough simulation of lighting-neutral images that can be fed into Unreal. As Aleena Chia found during her own investigations of the MetaHuman Creator, Epic developers would refer to these images as representing "the closest thing to 'ground truth'" one could find about the body and race.[42]

Neither the camera itself nor the gonioreflectometer approximations, however, represent neutral frames of reference to index skin. This is especially true when it comes to approximating light. Black cinematographers and lighting directors have long known about the "neutral" white cinematic apparatus and of the camera's inability to capture the darker highlights and shines of Black people's skin. The camera and the lighting setups it assumes will be present are designed to produce and preserve white understandings of flesh, and even "objective" systems such as an image-capturing rig and algorithmic light smoothing. Shine's presence and absence on Black skin has long been a site of white contestation and violence.[43]

Cinematographer Bradford Young argues that Black people's skin is treated in film as analogous to pure black fabrics and surfaces—a material that ravenously absorbs any light thrown at it.[44] Attempting to visually brighten dark skin so that it can be rendered as legible as white skin involves overlighting and blowing out the entire scene. Overlighting leads to the washed-out, flat tones of Black-led 1990s sitcoms like *The Cosby Show* and *The Fresh Prince of Bel-Air*.[45] Young observes, "Black skin has a very particular level of reflectance and specularity, so here it's actually the opposite: It also reflects light."[46] A solution to representing Black people's skin in a white cinematic apparatus is to hack the materiality of the apparatus itself to best capture its specularity. Ava Berkofsky, director of photography for Issa Rae's *Insecure*, notes that this hacking occurs across multiple sites; her own work on *Insecure* involves applying moisturizer or makeup with reflective minerals onto darker skinned actors, equipping the camera lens with a polarizer to lessen harsh reflections or overlit skin, and using bounced (rather than direct) lighting rigs.[47]

As art historian Krista Thompson argues, the interaction of *video light* and Black skin serves as a contemporary central axis for the coproduction of twenty-first-century ways of seeing and representing, particularly when seeing and representing the African diaspora.[48] Video light for Thompson is doubly deployed. First, it was a technique popularized in 1980s dancehalls by Jamaican videographer Jack Sowah, whose camera was affixed with a bright, unfiltered top-mounted light, creating a style whose "visual texture is harsh and burning white."[49] The proliferation of video light in the Caribbean, Thompson argues, contributed to practices of skin bleaching by dancehall participants in Kingston:

> This controversial practice, in which dancehall participants make their faces and other exposed parts of their bodies lighter and light sensitive through chemical means, stems in part from an effort to be more visible in the scope of video light, to be rendered legible through videographic technologies and technologies of light.[50]

Video light did more than just shine light on a recording surface. Rather, the videographic apparatus of video light created new material, embodied practices, that changed and diffracted the surfaces represented on video and film. Race simultaneously becomes materialized—and comes to matter[51]—through the entanglements of light and skin. This enacted practice foreshadows for us Thompson's second deployment of video light: the broader entanglements of visual surface, technological media, skin, and culture that permeate art worlds through their material practices. Here Thompson explores the historical and racial links between the Renaissance painting technique of surfacism and contemporary Black arts practices, ranging from Kehinde Wiley's illuminated paintings to "bling" fashion. Drawing from art historians John Berger and Svetlana Alpers, Thompson describes surfacism in Dutch and European portraiture as the combination of painting technique and medium that gives painted surfaces and subjects a bright, luminescent quality, which was used to connote wealth, prestige, and commodity status. In addition to the selection of objects painted—which came to include patterned marble floors, furs, and golden and metallic baubles—new attention was paid to sheen, shine, and glisten. Alpers argues that "Dutch painters, for the first time in the history of art, attempted to reproduce the optical effect of rays of light hitting the surfaces of the objects in their paintings."[52] The refractions of painted light were further augmented on the surface of the painting itself, as artists applied copious amounts of shellac to their canvases to increase their gloss and specularity.

Shine and specularity came to represent commodity status. The more present they were in the person's portrait, the more wealth and prestige the person held. Notably, Thompson observes, the only surface not commonly painted in the surfacist style was the white skin of the patrons themselves; patrons were represented in a warmer, less harsh, less glossy light, separating their humanity from that of the objects surrounding them. Representations of Black bodies in surfacist painting, on the other hand, were styled in the same techniques and media of shine and glisten as tradeable commodities, leading to "the bodies of persons defined as black not only literally circulated in a global economy as commodities but also were visually defined as such through the visual logic of surfacism."[53] The commodified shine and specularity depicted in surfacist art were replicated in the practices of African chattel slavery across Europe at the time, in which the skin and mouths of Black persons for sale were lathered in grease to give a commodified, shiny, "healthy" appearance.[54]

Even pre-film and video, the language and technique of light and specularity have been used to cast political, aesthetic, and ideological desire onto the surface of Black skin. These castings are not just visually representative; they directly impact practices of the body as well—representation both reflects and reflects on the body represented. As Thompson argues, "The bodies of men and women, manipulated to reflect light, become a new form of photographic surface, absorbing and reflecting light, appearing permanently marked by the light of representation."[55]

Thompson's articulations of the Blackness of video light were the start of a longer legacy of the interactions of Black skin and the camera lens. Genevieve Yue analyzes the "China Girls" film squares, images of upper bodies of (name notwithstanding) white women surrounded by blocks of color. These film squares were attached to the beginning of film projection strips, and were used in aiding projectionists' calibrations of light and picture.[56] Like the famous Kodak "Shirley cards" used to calibrate photographic printing, these "girl head" images centered whiteness and white femininity as a universally objective standard of quality measurement. A filmstrip or photo that was "color correct" matched the skin tones and color swatches on the girl head cards. Even films that intentionally adopted alternative or shifted color profiles—a color practice called "grading"—were measured by how many degrees of temperature "off center" they were from neutral calibration keys.

Just as we've seen in PBR, however, despite being deployed as a universal standard of visual measurement, China Girl "objective" skin color is also culturally manipulated. Yue quotes physicist David MacAdam, who, in his investigations of skin tone in color photography, notes that, "optimum reproduction of skin color is not 'exact' reproduction, [which] is rejected almost unanimously as 'beefy.' . . . When the print of the highest acceptance is compared with the original subject, it seems quite pale."[57] Proper white skin in photography, then, needed to appear even whiter than it did on the subject's flesh in order to appear to a white audience as "natural." The lighting techniques and film chemistry used to produce this whitening of skin have left lasting impressions on the quality of the "photorealism" of Black skin.

Media studies scholar Lorna Roth has analyzed how "diverse" Shirley cards in the 1990s that show different skin tones also highlight the white-centeredness of the photographic-filming apparatus.[58] In one Kodak card from 1996, three women—one white, one Black, and one east Asian—are pictured sit-standing in front of a gray background.[59] The skin and hair of the white model in the center of the picture features dynamic range; shadows provide depth to her features without losing detail, highlights and shine are dispersed to give shape to her face and detail to her hair while avoiding white blowout, and her fill light—a common lighting technique that brightens the back of the actor to "pop" her out of the background—sharpens the silhouette of her hair and shoulders. The east Asian model is similarly lit, although the camera begins to lose definition in her hair, giving it a dulled appearance. The Black model is less fortunate; her underlit hair has lost all definition, and her skin appears flat. Dull highlights muddle her features and poor lowlighting shift her skin's earthier tones toward gray. There is either no fill light or it is improperly used, as her upper silhouette emerges entirely from her bright white blouse while her arms fade into the background. In an attempt to light her as white, the shine and luster are removed from her skin.

We can see several of the above aesthetic and historical racialized moments reproduced through the Unreal MetaHuman Creator. Some of this production is in the choice of content; it is not a coincidence that across the MetaHuman demo, stream, and the "diverse" Shirley card, white, Asian, and Black bodies—real and virtual—are used to stand in relation to one another. Whiteness becomes framed as the default and dominant human image, with Blackness positioned as its opposite: a body that contradicts the logics and cultures of whiteness but that, with work, can be ultimately subsumed and appropriately metricized. The Asian body is used in a stereotypical Orientalist way: as a "middle ground" in terms of both skin tone and "Otherness" between the poles of whiteness and Blackness, a position of "not quite/not white"[60] that serves a different kind of decorative purpose to the white eye than Blackness does.[61]

Most of this production, however, boils down to the white desire for metricized and interoperable universality. For MetaHuman to function in the way it promises it can, there must be a universal index that can equally process multiple skin tones and embodied racial realties. The camera, we have seen, cannot do this—and in the case of correcting for white skin's "beefiness," it has quite literally been designed to reject certain kinds of color indices found offensive to the white eye. AI and machine learning, as it has been all-too-often contemporarily framed, has been posited as a solution to the issue. Perhaps the Live Link Face app, for example, if made aware of the historical centering of white desires of skin, could reverse engineer that bias.

Here again, however, whiteness's search for the universal representation, the universal body, emerges, even when produced in service of correcting previous missteps. For example, while computer graphics developers are now beginning to acknowledge the bias toward lighter skin that has been baked into photogrammetric systems,[62] there is still an ontological drive to reproduce the layered model of universal skin and light in photo capture that is entangled with whiteness and PBR in the first place. In attempting to correct for the problem, for example, Haiwen Feng and colleagues have proposed a dual algorithmic method for more accurately measuring skin albedo from photographic images.[63] Using methods called the FAIR (Facial Albedo Independent of Race) benchmark and TRUST (Towards Racially Unbiased Skin Tone estimation) neural network, Feng and colleagues attempt to read the color and light information of the entire background of the image and apply it to the extracted face texture. Even in the team's provided imagery, not only do the nonwhite faces still appear more flattened and gray than the white-aligned faces, but the solution itself replicates the epistemological valences of white photorealism. The camera image itself is still treated as an access to, quite literally, "ground truth," which has been polluted by colors of light. And the entire apparatus is still in service of white ways of knowing—how to make nonwhite bodies and faces better align with white technologies. Again, whiteness becomes double produced: it is a present "bias" in the technical system that should be corrected for, but that correction comes in the form of yet another whiteness, the pursuit of a universal skin and light model that can be made infinitely customizable and interoperable through computational systems.

Producing Melanin

The varying skin color, shine, and quality of look of 001 owe themselves to PBR's white photorealism. Theodore Kim has explored the historical making-invisible of Black (and, in general, melanated) skin in computer graphics, which, like photography, have over time come to universally enact "the body" as "the white body," particularly when it comes to the rendering of skin and hair.[64] Among the major technical contributors to this enactment is subsurface scattering—the rendering of diffuse light in skin—which contributes to the translucent quality of certain kinds of skin types. As Kim argues, the mathematically difficult, computationally intensive translucency problem "is only the dominating visual feature in *young, white* skin," and yet has taken up a vast majority of digital skin research over the past thirty years.[65] Reviewing the literature on skin rendering with this context "is a stomach-churning tour of whiteness."[66] Kim suggests that one possible solution to this issue, in addition to more research on different skin effects, is the production of more diverse Shirley cards for computer graphics, which would give digital artists a better frame of reference for lighting and calculating darker skin.[67] However, given the historical and material context of Shirley cards and PBR itself, we can see how the availability of a MetaHuman Shirley or better albedo measurement wouldn't have saved 001.

I wrote in chapter 4 that the two core techniques that unify the varied practices of PBR are microfacet theory and the conservation of energy: how light bounces off a surface and how it penetrates and diffuses within a surface, respectively. In their application toward photorealistic rendering, these abstractions of physics—themselves already entangled with white empiricism—become further entangled with white histories and practices of photography and cinema to produce a photoreality that feels "real" only to the white eye. The "eyeball test" diffracts throughout the current ontologies of matter baked into Unreal's PBR, which countermand the material condition of dark skin. The embedded conservation of energy reflectance/diffusion model fundamental to PBR states that the more specular a surface is, the less diffuse color a surface exhibits; as materials get shinier, they also get darker. This rough calculation already introduces aesthetic concerns in rendering darker skin, in which both shine and range of color expression are key elements. Even more fundamental, though, is the ontology of metalness in PBR's conservation of energy. As noted above, metals are conductors. Their electroconductive properties make them visually behave in notably different ways than dielectric, or insulating, materials. They are highly reflective, exhibit little to no subsurface scattering, and their specular highlights and reflections can have a colored tint. This last feature, especially, makes conductors oddities in PBR, which by default renders specular values as "neutral" white light. As such, physically based renders need to determine whether a material is conductive or insulating in order to appropriately calculate light and shading. As most everyday conductors are metals, artist-friendly principled shading models use the binary "metalness" property as a proxy for conductivity, allowing artists to select which rendering model to use.

The metalness attribute, however, makes invisible one of the most common, everyday conductors that we encounter in the human world:

melanin. Melanin—present in all human skin, hair, and in the human brain—is one of the only known biological materials that exhibits conductive properties; its potential use as an energy-efficient conductor in architecture, biomaterials, and green energy is only beginning to be explored.[68] Western science has known for some time that melanin concentrations impact the diffusion and scattering of non-ultraviolet light. But for all its universality in the human body, melanin's visual properties—and particularly its properties when present in high concentrations of melanocytes that result in darker skin—have been shockingly understudied. This understudy of the visual effects melanin, coupled with a general lack of attentiveness to the needs of dark skin, has already contributed to public— and embarrassing—faux pas by technology companies. They include the now famous "green light" problem in smartwatches and health trackers, in which optical sensors using green LED light reflectance as a measuring tool fail on darker skin due to melanin's high green absorption index. Even user-made modifications to the Unreal skin shaders to introduce melanin properties tend to model melanin as "brownness." These properties lead to skin simulations that render Black people's skin as under-specular and reddened, and fail at introducing the blue undertones featured in some dark skin.[69] Curiously, while the default MetaHuman skin shader does not feature a "melanin" property, their hair shaders *do*, although even here "melanin" is again treated simply as a color control slider for "gray-blonde-brown."

The invisibility of melanin in white photorealism leads artists and developers to treat darker skin as simply darker or dyed white skin, rather than as a surface with unique material and visual needs. When coupled with the eyeball test, this invisibility manifests in multiple ways. First, as seen in the "diverse" Shirley cards of the 1990s, what counts as an accurate representation of human skin depends on who is providing the card. I doubt, for example, that Kodak producers intentionally underlit and grayed out the Black model on their 1996 card. Rather, the color of the model's skin, as produced by her skin tone, the lighting in the studio, the camera settings, and the printers and ink—all of which were designed to first replicate white skin—never stood a chance. Importantly however, this is not to absolve the human element—before distribution, some producer had to look at the card and its lighting conditions and shrug, "Yeah, that looks about right."

The "about-rightness" of Black skin in white photorealism still pervades photography. It was evident in Annie Leibovitz's controversial 2020 *Vogue* photoshoot of gymnast Simone Biles, which left Biles underlit and flattened. It could be seen in Australian cosmetic company BECCA's advertisements of Black-skintone-friendly foundation, featuring the hand of a white model digitally manipulated to look Black. Not only did the company choose not to hire Black models for their shoot, they also miscolored the manipulated hand, making the palm and back-of-the-hand skin tone the same color—as it appears for pale white skin—rather than rendering the hand in gradient tones more common to melanated skin. Here again the logics of the appearance of white skin were assumed to be easily portable to other skin tones and skin types.

Second, in addition to the white historical conditions of the photographic apparatus, PBR's reliance on white empiricism for its cultural cache contrasts with the material realities of photographically representing skin. PBR represents the promise of a universal rendering process capable of producing shaders that visibly work across varying lighting conditions; the claim that human skin is not algorithmically universalizeable contradicts PBR's core narrative. Kim, upon presenting his research for review at a top computer graphics conference, even got the feedback that pointing out that different skin tones have different rendering needs was itself racist.[70] In arguing that all skin must, by definition, have universal lighting conditions, white skin becomes "rendered technical."[71] It is rendered neutral and objective, giving white skin the mathematical prestige of universal skin. The invoking of Black people's skin as having distinct needs thus brings a "bias" into the world of computer graphics, and therefore is perceived as racist. The correct approach to rendering color, to engineers, is to remain colorblind.

Though Unreal's PBR inherits the white bias of the cinematic apparatus, its use cases, technical capacities, and ontological positions make it difficult to replicate the specular hacks used to better light darker skin. First, the lighting schema in a real-time, interactive 3D scene in a digital game doesn't accommodate the just-off-screen lighting rig tricks available to photography and cinema. Thanks to relatively static traditional camera setups, it is possible to create essentially two completely different lighting conditions for each actor in the shot, while also making it convincingly appear as though both actors are occupying the same lightspace. This tight control of actor position, camera frame, and spatial configuration allows cinematographers like Berkofsky to differently light multiple skin tones and set pieces while preserving visual coherence. In an interactive gaming space, where the player has the ability to move throughout the scene, multiple lighting setups would quickly become obvious, while also making the scene visually disorienting. Lighting setups must then work universally for the multiple actors and set objects in a scene. The practices of white photorealism from film and photography and cinema are then reenacted, when universal lighting conditions most adversely affect darker, more reflective skin.

The white photoreal assemblage diffracts color biases against dark skin even when the texture maps of a character's skin are more or less color accurate. We can see this with 001: while her diffuse skin pattern is appropriate, the bright, universal lights of the Materials Editor space render her whiter. Conversely, in the "Meet the MetaHumans" animatic, the lighting scheme and skin shaders for 004 underlight and flatten 001. Diffractions of whiteness are evident in more popular PBR-based media as well. Gaming communities voiced concern over the whitewashing of Barret Wallace, a main character in *Final Fantasy VII* and one of the only Black characters in the *Final Fantasy* game series, after promotional screenshots of 2020's *Final Fantasy VII: Remake*—a UE4-created remaster of 1997's *VII*—showed a Barret with noticeably lighter skin. Similar concerns were voiced over Disney's 3D animated series *Star Wars: The Bad Batch*, in which animated clone soldier characters based off Māori actor Temuera Morrison were rendered with pale skin.[72] Accusations of whitewashing were only compounded by *The Bad Batch*'s casting of a white voice actor for Morrison's roles, and by Disney Animation's history of drawing and rendering characters lighter as an art-direction decision.[73] Though *The Bad Batch* is pre-rendered animation, it uses the same Disney Principled Shader from which Unreal's PBR shaders are derived.

In both instances, developers and supporters have blamed the lighting system rather than the artists. Reddit threads filled with vitriol against "race baiting" cultural critics consistently pointed to Unreal to justify Barret's skin tone, arguing that his whitewashing is merely a "trick of the light" in the in-game lighting engine. Disney, to its credit, altered the appearance of the clone soldiers to better reflect Morrison's appearance, but was also very careful to avoid the use of any body- or skin-centered language. Instead, they identified lighting schema as the cause of audiences' concerns. Geek culture website io9 reported:

> A source familiar with production of *The Bad Batch* told io9 that in in the run-up to its premiere this week, changes to the lighting tools utilized by the animation team were made to moderate their effects in the premiere episode's starkly-lit primary settings. Such tweaks will also be made in future episodes of the series.[74]

PBR here plays a shifting cultural role in white photorealism. It is at times discussed as sacrosanct, a neutral, objective system of mimesis whose errors are only in the eye of the viewer—"a trick of the light." At other times, it is invoked as a system-in-progress, an apparatus approaching universal truth but which still has unintended consequences. In both cases, PBR is articulated in a way that absolves digital artists and programmers from accusations of an anti-Black aesthetic bias, or what Imani Perry has called "post-intentional" racism.[75] No individual artist lightened or faded 001's, Barret's, or clone soldiers' skin, the argument goes. Rather, variables spread throughout the renderer produce paler skin regardless of artist intent. By this argument, whitewashing was a systemic product rather than an intentional aesthetic choice. There is certainly some truth to this narrative, especially since PBR reduces artists' control over "minor" details like specular highlights and Fresnel reflections. Only artists with a deep understanding of Unreal's codebase, or major studios, have the capacity to edit specularity at a shader-level scale. Even still, Disney not seeing the problem in the first place reinforces white photorealisms' reliance on "good enough" when it comes to darker skin. As Young has argued, we should not render the cinematic apparatus's problems with race as purely technical:

> I don't think it's about a technical deficit; it's an emotional deficit. It's consciousness that's missing in the equation. The way the story is being told trickles down to the way people are being photographed. If you don't know or care about the people in front of the camera, I don't expect you to be very meticulous about how you capture them on film.[76]

Despite PBR's mimicry of the photographic apparatus, not all the hacks deployed by figures like Young and Berkofsky are viable in the apparatus of real-time rendering. Using polarizers to better capture bounced light, for example, is currently impossible in Unreal. Since PBR abstracts light as rays rather than as waves, cinematic phenomena that derive from light's wave-like features—such as polarization—are nearly impossible to currently simulate. There are some editable properties on Light actors,[77] such as multiplying specular scale, that can mildly mimic polarization techniques. However, even these properties are accompanied by strong warnings on both Unreal forums and in Unreal's technical documentation: "Use only with great care! Any value besides 1 is not physical!"[78]

Mimetically, nonwhite skin just doesn't *look* right. Cinematically, lighting practices that can help better represent Blackness are either underutilized or discouraged. Ontologically, how skin is materialized dismisses one of the most important factors in skin color and specularity for anyone not white. PBR's borrowing of the cultural cache of physics allows for these political and aesthetic issues to be either rendered invisible (critics just aren't "looking" correctly) or rendered technical, in that the problem will be automatically solved as universal skin and lighting models advance. Thus, no special attention is paid to darker skin tones. Ironically, one possible technical remedy—the incorporation of melanin's conductivity into skin shaders—is already fraught with epistemic and political tension. Like the surfacist art projects highlighted by Thompson, ways of representing Blackness are already entangled with representing minerality and commodity. In PBR, to make Black skin more electroconductive, more absorbent, and more *visible*, may be to make it more metal.

Conclusion

"Friendly reminder that *Horizon Zero West* nailed Black People <3,"[79] computer graphics artist Jeryce Dianingana tweeted in late December 2022. Accompanying his tweet were six images Dianingana captured from the PlayStation 5 version of the game, each featuring a well-rendered image of a Black digital character. Responses to the thread were mixed, with some commenters celebrating the game's character art direction and mocking the current state of Black skin rendering in other contemporary games. Others expressed hesitation, noting that the hair rendering in the game of Black hair was still suspect, with most of the Black character's heads covered with helmets or hats so as to not have to render their hairstyles.

Among the other respondents was Jan-Bart van Beek, the studio and art director of Guerrilla Games, the developers of the *Horizon* series: "Thanks Jeryce! *HFW* skin shading system used a novel approach where we modeled melatonin [*sic*] and blood distribution in the skin, so characters of any ethnicity could have correct skin complexion while also showing emotional effects like anger and blushing."[80]

The skin effects in *Horizon Forbidden West*, developed using Guerrilla's proprietary Decima Engine, still use physically based rendering, but coupled with a skin shader system that imagines skin differently, as a fluid collection of blood and melanin, rather than as a series of layered strata. The results were striking, and while issues still persist with this model—nonwhite skin throughout the game still almost exclusively leans toward the red end of the spectrum associated with that of white skin, almost certainly due to the centering of blood as a major coloring agent—*Horizon* demonstrates some of the kinds of work that can be produced with thoughtfulness and care for nonwhite skin. Replies to van Beek's explanation tweet also included the typical internet white supremacist trolls, arguing that the time spent on rendering Black skin was the reason *Horizon* didn't win any Game of the Year awards. Emma Vossen's 2019 quip, that "Gamers are still convinced that there are only two races: white and 'political,'"[81] still rings true.

Still, *Horizon*, van Beek, and Dianingana remind us that just as race is not an essential quality but rather an ongoing, contested historical and ontological practice, so too are PBR and computer graphics human practices and techniques that are entangled in various and conflicting ways with longer histories of race and vision. PBR need not forever be aligned with white photorealism; just as Black artists and cinematographers hacked and re-created a camera and cinematic apparatus that was not created for them, so too can computer graphics be made otherwise. *Horizon* and Decima play this out with photorealism, offering new ways of imagining human bodies that leave more room open for multiple kinds of skin. In other parts of the game arts community, A. M. Darke's curated Open Source Afro Hair Library takes a different tack. Rather than embracing photorealistic styles as *Horizon* does, or rejecting them, as Miner's illustration of low-res indigenous projects do, Darke's Library operates indifferently to them, allowing for the production and mixing of photoreal and low res to create new kinds of imaginations and representations of Blackness in digital spaces.

Changes to Epic's MetaHuman Creator, then, need not be to seek ever more for a "ground truth" representation of human skin, an epistemological project that both centers whiteness and also would be never-ending. MetaHuman could instead explore radical forms of nonconformity and disunity, embracing how multiple and conflicting rendering styles, lighting rigs, and cinematic simulations could be hacked together to model the epistemic and ontological plurality threaded throughout humanity. Such a project, however, would demand a break from Epic's search for easily modifiable uniformity, and its associated impacts on automation of artist labor.

Conclusion

Resource Materialities, *Fortnite*, and the Metaverse

This book has confronted how feminist technoscience studies, when interpreted through theories of queer and raced experiences, can change game studies' analyses of game engines and platforms. Platform studies' language of "layers" and its implicit ontology of "brackets"[1] breaks our analytic lens separately into questions of material affordance and of culture. By contrast, feminist technoscience studies—and feminist science and technology studies (STS) more broadly—highlights how material and cultural realties are always bound up together. Moments of apparent division or unity between the two are made real through human practices. Analytic questions are therefore always enmeshed with questions of ontology, and questions of ontology always reflect social, institutional, and cultural systems of power.

The multiplicity of game engines is a useful lens through which to examine the tensions between feminist STS and platform studies. Their capacities to integrate external assets and translate digital narratives across diverse hardware configurations call into question the very boundaries of the concept of platform itself. Game engines integrate and shape industrial and academic contexts, and produce agency across human and technological spaces, acting as fractional coherences.[2] Bricoleur material practices unite a heterogeneous network of texts, histories, materialities, and cultures.

Knowing and theorizing a game engine thus requires drawing agential cuts[3]—folding a complex and ever-extending situation[4] to enact the object that can be studied: platform studies. Jussi Parikka and Thomas Apperley have argued that platform studies works to produce a given platform as a stable object on which analyses can be leveled. Further, the coproductive relationship between a game engine and the games it is used to make—particularly in the case of Unreal—provides a helpful counter-framing. Games studies conceptualizes game engines either as underlying systems of affordances and constraints or media of transmission that shape game narratives or control the labor of workers. However, I have argued that games also shape the engines used to produce them, as do industrial, military, raced, and gendered power structures. These structures are, too, shaped in turn. Game engines like Unreal do not operate within social or cultural contexts, but rather are a part of the production of context and social space itself.

Throughout this book I have used situational analysis to trace the Unreal assemblage, highlighting how Unreal has been enacted with and through questions of race, gender, and power. I opened by followed Epic Games and Unreal's early history, and how the early design of the engine was shaped by competitors in the games industry and interactions with the US military. From early days, Epic framed Unreal as a democratizing force for game development, while also producing Unreal as a flexible toolset for army simulation, training, and recruitment. The computational dimensions of the engine were only a part of this toolset; Epic and the army also envisioned Unreal as the connective tissue between the US government and the interactive entertainment industry at large. In so doing, Unreal became part of the production of computation and engineering culture as masculinized and militaristic. It wasn't physically strong and reckless like the hypermasculine Rambo films would have potential army recruits believe, but rather militarist masculinity as "reasoned" and "analytic."

The first major arc of this book traced how Unreal queers our analysis of game narrative, agency, and bodily presence in games and software. An examination of the orientation of 3D space in Unreal showed how its programming belies disciplinary and epistemic framings of the body. Orientations of the X, Y, and Z axes served as proxies for the body itself. Beyond just controlling bodily avatars in 3D space, the body emerged in Unreal as a set of labor relations—systems of learning and spatial guidance—and as the intermediary between Unreal's dataspace and worldspace. Next, through a queer reading of the relationship between *BioShock Infinite*'s Elizabeth character and Unreal's Kismet visual programming language used to create her, Elizbeth's narrative agency was cast as being *intra-active*—that is, it emerged from the mutual entanglement and care among Liz, developers, and extended components of the game's engine—rather than interactive, framed as a kind of conflict-based, neoliberal subjectivity. Elizabeth is powerful in the game's system and the game's narrative because of her dependency on and care for the gameworld and the engine, not because of her ability to resist or exert her will on the player or the game.

The second arc explored how race was produced with and though Unreal, particularly by forming whiteness as universal and objective and situating Blackness as a derivation. This enactment of race, which I labeled "white photorealism," was practiced through physically based rendering (PBR). PBR borrowed the epistemic authority of physics and of white cinema to make claims about its mimetic relationship to our lived reality. I traced two examples of how whiteness was enacted as natural and objective. First, I discussed the entangling of Unreal's PBR and scientific objectivity in the NVIDIA moon landing demo with longer histories of cinematic photorealism, and how whiteness has played a role in naturalizing both science and cinematic affect. Second, Unreal calculated the skin tone of dark skin, thus participating in a longer history of dark skin being derived from or representing an insufficient version of whiteness. Both cases showed how Unreal, as a part of the gaming community's larger "quest for realism," implicitly produced white ontologies and ways of seeing—the objective eye that determined the "rightness" of a renderer's realism.

Unreal represents a historical accretion of techniques, technologies, and ideologies, so continues to be both part and parcel of gaming's future. As the games situation shifts over time, so will the theories and perspectives scholars and analysts bring to game platforms. These analyses are themselves fundamentally a part of gaming's situatedness. Future studies of game engines as platforms, I suspect, will dovetail with what appears to be the near future of Epic and Unreal—a continuing move toward platformization. Platformization in this sense refers not to the Bogost and Montfort conceptual genealogy critiqued throughout this text, but rather to the transformation of legacy media and pop culture institutions into online, data-driven, networked social media platforms, such as Facebook (Meta), TikTok, and Twitter.[5] While this data-driven shift promises more user control and democratic distribution of voices than legacy media, the manipulation of posted content, consolidation through monopolistic mergers and alliances, and extraction and sale of user data serves only to accelerate capital's control over the state and society.[6]

Game studies scholars have already begun to weave together these two strands of platform studies theory. They have examined the beneficial relationship between social media companies and online gaming/gambling companies, with a particular focus on the closeness between Zynga and Facebook that led to microtransaction windfalls for both companies.[7]

Scholars have also considered how game engines like Unity have started to create their own social production platforms through a combination of free game assets, developer storefronts, and investments in university and online training programs.[8] Further, as Benjamin Nicoll and Brendan Keogh note, the "indie" spirit that Unity advertises of their non-AAA userbase[9] mimics the "authenticity of the ordinary"[10]—the "person next door" aesthetic carefully crafted and leveraged by influencer and other social media personalities to connect with their networked audiences, while also rendering invisible the tremendous investments of capital necessary to continually produce their content. Epic Games is certainly moving in similar directions. Though still a privately owned company, the $US330 million purchase of 40 percent of Epic's share capital by Chinese technology mega-conglomerate Tencent in 2012 signaled the tech industry's recognition of Epic's future monetization potential.

To conclude this book, I take a brief tour of Epic's ongoing role in the platformization of the games industry. This platformization, through imaginations of a "Metaverse," makes financial sense only insofar as games can produce new sources of revenue. Server space, content moderation, and the transition from title-based, staggered game development cycles to a continuous need for new content are all massively expensive. Future research, I argue, should approach game engines and their central role in the platformization of game companies through their capacity to produce "resource materialities"—the coalescence of practices, materials, and epistemes that produce a stable object that can be operationalized by capital for value extraction.[11]

"Ask That Question Again in 12 Months"

Over the past three years, a conversational Twitter thread among *Fortnite* fans, angel investors, and Epic Games CEO Tim Sweeney inadvertently documented both the aims and failed promises of the platformization of persistent real-time multiuser 3D environments marketed as "the Metaverse." In 2019, as part of an "Ask a famous person one question" Twitter thread, securities trader and Roundhill CEO Will Hershey asked Sweeney whether he believed that *Fortnite* was more of a game or more of a platform.[12] The question was a prescient one; in the prior year, Epic had quietly started platformizing *Fortnite*, their massively successful third-person shooter battle-royale game. While *Fortnite* and its estimated $5 billion monthly profit[13] was as important to Epic's resurgent market successes in the mid-2010s as further refinements to the Unreal Engine were, Sweeney and the Epic team understood that player interest in the game would eventually wane. One of the game's most important demographics—the Twitch-streaming Generation Z—would eventually age out of *Fortnite*'s fast-twitch, meme-culture-inundated gameplay. Epic thus embarked on a hybrid technical-marketing endeavor to retain the game's 250 million registered players. As it continued to release game updates, including new levels, challenges, and player avatar skins, Epic was interested in turning *Fortnite* into a more general-purpose online hangout and event space. They wanted a space for players of all ages to socialize, stream, and participate in cross-corporate events, such as rapper Travis Scott's in-game March 2020 "Astronomical" concert.

In anticipation of *Fortnite*'s new direction, Sweeney answered Hershey: "*Fortnite* is a game. But please ask that question again in 12 months."[14] The internet never forgets. A year later, user "Bert" again asked Sweeney about *Fortnite*'s game/platform status, with Sweeney confirming that "*Fortnite* is a game . . . primarily," but that new updates and functionality in the coming year would push the shooter much closer to what a Metaverse platform should be.[15] Not to be deterred, venture capitalist and Metaverse hype man Matthew Ball would ask the same question again (in a now-deleted tweet) at the end of 2021. "Wish I could say platform," Sweeney replied, "but we need to do a lot more with the tools and economy to actually be there."

The recent barrages of Metaverse marketing by Silicon Valley and tech venture capitalists demonstrate that the tools and economy of the Metaverse are closely coupled. Blockchain and Web3 could be loosely—if generously—described as technical innovations for digital security, but their public hype has centered on their monetary value—the Metaverse as speculative investment. Similarly, Meta (Facebook) CEO Mark Zuckerberg tightly couples his visions for monetizable 3D space to Meta's investments in virtual reality, motion tracking, and haptics technology, investments that have totaled over $US15 billion. Meta's $15 billion investment has not only gone toward an aesthetically boring virtual world, but also toward lobbying efforts, industry partnerships, and externally funded research and development of software standards and protocols. Given the crashes of Bitcoin gaming marketplaces, the sparsely populated horizons of Web3 online worlds, and the embarrassing rollout of Facebook's Metaverse VR social media network, it may be tempting to cast this era of "Metaverse" technologies as merely an overhyped, techno-capitalist bust. But while it is true that its consumer-facing technologies and platforms are currently underwhelming, the Metaverse as rhetoric has been leveraged by tech companies to heavily invest in physical, digital, and institutional platforms and infrastructures on which the next era of online presence and governance may be built.

Further, hardware, software, and gaming companies such as NVIDIA, Intel, Apple, Unity, and Epic Games too have invested billions in internal and external projects aiming to shape the underlying legal and technical platforms of the future of digital communication. Following the Adobe and Autodesk models of the mid-2000s, Unity has sought to become a major driver of the 3D web by producing spin-off products of its main engine catering to automotive, simulation, and medical industries, and purchasing media graphics companies like Wētā Workshop. These companies bring with them not only their visual effects expertise but also their databases of 3D scans, prior created assets, and interpersonal connections to industries beyond gaming.

The current Metaverse—particularly the version envisioned by Facebook and Unity—operates as what Kline, Dyer-Witheford, and de Peuter have called a mutually constitutive circuit of technology, marketing, and culture.[16] Mimicking similar patterns in the cryptocurrency space,[17] capital flows into the Metaverse, backed by a series of "just around the corner" promises of full platformization of new or existing 3D environments dependent on new technological infrastructure. Rather than investing only in their own technical research and development, games and platform companies are attempting to buy their way to the Metaverse by acquiring media and software companies. Epic itself has, over the past several years, purchased volumetric scanning companies, environmental asset databases, motion tracking and animation companies, and the indie music streaming service BandCamp. They're betting that integrating software tools and datasets will provide footholds in this new digital ground, eventually allowing them to outpace their competitors.

Sweeney has been talking about "the Metaverse" since at least 2018,[18] long before Facebook and cryptocurrency companies seized on the term. For years he has been open about his plans to transform *Fortnite* into a platform for persistent online 3D socialization. Yet Epic and *Fortnite* can be distinguished from both Unity's platform model and Facebook (Meta's) attempts at building persistent VR Metaverse worlds. Epic's dual status as a game developer and an engine developer not only gives them expertise in both content development and software development, it also affords them the ability to blend the two practices. Not only is the Unreal Engine an industry standard in games and animation content development, but it is also deeply tied into the Epic Game Store, Epic's player-facing storefront that sells games made in Unreal alongside assets, plug-ins, and extensions to Unreal itself. In this sense, Epic is already ahead of Metaverse competitors like Meta (Facebook), whose business model has long relied on users and other developers for content to be deployed on their platforms. Unreal's infrastructural blurring of online storefront and warehouse also provides a technical advantage to Epic's Metaverse ambitions, as well as a legal and monetary incentive to "open up" other platforms' payment methods.

At the heart of Sweeney's Metaverse dreams lies the expansion of *Fortnite*'s Creative Mode, an in-game level builder and editor. Creative Mode presently operates through in-game mechanics; players walk around a 3D space with their avatars and can "shoot" game-used tiles and assets to create custom levels and architecture. However, Sweeney's ultimate goals would result in what games scholars would experience as a figure-ground swap; creative and design elements of the Unreal Engine would be repurposed into gameplay and player-led content creations assets brough into *Fortnite*. Here we see the classical platform studies layers model defied: the game has become the substrate for the engine. First announced in May of 2022, "Unreal Engine for *Fortnite*" (UEFN), which has since been more popularly referred to as *Fortnite*'s "Creative Mode 2.0" (FC2), brings functionality and widgets from Unreal Engine 5 directly into *Fortnite*'s interface. Though as of this writing not all initial features of FC2 have been rolled out, during a monthly Twitch stream, Epic's development team revealed a live demo that showed the UE5 interface inside of *Fortnite*. They also used UE5's scripting and geometry brush tools to create new models, AI behaviors, and visual effects. Online rumors and leaks also suggest the possibility of non-player character and player character spawners—which would allow for new kinds of multiplayer and phase-based gameplay—and a debugging tool that could theoretically produce more polished games. The introduction of behavioral scripting and geometry creation is a vast leap in functionality for Creative Mode, which has traditionally operated by allowing players to recombine various prebuilt assets. Further, FC2 features integration with the Epic Games store, a move designed to provide creators the ability to monetize their creations "without having to do a deal with us (Epic)."[19] Unreal 5 integration would thus provide players with access to both technical and economic capital.

Epic's status as a private company gives Sweeney a level of control to experiment with smaller and more creatively distinct visions of Metaverse spaces than designers at Meta and Unity, whose publicly traded status demands prioritizing growth and user enrollment. We are already seeing these distinct approaches play out. Meta's need for cross-sector growth has resulted in a pitch of "Metaverse-as-neutral space." VR and persistent 3D worlds are sold as infinitely malleable spaces suitable for productivity, socialization, virtual production, education, and play. Yet the end result is a dreary aesthetic sludge, where the space's demanded flexibility produces a virtual world good at *nothing in particular*. Advertising campaigns attempt to pitch the excitement of moving one's office meeting into a virtual space. Epic Games, on the other hand, appears to be pitching the Metaverse as a series of federated, interlinked spaces, each one with the aesthetic and functional character of a particular brand. *Fortnite*-as-Metaverse is clearly being sold to a tween/young adult audience; corporate-branded avatar skins are sourced from popular youth media such as *Naruto*, *Dragonball*, and the Marvel Cinematic Universe. Its virtual concert series features pop musicians like Travis Scott and Ariana Grande. These external corporate partnerships aesthetically align with *Fortnite*'s semi-cartoon style; no matter the activity, players still feel as though they are "within" the game. Similarly, Epic has recently begun a partnership with LEGO to build a build-and-play Metaverse distinct from *Fortnite*, targeted at younger children.[20] A successful launch of this virtual space would allow Epic to capture two major gaming age groups in its Metaverse spaces, while maintaining distinct aesthetic, gameplay, and marketing identities for each.

Successfully building UEFN could provide a proof-of-concept for smaller-scale engine integration into other game-Metaverse platforms, such as Epic's planned LEGO partnership. One could imagine a long-term strategy in which young game players are introduced to Unreal-style game development practices through a LEGO-branded, *Roblox*-style Creative Mode; advance to developing levels in *Fortnite* through its Unreal-powered FC2; and then "graduate" to developing fully independent games through Unreal's free licensing. Such a pipeline would be a twenty-first-century mirror of the modder-turned-developer model enabled by the packaging of Unreal Editor with *Unreal* and *America's Army* in the 1990s and early 2000s.

While we should always take public tech demos like the UEFN Twitch stream with a grain of salt, a game "underpinning" a game engine highlights the ontological uncertainties facing platform studies and game studies in the coming decade, as the "layers" model of production becomes increasingly untenable. Further, the use of game engines to transform games into platforms complicates the relationship between content production and data extraction. The 2000s model of using game engines to mod existing games was tied to an explicitly nonmonetizable model. As with fan fiction, game developers profited from encouraging fan bases using tools to create new modes and experiences for their games. Modders attempted to profit from their work, but were likely to get sued by those same companies.[21] Social media platforms are successful inversely, because their user-generated content and monetization infrastructures are intrinsic and coproductive. Creators *expect* to be able to monetize their work, and tailor their content to be better advertised and distributed by algorithms. Monetization on networked platforms occurs not only through the sale of content, but also through the production of the social network *itself* as a resource to be mined. It is designed to produce and extract data that can be used for improving user experience and selling to advertisers, governments, and other capital interests. Not only are the analytic boundaries between games and game engines being continually challenged, but as game engines gradually transform from software environments into the plumbing of Metaverse technologies,[22] games and platform studies scholars will need to increasingly turn to theories of infrastructure and large-scale heterogeneous systems.

The transformation of hybrid entertainment/production software like *Fortnite*/Unreal into a platform Metaverse too will require more than just plugging engine tools into games and expanding Epic's Game Store. It will require long-term, large-scale reorganization of the games industry at technical, organizational, and governmental scales. The games industry will need to produce both enticing legal and monetization models to encourage content creation and new infrastructures for measuring, extracting, and selling data from Metaverse player bases. Further, keeping players continually locked into the Metaverse requires the ability to access it across multiple device paradigms; while Meta hypes VR as the future of Metaverse human-computer interaction, current evidence suggests that the Metaverse will be much more mobile, accessible through user's phones and other personal devices. As such, the resources needed to power the Metaverse extend beyond leveraging players' creative capital; managing new technical and infrastructural resources will be required. Rather than tying the Metaverse to a singular digital mediation platform, the Metaverse may be better thought of as a "working object"[23] through which Epic and other major techno-capital concerns of Big Tech—including barriers to retaining and extracting data from users, manufacturing and microchip shortages, peer competition, and increasing regulatory scrutiny—are worked through.

I see the beginnings of this process in the use of game engines to fashion these concerns into "resource materialities." This term comes from anthropology and STS studies of the underground, and advocates for a move away from viewing natural resources as substances with essential qualities that exist, ready to be extracted. It advances us toward the study of resource materialities as "complex arrangements of physical stuff, extractive infrastructures, calculative devices, discourses of the market and development, the nation and the corporation, everyday practices, and so on, that allow those substances to exist as resources."[24] Resources, in other words, are not pregiven items available to be extracted from the ground. Rather, they themselves are end products of a long chain of material, political, and institutional systems that produce extractability and mobility. Mineral slurry—the mix of particulate matter, water, and solvent through which ore such as coal and iron are mined and moved—provides an excellent illustration. Iron is not generally found in ready-made chunks brought out of the earth; it is produced through crushing and grinding of heterogeneous rock formations. The resulting particulate matter can be combined with liquids and frothed, coarsely separating different ores. This liquid froth is also a transit medium, as it is more cost-effective to build a network of pipes through which liquid iron ore slurry can be pumped than to pay truck drivers to haul reconstituted rock. Iron can be extracted and valued *as* iron only through a combination of industrial processes, labor circumvention, mass infrastructural proliferation, inter-and intra-national commerce treaties and regulations, and the alchemical transformation of a distributed, solid rock into a free-flowing liquid.

If we continue to apply extracting, mining, and capturing metaphors to the relationship between platform capital and a platform's users, the lens of resource materialities allows us to see beyond how game engines will be used to extract new sources of user value in the Metaverse. We can also understand why game engines and their ownership groups will be responsible for transmuting users, technologies, and legal systems into infrastructures of extraction.

Scholars have long noted how game engines produce an ideal body. An ideal body produces a standardized subject[25] not only in terms of bodily orientation and capacity,[26] but also in terms of raced and gendered subjectivities that assume a white neoliberal subject.[27] Game engines in the Metaverse, however, move beyond representational and mimetic practices of the body, toward producing the user and their body as a resource through which data can be harvested and put to use. Initially, these data "phantasms"—digital traces of a human subject that come to take on a life of their own—were primarily put to use as marketing and targeted advertising materials.[28] Increasingly, however, the use of photogrammetric tracking and capture technology built into hardware interfaces like Meta's Quest Pro are being piped into neural network heuristics. These networks produce new representations of human bodies and practices that can be further deployed and monetized in Metaverse spaces. These representations both siphon value away from digital artists and designers and reproduce the white male abled body as the standard from which all others are marked as deviant.[29]

The need for a platform like *Fortnite* to function mechanically and aesthetically across a diverse array of hardware configurations—VR, powerful desktop computers, and light mobile phones—requires copious amounts of computing power and the skilled craftsmanship and expertise of engine developers and game optimization workers. The diminishing returns on increasing hardware power, however, have created a bottle-neck for the Metaverse: the need for more efficient rendering and net-working software techniques. Infrastructurally, game engines will serve as the content "plumbing" of the Metaverse[30] that translate computational processes across hardware platforms, helping to ensure that the same digital content can simultaneously run across multiple devices. Consis-tent processing speed across device scales was once sought through mate-rial means, such as increasing the density of transistors or heatsinks on a microchip. However, global labor and mining shortages coupled with the physical properties of silicon mean that we are rapidly approaching the limits of Moore's Law.[31] As such, the advances in computing power needed to build shared, cross-platform digital environments will instead come from software practices and algorithmic efficiency. Game engines such as Unreal advance toward this efficiency by producing "heat itself" as a resource, further translated across an array of other resource pro-ductions. Heat becomes made knowable through a multitude of affective and phenomenological indices: the affective measurement of heat via "frames per second" metrics, internal tracking of computational "opera-tions per tick," thermo-readings of video cards and their heat syncs, and fan and case management. Metaverse developers will use game engines to play with heat; using internal tools, third-party software, and techni-cal tricks of the trade to minimize software computations and distribute heat across components of a computer's hardware, so that environments run equally smoothly for simultaneous, heterogeneous user configura-tions. Game engines are thus positioned to operate as the future plumb-ing point in a broader flow of heat across bodies, electronics, indices, and user experiences.[32]

Institutionally, game engine companies are part of a larger legal and institutional project aimed at standardizing and consolidating the techni-cal and commercial practices. These efforts generally benefit the major tech corporations who already exert hegemonic control over digital com-munication policy. The integration of monetization systems into games such as *Fortnite* has technical, legal, and political ramifications that have metastasized in the form of ongoing lawsuits between Epic Games, Google, and Apple over the rights of media platform distributors to monopolize access to software and hardware platforms.[33] While the major arguments in these cases center on antitrust and anticompetitiveness claims, hidden in court transcripts the ontological foundations are being laid as well. Of particular interest, revealed in court's findings, is Epic's efforts to create a legal distinction between "a game" and "a Metaverse." Though Epic will likely lose its lawsuit against Apple, on this definitional front the gaming company successfully created a foothold of precedent that categorized games and Metaverses separately. From Judge Yvonne Gonzalez Rogers's injunction,

> The Court understands that, based on the record, the concept of a Metaverse is a digital virtual world where individuals can create character avatars and play them through interactive programmed and created experiences. In Mr. Sweeney's own words, a Metaverse is "a realistic 3D work in which participants have both social experiences, like sitting in a bar and talking, and also game experiences." In short, a Metaverse both mimics the real world by providing virtual social possibilities, while simultaneously incorporating gaming or simulation type of experiences for players to enjoy. Epic Games' and Mr. Sweeney's plans for *Fortnite* and its Metaverse involved shifting the video game from primarily relying on the former modes (*i.e.*, developer designed, traditionally gaming, and competitive modes) to the latter modes (*i.e.*, social and creative modes), where users-becoming-creators would themselves be rewarded and enriched. The Court general finds Mr. Sweeney's personal beliefs about the future of the Metaverse are sincerely held.[34]

Such a definition creates a distinction between a game—defined as a particular artistic or media element, akin to a movie or a book—from a Metaverse. The latter is now defined as a *social space* within which media experiences, such as a mall or a public event, can occur. As such, future legal cases may have standing to judge Metaverse disputes by taking into account consumer agency (what is a user allowed to do within a social space?) rather than solely on author agency (what rights does an author have over the control of their creative work?).

Finally, while on this particular legal front Epic and Apple were competitors—each aiming to produce legal precedents for control over Metaverse standards—on other fronts the two companies operate in concert. Through their participation in the Khronos Group—an industry consortium of over 150 game developers, hardware manufacturers, and publishers—these companies work to advance industry "open" standards for the 3D web. Pursuit of these standards is often framed in terms of efficiently creating technical compatibility, such as through the Vulkan heat-management API or the OpenGL web graphics standard. Yet Khronos primarily advances standards that benefit its most well-funded consortium members. This favoritism can sometimes take the form of advancing standards that favor member hardware and processing architectures over others, or creating inefficiencies in "open" technical standards that accommodate private technical standards, such as Vulkan's accommodation of Apple's proprietary Metal API. Further, Khronos and its member organizations will partner with new and legacy lobbying groups—such as the Metaverse Forum and the Computer & Communications Industry Association (CCIA)—to prepare briefs and testimonials aimed at authoring industry-favorable US legislation. Like Khronos, while groups like the CCIA outwardly project a collective goal of efficient industry-government collaboration, a closer examination of their legislative priorities reveals a "pay-to-play" model in which lobby groups are willing to contradict their prior stances and undermine democratic and open standards to suit the interests of their most monied members.

The diverging corporate strategies of "Metaverse as productivity tool" versus "Metaverse as licensed hangout space" continue to play out. We have already witnessed the spectacular failures of janky real-time 3D social networking spaces alongside the crumbling scams of cryptocurrencies and blockchain-centered Metaverse real-estate-like "investment." These prominent, public-facing collapses and overall vagueness of vision create a narrative of a fizzled tech bubble, a Silicon Valley fever dream that never quite took off. But the infrastructures, codebases, legal precedents, and actors from this bubble remain, both as ready-at-hand resources to be integrated into a future 3D web and as active development practices producing bodies and nation-states calling for new methods and forms of extractive capital. In continuing to break down the artificially constructed "surface-depth" divide between content/culture and technology/platform, game studies scholars must also illuminate the infrastructural and institutional processes that produce games and their users. Though it is unclear what shapes and qualities the intertwined futures of gaming and the web/Metaverse will have, it remains clear that game engines—and Unreal—will play central roles in crafting that future.

Notes

Introduction

1. Matthew Gault, "The Weather Channel Is Using Unreal Engine to Show How Dangerous Hurricane Florence Is," *Motherboard*, September 14, 2018, https://www.vice.com/en/article/7xjv9x/the-weather-channel-using-unreal-engine-to-show-hurricane-florence.
2. Matthew Gault, "Weather Channel Is Using Unreal Engine."
3. Lars Doucet and Anthony Pecorella, "Game Engines on Steam: The Definitive Breakdown," *Game Developer*, September 2, 2021, https://www.gamedeveloper.com/business/game-engines-on-steam-the-definitive-breakdown.
4. Stefan Werning, *Making Games: The Politics and Poetics of Game Creation Tools* (Cambridge, MA: MIT Press, 2021), 26.
5. For more on Sierra's AGI engine and its place in history as arguably the first game engine, see Laine Nooney, "Let's Begin Again: Sierra On-Line and the Origins of the Graphical Adventure Game," *American Journal of Play* 10, no. 1 (2017): 71–98.
6. Thomas H. Apperley and Darshana Jayemane, "Game Studies' Material Turn," *Westminster Papers in Communication and Culture* 9, no. 1 (2012): 5–25.
7. John Banks, *Co-Creating Videogames* (New York: Bloomsbury, 2013).
8. Banks, *Co-Creating Videogames*.
9. Casey O'Donnell, "Platforms in the Cloud: On the Ephemerality of Platforms," *Digital Culture & Education* 8(2), 185–190 (2016).
10. John Law, *Aircraft Stories: Decentering the Object in Technoscience* (Durham, NC: Duke University Press, 2002), 3.
11. Law, *Aircraft Stories*, 2.
12. Law, *Aircraft Stories*, 2.
13. Malout Juelskjær and Nete Schwennesen, "Intra-Active Entanglements—An Interview with Karen Barad," *Kvinder, Køn & Forskning* 1–2 (2012).
14. For more on this, see Thomas Apperley and Jussi Parikka, "Platform Studies' Epistemic Threshold," *Games and Culture* 13, no. 4 (2018): 349–369; and

Benjamin Nicoll, "A Dialectic of Obsolescence? The Sega Saturn as a Residual Platform," in *Minor Platforms in Videogame History* (Amsterdam: Amsterdam University Press, 2019), 133–156.

15. Alexander Galloway, *Gaming: Essays on Algorithmic Culture* (Minneapolis: University of Minnesota Press, 2006), 12.

16. Benjamin Nicoll and Brendan Keogh, *The Unity Game Engine and the Circuits of Cultural Software* (London: Palgrave Pivot, 2019).

17. Werning, *Making Games*.

18. Sandra Harding, "Rethinking Standpoint Epistemology: What Is 'Strong Objectivity?'" in *Feminist Epistemologies*, ed. Linda Alcoff and Elizabeth Potter (New York: Routledge, 2013), 49–82.

19. This is not to say that games and engines have no material or structural factors when provided with capital (the 2020s shortage of graphics cards due to cryptocurrency mining is a recent example), but rather that the logic and ontologies of game development are substantively different than they are for players, consumers, and small companies.

20. Eric Freedman, *The Persistence of Code in Game Engine Culture* (New York: Routledge, 2020), 12, citing P. Paul Dourish, *The Stuff of Bits: An Essay on the Materiality of Information* (Cambridge, MA: MIT Press, 2017), 57.

21. Tara McPherson, "Designing for Difference," *Differences* 25, no. 1 (2014): 177–188.

22. Annemarie Mol, *The Body Multiple: Ontology in Medical Practice* (Durham, NC: Duke University Press, 2002).

23. For broader histories and debates surrounding feminist technoscience studies, some of the work I find most useful includes Donna Jeanne Haraway, "A Game of Cat's Cradle: Science Studies, Feminist Theory, Cultural Studies," *Configurations* 2, no. 1 (1994): 59–71; Cecilia Åsberg, "Enter Cyborg: Tracing the Historiography and Ontological Turn of Feminist Technoscience Studies," *International Journal of Feminist Technoscience* 1, no. 1 (2010): 1–25; Judy Wajcman, "Feminist Theories of Technology," *Cambridge Journal of Economics* 34, no. 1 (2010): 143–152; and Katherine McKittrick, *Dear Science and Other Stories* (Durham, NC: Duke University Press, 2020).

24. Judy Wajcman, *Feminism Confronts Technology* (University Park, PA: Penn State Press, 1991).

25. Constance Penley, Andrew Ross, and Donna Haraway, "Cyborgs at Large: Interview with Donna Haraway," *Social Text* 25/26 (1990): 8–23.

26. Donna Haraway, *Staying with the Trouble: Making Kin in the Chthulucene* (Durham, NC: Duke University Press, 2016).

27. John Law and Annemarie Mol, "Notes on Materiality and Sociality," *Sociological Review* 43, no. 2 (1995): 274–294.

28. Catherine Knight Steele, *Digital Black Feminism* (New York: New York University Press, 2021).

29. Ruha Benjamin, *Race after Technology: Abolitionist Tools for the New Jim Code* (Medford, MA: Polity Press, 2019).

30. Kishonna L. Gray, *Intersectional Tech: Black Users in Digital Gaming* (Baton Rouge, LA: LSU Press, 2020).

31. Jennifer Malkowski and TreaAndrea M. Russworm, *Gaming Representation* (Bloomington: Indiana University Press, 2017).

32. Amanda Phillips, *Gamer Trouble: Feminist Confrontations in Digital Culture* (New York: New York University Press, 2020).

33. John Law and Marianne Elisabeth Lien, "Slippery: Field Notes in Empirical Ontology," *Social Studies of Science* 43, no. 3 (2013): 363–378, 365.

34. Steven E. Jones and George K. Thiruvathukal, *Codename Revolution: The Nintendo Wii Platform* (Cambridge, MA: MIT Press, 2012), 27, Quoted in Dale Leorke, "Rebranding the Platform: The Limitations of 'Platform Studies,'" *Digital Culture and Education* 4, no. 3 (2012): 257–268(emphasis in the original).

35. Nick Srnicek, *Platform Capitalism* (Hoboken, NJ: John Wiley & Sons, 2017).

36. Ariadna Matamoros-Fernández, "Platformed Racism: The Mediation and Circulation of an Australian Race-Based Controversy on Twitter, Facebook and YouTube," *Information, Communication & Society* 20, no. 6 (2017): 930–946.

37. Jean Burgess and Nancy K. Baym, *Twitter: A Biography* (New York: New York University Press, 2020).

38. Safiya Umoja Noble, *Algorithms of Oppression: How Search Engines Reinforce Racism* (New York: New York University Press, 2018).

39. Ian Bogost and Nick Montfort, "Platform Studies: Frequently Questioned Answers," paper written for Digital Arts and Culture 2009 Conference, December 12–15, 2009, Irvine, CA.

40. Anastasia Salter and John Murray, *Flash: Building the Interactive Web* (Cambridge, MA: MIT Press, 2014).

41. Zabet Patterson, *Peripheral Vision: Bell Labs, the SC 4020, and the Origins of Computer Art* (Cambridge, MA: MIT Press, 2015).

42. J. Svelch, "Platform Studies, Computational Essentialism, and Magic: The Gathering," *Analog Game Studies* 3, no. 5 (2016).

43. Lars Konzack, "Computer Game Criticism: A Method for Computer Game Analysis," Proceedings of Computer Games and Digital Cultures Conference, ed. Frans Mäyrä. Tampere: Tampere University Press, 2002.

44. Nick Montfort, "Combat in Context," *Game Studies* 6, no. 1 (2006): 1.

45. "Levels of Platform Studies," Platform Studies, accessed October 24, 2021, http://platformstudies.org/levels.html.

46. Montfort, "Combat in Context."

47. Montfort, "Combat in Context."

48. Dale Leorke, "Rebranding the Platform: The Limitations of 'Platform Studies,'" *Digital Culture and Education* 4, no. 3 (2012): 257–268.

49. Montfort, "Combat in Context."

50. Montfort, "Combat in Context," endnote 3.

51. Paul Dourish, "What We Talk about When We Talk about Context," *Personal and Ubiquitous Computing* 8, no. 1 (2004): 19–30.

52. Bruno Latour, "Drawing Things Together," in *The Map Reader: Theories of Mapping Practice and Cartographic Representation*, ed. Martin Dodge, Rob Kitchin, and Chris Perkins (Hoboken, NJ: Wiley, 2011), 65–72.

53. Nick Montfort and Ian Bogost, *Racing the Beam: The Atari Video Computer System* (Cambridge, MA: MIT Press, 2009), 42.

54. Epic Games, "Unreal Engine FAQs: What Platforms Are Supported?" https://www.unrealengine.com/en-US/faq.

55. Ian Bogost and Nick Montfort, "Platform Studies: Frequently Questioned Answers," *Digital Arts and Culture* (December, 2009): 12–15.

56. Marc Andreessen, "Analyzing the Facebook Platform, Three Weeks In," *Pmarca*, blog post, June 2007, http://web.archive.org/web/20071021003047/blog.pmarca.com/2007/06/analyzing_the_f.html, cited in Nick Montfort and Ian Bogost, *Racing the Beam: The Atari Video Computer System* (Cambridge, MA: MIT Press, 2009).

57. M. Andreessen, "The Three Kinds of Platforms You Meet on the Internet," *Pmarca*, blog post, September 2007, http://web.archive.org/web/20071018161644/http://blog.pmarca.com/2007/09/the-three-kinds.html, cited in Montfort and Bogost, *Racing the Beam*.

58. Bogost and Montfort. "Platform Studies: Frequently Questioned Answers."

59. Bogost and Montfort. "Platform Studies: Frequently Questioned Answers." 4.

60. Bogost and Montfort. "Platform Studies: Frequently Questioned Answers." 4.

61. Bogost and Montfort. "Platform Studies: Frequently Questioned Answers." , 4

62. Montfort "Combat in Context."

63. Lisa Nakamura, "Indigenous Circuits: Navajo Women and the Racialization of Early Electronic Manufacture," *American Quarterly* 66, no. 4 (2014): 919–941.

64. Aubrey Anable, "Platform Studies," *Feminist Media Histories* 4, no. 2 (2018): 135–140.

65. Aubrey Anable, *Playing with Feelings: Video Games and Affect* (Minneapolis: University of Minnesota Press, 2018).

66. Anable, *Playing with Feelings*, 137.

67. Constance Penley, *The Future of an Illusion: Film, Feminism, and Psychoanalysis* (Minneapolis: University of Minnesota Press, 1989).

68. Nakamura, "Indigenous Circuits."

69. Anable, "Platform Studies," citing Nakamura, "Indigenous Circuits."

70. McPherson, "Designing for Difference."

71. Nick Montfort, "Platform Studies at 10," *nickm*, blog post, July 2018 (emphasis original), https://nickm.com/post/2018/07/platform-studies-at-10/,

72. Montfort and Bogost, *Racing the Beam*.

73. Alex Custodio, *Who Are You?: Nintendo's Game Boy Advance Platform* (Cambridge, MA: MIT Press, 2020).

74. Apperley and Jayemane, "Games Studies' Material Turn," 12.

75. O'Donnell, "Platforms in the Cloud," 188.

76. Marilyn Strathern, "On Space and Depth," in *Complexities: Social Studies of Knowledge Practices*, ed. John Law and Annemarie Mol (Durham, NC: Duke University Press, 2002), 88.

77. Thomas Apperley and Jussi Parikka, "Platform Studies' Epistemic Threshold," *Games and Culture* 13, no. 4 (2018): 349–369.

78. Karen Barad, *Meeting the Universe Halfway: Quantum Physics and the Entanglement of Matter and Meaning* (Durham, NC: Duke University Press, 2007).

79. Pheng Cheah, "Mattering," *Diacritics* 26, no. 1 (1996): 108–139.

80. Anable, "Platform Studies," 137.

81. Mol, The Body Multiple, 4.

82. Mol, The Body Multiple, 5.

83. Bruno Latour, *Reassembling the Social: An Introduction to Actor-Network-Theory* (Oxford: Oxford University Press, 2007).

84. Judith Butler, Bodies that Matter: On the Discursive Limits of "Sex." (New York: Routledge, 1993).

85. Mol, The Body Multiple, 7.

86. Tim Lenoir, "All but War Is Simulation: The Military-Entertainment Complex," *Configurations* 8, no. 3 (2000): 289–335.

87. Aleena Chia, "The Artist and the Automaton in Digital Game Production," *Convergence* 28, no. 2 (2022). 389–412.

88. Tanya Richardson and Gisa Weszkalnys, "Introduction: Resource Materialities," *Anthropological Quarterly* 87, no. 1 (2014): 5–30.

Chapter 1

1. Beth J. Asch, James Hosek, Jeremy Arkes, C. Christine Fair, Jennifer Sharp, and Mark E. Totten, "Have Improved Resources Increased Military Recruiting and Retention?" *RAND Corporation*, 2004, https://www.rand.org/pubs/research_briefs/RB7556.html.

2. US Army, "The Army Values," *Army.mil*, accessed July 10, 2021, https://www.army.mil/values/.

3. For US casualties, Seymour Hersh, *Chain of Command* (New York: Penguin Books, 2005), 181; for Iraqi casualties, Thomas A. Keaney and Eliot A. Cohen, "Gulf War Air Power Survey," *Report Commissioned by the U.S. Air Force* (1993).

4. Douglas Kellner, "The Persian Gulf TV War Revisited," in *Reporting War* ed. Stuart Allan and Barbie Zelizer (New York: Routledge, 2004), 146–164; and Jean Baudrillard, *The Gulf War Did Not Take Place* (Bloomington: Indiana University Press, 1995).

5. Ed Halter, *From Sun Tzu to Xbox: War and Video Games* (New York: Thunder's Mouth Press, 2006).

6. Raiford Guins and Henry Lowood, "Atari's Army Battlezone Project," *ROMchip* 2, no. 1 (2020).

7. Halter, *From Sun Tzu to Xbox*. One of these contemporaries was Mike Macedonia.

8. "America's Army Game Sets Five Guinness World Records," *U.S. Army*, accessed July 24, 2021, https://www.army.mil/article/16678/americas_army_game_sets_five_guinness_world_records.

9. Laine Nooney, "A Pedestal, a Table, a Love Letter: Archaeologies of Gender in Videogame History," *Game Studies* 13, no. 2 (2013).

10. John Law, *Aircraft Stories: Decentering the Object in Technoscience* (Durham, NC: Duke University Press, 2002), 2.

11. Senate Sessions, "Floor Statements by Senator Sessions," 1993, archived December 12, 2016, http://www.sessions.senate.gov/public/index.cfm/floor-statements?ID=ADA43A1E-7E9C-9AF9-7EF1-9F3BEAE3E1BE.

12. Senate Sessions "Floor Statements."

13. Nigel Cross, "Designerly Ways of Knowing: Design Discipline Versus Design Science," *Design Issues* 17, no. 3 (2001): 49–55.

14. Eric Freedman, *The Persistence of Code in Game Engine Culture* (New York: Routledge, 2020).

15. Edward S. Herman and Noam Chomsky, *Manufacturing Consent: The Political Economy of the Mass Media* (New York: Random House, 2010).

16. Tara McPherson, "US Operating Systems at Mid-Century: The Intertwining of Race and UNIX," in *Race after the Internet*, ed. Lisa Nakamura and Peter Chow-White (New York: Routledge, 2013), 21–37.

17. Tim Lenoir, "All but War Is Simulation," *Configurations* 8, no. 3 (2000): 289–335.

18. Shenja Van der Graaf and David B. Nieborg, "Together We Brand: America's Army," DiGRA Conference 2009, "Breaking New Ground: Innovation in Games, Play, Practice and Theory," September 1–4, West London, UK.

19. Herman and Chomsky, *Manufacturing Consent*.

20. Marcus Power, "Digitized Virtuosity: Video War Games and Post-9/11 Cyber-Deterrence," *Security Dialogue* 38, no. 2 (2007): 271–288.

21. Robertson Allen, *America's Digital Army: Games at Work and War* (Lincoln: University of Nebraska Press, 2017).

22. David B. Nieborg, "Empower yourself, defend freedom! Playing games during times of war," in Digital material: tracing new media in everyday life and technology, ed. M. van den Boomen, S. Lammes, A-S. Lehmann, J. Raessens, and M. T. Schäfer (Amsterdam, Netherlands:Amsterdam University Press, 2009), 35-47.

23. Tim Lenoir and Luke Caldwell, *The Military-Entertainment Complex* (Cambridge, MA: Harvard University Press, 2018), 73.

24. Allen, *America's Digital Army*, 125.

25. Lisa Nakamura, "Indigenous Circuits: Navajo Women and the Racialization of Early Electronic Manufacture," *American Quarterly* 66, no. 4 (2014): 919–941.

26. James Malazita, Alexander Nikolaev, and Douglas Porpora, "Moral Argument in the Public Sphere: The Case of Bosnia," *Review of Communication* 14, no. 3/4 (2014): 229–244.

27. Bluesnews, "Stardock Games, IGDA Announce Game::Business: Law Summit," May 21, 2002, https://www.bluesnews.com/a/365.

28. Judy Wajcman, *Feminism Confronts Technology* (University Park, PA: Penn State Press, 1991).

29. Phil Salvador, "The Obscuritory—John Hiles Interview," *Obscuritory*, August 26, 2016, https://obscuritory.com/software/john-hiles-interview/.

30. James Der Derian, "Cyberspace as Battlespace: The New Virtual Alliance of the Military, the Media, and the Entertainment Industry," in *Living with Cyberspace: Technology & Societies in the 21st Century*, ed. John Armitage and Joanne Roberts(2002): 61–71.

31. Ronald J. Roland, "Panel: The Future of Military Simulation," *Proceedings of the 1998 Winter Simulation Conference*, ed. D. J. Medeiros, E. F. Watson, J. S. Carson, and M. S. Manivannan (1998), https://repository.lib.ncsu.edu/bitstream/handle/1840.4/6727/1998_0109.pdf?sequence=1.

32. University of Central Florida, "UCF Hires Assistant VP for Research to Build Funding Base," August 27, 2013, https://www.ucf.edu/news/ucf-hires-assistant-vp-for-research-to-build-funding-base/.

33. For more, see, P. Harrigan and M. G. Kirschenbaum, eds., *Zones of Control: Perspectives on Wargaming* (Cambridge, MA: MIT Press, 2016).

34. Robert Moran, "A Playful Army Experience at Franklin Mills," *Philadelphia Inquirer*, August 8, 2008, https://www.inquirer.com/philly/news/breaking/20080829_A_playful_Army_experience_at_Franklin_Mills.html; Allen, *America's Digital Army*; and Pat Elder, "Army Vans Equipped for Recruiting," *Military Trader*, July 14, 2008, https://www.militarytrader.com/mv-101/army-vans-equipped-for-recruiting.

35. Brian Sutton-Smith Library and Archives of Play at The Strong: America's Army Collection, Series I: Administrative History, 1999–2018, I—Folder 05_Emails.

36. John Hiles, Mike Zyda, and Mike Capps, "US Army and MOVES Research Proposal: You're in the Army Now!," Brian Sutton-Smith Library and Archives of

Play at The Strong America's Army Collection Series I: Administrative History, 1999–2018, I—Folder 02_Scope of work—01_Army Recruit MOU, 11.

37. Mihaly Csikszentmihalyi, Sami Abuhamdeh, and Jeanne Nakamura, "Flow," in *Handbook of Competence and Motivation* (New York: Guilford Press, 2005), 598–608.

38. Braxton Soderman, *Against Flow: Video Games and the Flowing Subject* (Cambridge, MA: MIT Press, 2021).

39. "Information Extraction," PowerPoint slides, Naval Postgraduate School MOVES Institute, archived at the Brian Sutton-Smith Library and Archives of Play at The Strong, America's Army Collection Series I: Administrative History, 1999–2018, I—Folder 02_Scope of work—01_Army Recruit MOU.

40. Multiple iterations of this story were found throughout the archive, and it would eventually be updated and released in print as Matthew J. Caffrey Jr., *On Wargaming* (Newport, RI: US Naval War College Press, 2019).

41. "About NDL Overview," *Gamebryo*, June 9, 2003, https://web.archive.org/web/20030609161531/http://www.ndl.com/about_overview.cfm.

42. Hiles et al., "You're in the Army Now," 11.

43. Bleszinski quote taken from Tycho, "The History of Unreal Technology Part 3," *UnrealOps*, January 2, 2005, http://www.barbos.net/unrealops/modules.php?op=modload&name=Reviews&file=index&req=showcontent&id=162.

44. Tim Sweeney, quotes from Benj Edwards, "From the Past to the Future: Tim Sweeney Talks," *Game Developer*, May 25, 2009, https://www.gamedeveloper.com/design/from-the-past-to-the-future-tim-sweeney-talks.

45. Mike Thomsen, "The History of Unreal Engine," *IGN*, February 23, 2010, https://www.ign.com/articles/2010/02/23/history-of-the-unreal-engine.

46. Thomsen, "History of Unreal Engine."

47. Edwards, "From the Past to the Future."

48. Thomsen, "History of Unreal Engine."

49. ZZT still has a thriving online mod community.

50. ZZT would be later retconned to stand for "Zoo of Zero Tolerance": see Dr. Dos, "Livestream—The Joy of ZZT Ep. 6: Squashing Bugs and One More Puzzle," *Museum of ZZT*, March 26, 2020, https://www.museumofzzt.com/article/463/zzt-and-epic-newsletter-scans.

51. Thomas Poell, David B. Nieborg, and Brooke Erin Duffy, *Platforms and Cultural Production* (Hoboken, NJ: John Wiley & Sons, 2021).

52. Thomsen, "History of Unreal Engine."

53. Brian Crecente, "Better with Age: A History of Epic Games," *Polygon*, October 1, 2012, https://www.polygon.com/2012/10/1/3438196/better-with-age-a-history-of-epic-games.

54. Crecente, "Better with Age."

55. Matt Tagliaferri, *Unreal: The Official Strategy Guide* (New York: GT Interactive Software, 1998).

56. Robertson Allen would note that during his interviews with AA developers, many of them would come to work dressed in fatigues and military-themed t-shirts, to the point that Allen had thought many of them were enlisted men. They weren't, but several of the developers described themselves as essentially military cosplayers.

57. The army, however, was careful to never use the term "shooter" in its official materials, instead calling the game genre either "First Person Perspective" or

"First Person Perspective Action." Non-official material, such as MOVES development team emails, however, regularly use "FPS" nomenclature.

58. Crecente, "Better with Age."

59. IGN Staff, "Jay Wilbur Joins Epic MegaGames," *IGN*, March 8, 1997, https://www.ign.com/articles/1997/03/08/jay-wilbur-joins-epic-megagames.

60. Email from July 10, 2002, between Mike Capps, Mike Zyda, Alex Mayberry, Brian Sutton-Smith Library and Archives of Play at The Strong; America's Army Collection; Series I: Administrative History, 1999–2018, I—Folder 05_Emails.

61. From: Epic MegaGames/MOVES Licensing Agreement: Brian Sutton-Smith Library and Archives of Play at The Strong; America's Army collection, Series I: Administrative History, 1999–2018, I—Folder 03_Licenses and agreements—01_Admin.

62. "Army Game Plan" master document, Brian Sutton-Smith Library and Archives of Play at The Strong; America's Army Collection Series II: Game Design Documentation, 1999–2005.

63. Freedman, *Persistence of Code*.

64. Epic MegaGames/MOVES Licensing Agreement: Brian Sutton-Smith Library and Archives of Play at The Strong; America's Army Collection, Series I: Administrative History, 1999–2018, I—Folder 03_Licenses and agreements—01_Admin.

65. Casey O'Donnell, "Platforms in the Cloud: On the Ephemerality of Platforms," *Digital Culture & Education* 8 (2016): 47–59.

66. Epic MegaGames/MOVES Licensing Agreement: Brian Sutton-Smith Library and Archives of Play at The Strong; America's Army Collection, Series I: Administrative History, 1999–2018, I—Folder 03_Licenses and agreements—01_Admin.

67. Damien Chambers, "Interview: John Gibson (TripWire Interactive)," *Geeks under Grace*, December 17, 2016, https://geeksundergrace.com/gaming/interview-john-gibson-tripwire-interactive/. Gibson would later go on to form TripWire studios and spend his career making games that combined evangelical Christianity with blood-and-gore shoot-em-ups, before being let go from TripWire for publicly supporting Texas Governor Abbot's antiabortion laws in 2021.

68. Michael Zyda, Alex Mayberry, Casey Wardynski, Russell Shilling, and Margaret Davis, "The MOVES Institute's America's Army Operations Game," *Proceedings of the ACM SIGGRAPH 2003 Symposium on Interactive 3D Graphics*, April 28–30, 2003, pp. 217–218, color plate pp. 252, http://hdl.handle.net/10945/41556.

69. Crecente, "Better with Age."

70. "Homelanfed.com: News: 'America's Army' Exclusive Interview Part 2," Homelanfed.com, June 18, 2003, http://web.archive.org/web/20030618075852/http://www.homelanfed.com/index.php?id=13554.

71. Email from Jay Wilbur to Mike Zyda, June 16, 2003, Brian Sutton-Smith Library and Archives of Play at The Strong; America's Army Collection; Series I: Administrative History, 1999–2018, I—Folder 05_Emails.

72. Law, *Aircraft Stories*.

73. Mike Zyda "Post Mortem Memo," Brian Sutton-Smith Library and Archives of Play at The Strong; America's Army Collection, Series I: Administrative History, 1999–2018, I—Folder 08_Project conclusion and analysis—03_Separate file.

74. Allen, *America's Digital Army*.

75. See, Brian Sutton-Smith Library and Archives of Play at The Strong; America's Army Collection, and Allen America's Digital Army.

76. Allen's book provides a wonderful ethnographic exploration of post-MOVES *AA* life after 2006.

77. Owen S. Good, "America's Army Going Dark after 20 Years," *Polygon*, February 8, 2022, https://www.polygon.com/22924209/americas-army-proving-grounds-shut down-servers-sunset-pc-ps4.

78. James Barlow, "Epic Games Targets the Military, Government as Growth Areas," *Triangle Business Journal*, December 4, 2015, https://www.bizjournals .com/triangle/blog/techflash/2015/12/epic-games-targets-the-military -government.html.

79. Barlow, "Epic Games Targets the Military."

80. Sara Ahmed, *Queer Phenomenology: Orientations, Objects, Others* (Durham, NC: Duke University Press, 2006).

81. Yvonne Tasker, *Spectacular Bodies: Gender, Genre, and the Action Cinema* (New York: Routledge, 1993).

Chapter 2

1. Jennifer R. Whitson, "Voodoo Software and Boundary Objects in Game Development: How Developers Collaborate and Conflict with Game Engines and Art Tools," *New Media & Society* 20, no. 7 (2018): 2315–2332.

2. Brendan Keogh, *A Play of Bodies: How We Perceive Videogames* (Cambridge, MA: MIT Press, 2018).

3. James Ash, "Technologies of Captivation: Videogames and the Attunement of Affect," *Body & Society* 19, no. 1 (2013): 27–51.

4. Keogh, *A Play of Bodies*, 33.

5. See, Anne Friedberg, *The Virtual Window: From Alberti to Microsoft* (Cambridge, MA: MIT Press, 2009); Jonathan Crary, *Techniques of the Observer: On Vision and Modernity in the Nineteenth Century* (Cambridge, MA: MIT Press, 1992).

6. Steve Swink, *Game Feel: A Game Designer's Guide to Virtual Sensation* (Boca Raton, FL: CRC Press, 2008).

7. There is a deeper distinction to this software as well, as CAM may be used to refer more specifically to "post-design" software that serves as a direct interface between a completed 3D model and the machines on the factory floor.

8. Marc Steinberg, "From Automobile Capitalism to Platform Capitalism: Toyotism as a Prehistory of Digital Platforms," *Organization Studies* 43, no. 7 (2022): 1069–1090.

9. Tim Sweeney, Twitter, September 11, 2015, 6:50 pm, https://twitter.com /TimSweeneyEpic/status/642470320763469824. The Unreal forum community conversation referenced by Sweeney is now offline, but is archived by the Wayback Machine at https://web.archive.org/web/20191007215605/https://forums .unrealengine.com/community/general-discussion/46691-z-up-vs-y-up-the -solution-to-the-debate-lies-within?75420-Z-Up-vs-Y-Up-the-solution-to-the -debate-lies-within=.

10. Dylan Mulvin, *Proxies: The Cultural Work of Standing In* (Cambridge, MA: MIT Press, 2021).

11. Mulvin, *Proxies*, 8.

12. Jean Baudrillard, *Simulacra and Simulation* (Ann Arbor: University of Michigan Press, 1994).

13. Mulvin, *Proxies*, 19.
14. Sara Ahmed, *Queer Phenomenology: Orientations, Objects, Others* (Durham, NC: Duke University Press, 2006), 7.
15. Ahmed, *Queer Phenomenology*, 11.
16. Ahmed, *Queer Phenomenology*, 60.
17. Ahmed, *Queer Phenomenology*, 92.
18. David Nieborg, "From Premium to Freemium: The Political Economy of the App," in *Social, Casual and Mobile Games: The Changing Gaming Landscape*, ed. T. Leaver and M. Willson(Amsterdam: Amsterdam University Press, 2016), 225–240.
19. Karen Barad, "Posthumanist Performativity: Toward an Understanding of How Matter Comes to Matter," *Signs: Journal of Women in Culture and Society* 28, no. 3 (2003): 801–831.
20. Steve Woolgar, "Configuring the User: The Case of Usability Trials," *Sociological Review* 38, no. 1 suppl (1990): 58–99.
21. Mathew Wadstein, "Your First Hour in Unreal Engine 5," *Unreal Engine*, April 2, 2022 (updated March 22, 2023), https://dev.epicgames.com/community/learning /courses/ZpX/your-first-hour-in-unreal-engine-5/OEa/unreal-engine-creating -your-first-project.
22. Wadstein, "Your First Hour in Unreal."
23. Vivian Sobchack, *The Address of the Eye: A Phenomenology of Film Experience* (Princeton, NJ: Princeton University Press, 1992), 23 (emphasis in the original).
24. Tyler Wilde, "How WASD Became the Standard PC Control Scheme," *PC Gamer*, February 4, 2021, https://www.pcgamer.com/how-wasd-became-the-standard -pc-control-scheme/.
25. Mark J. P. Wolf, "Z-Axis Development in the Video Game," in *The Video Game Theory Reader 2*, ed. Bernard Perron, and Mark J. P. Wolf (New York: Routledge, 2008), 173–190.
26. Wilde, "How WASD Became the Standard."
27. Gary Lee Downey, *The Machine in Me: An Anthropologist Sits among Computer Engineers* (New York: Routledge, 1998).
28. Keogh, *Play of Bodies*; and Ash "Technologies of Captivation."
29. Bruno Latour, "Visualization and Cognition," *Knowledge and Society* 6, no. 6 (1986): 1–40.
30. Latour, "Visualization and Cognition," 5 (emphasis in the original).
31. Michael Alba, "Unreal Engine, Very Real Renders: Ray Tracing for Engineers," Engineering.com, November 15, 2019, https://www.engineering.com/story /unreal-engine-very-real-renders-ray-tracing-for-engineers.
32. Unreal Engine, "Creating a Digital Showroom: Audi and Mackevision Choose UE4," Unreal Engine.com, July 15, 2019, https://www.unrealengine.com/en-US /spotlights/creating-a-digital-showroom-audi-and-mackevision-choose-ue4.
33. The term "remediation" comes from J. David Bolter and Richard A. Grusin, "Remediation," *Configurations* 4, no. 3 (1996): 311–358. The quoted text can be found in Unreal Engine, "Creating a Digital Showroom."
34. Doug Wolff, "Real-Time Visualization Transforms Daimler's Engineering Pipeline," Unreal Engine.com, November 26, 2019, https://www.unrealengine.com /en-US/spotlights/real-time-visualization-transforms-daimler-s-engineering -pipeline.
35. Wolff, "Real-Time Visualization."

36. Wolf, "Z-Axis Development in the Video Game," (emphasis in the original).

37. Downey, *The Machine in Me*.

38. Dean Nieusma and James W. Malazita, "'Making' a Bridge: Critical Making as Synthesized Engineering/Humanistic Inquiry," 2016 ASEE Annual Conference & Exposition, June 26–29, 2016; and James W. Malazita and Korryn Resetar, "Infrastructures of Abstraction: How Computer Science Education Produces Anti-Political Subjects," *Digital Creativity* 30, no. 4 (2019): 300–312.

39. Downey, *The Machine in Me*, 163–164.

40. Downey, *The Machine in Me*, 176.

41. NASA Goddard Space Flight Center, "Coordinated Earth: Measuring Space in the Near-Earth Environment," October 8, 2014 (updated January 8, 2015), https://svs.gsfc.nasa.gov/4217.

42. Tim Sweeney, Twitter, January 14, 2018, 2:29 pm, https://twitter.com/TimSweeneyEpic/status/952661474501111808.

43. Jacob Gaboury, "Hidden Surface Problems: On the Digital Image as Material Object," *Journal of Visual Culture* 14, no. 1 (2015): 40–60.

44. Keogh, *Play of Bodies*, 24.

45. Saumya Malviya, "Symbol as Metonymy and Metaphor: A Sociological Perspective on Mathematical Symbolism," *Science, Technology and Society* 24, no. 1 (2019): 53–72.

46. Malviya, "Symbol as Metonymy and Metaphor," 67.

47. Jara Rocha and Femke Snelting, "Dis-Orientation and Its Aftermath," in *Volumetric Regimes: Material Cultures of Quantified Presence*, ed. Jara Rocha and Femke Snelting (London: Open Humanities Press, 2022), 57–75.

48. James Malazita, Dominic Francis Gelfuso, and Dean Nieusma, "Contextualizing 3D Printing's and Photosculpture's Contributions to Techno-Creative Literacies," 2016 ASEE Annual Conference & Exposition, June 26–29, 2016.

49. "Why Is the Origin in Computer Graphics Coordinates at the Top Left?" *Game Development Stack Exchange*, September 19, 2014, https://gamedev.stackexchange.com/questions/83570/why-is-the-origin-in-computer-graphics-coordinates-at-the-top-left.

50. Gaboury, "Hidden Surface Problems," 41.

51. Jack Halberstam, *The Queer Art of Failure* (Durham, NC: Duke University Press, 2011), https://doi.org/10.2307/j.ctv11sn283.

52. Jenny Sundén, "On Trans-, Glitch, and Gender as Machinery of Failure," *First Monday* (2015); Legacy Russell, "Elsewhere, After the Flood: Glitch Feminism and the Genesis of the Glitch Body Politic," *Rhizome*, March 12, 2013, http://rhizome.org/editorial/2013/mar/12/glitch-body-politic/; and Arianna Gass, "The Body in Play: Performance in and through Video Games," dissertation, University of Chicago, 2022.

53. Tony Bonilla, Twitter. March 7, 2023, 5:55 PM. https://twitter.com/Tonymation/status/1633239873992953856

Chapter 3

1. Katharina Emmerich, Patrizia Ring, and Maic Masuch, "I'm Glad You Are on My Side: How to Design Compelling Game Companions," in *Proceedings of the 2018 Annual Symposium on Computer-Human Interaction in Play* (2018), 141–152.

2. Stephanie C. Jennings, "A Meta-Synthesis of Agency in Game Studies: Trends, Troubles, Trajectories," G| A| M| E: Games as Art, Media, Entertainment 1, no. 8 (2019): 85-106.

3. Janet H. Murray, Hamlet on the Holodeck, Updated Edition: The Future of Narrative in Cyberspace (Cambridge, MA: MIT Press, 2017).

4. Murray, Hamlet on the Holodeck, 161.

5. TreaAndrea M. Russworm, "Dystopian Blackness and the Limits of Racial Empathy in The Walking Dead and The Last of Us," in Gaming Representation: Race, Gender, and Sexuality in Video Games, ed. Jennifer Malkowski and TreaAndrea M. Russworm (Bloomington: Indiana University Press, 2017), 109–128.

6. Stephanie Jennings, "Only You Can Save the World (of Videogames): Authoritarian Agencies in the Heroism of Videogame Design, Play, and Culture," Convergence 28, no. 2 (2022): 320-344

7. Jennings, "A Meta-Synthesis of Agency."

8. D. Fox Harrell and Jichen Zhu, "Agency Play: Dimensions of Agency for Interactive Narrative Design," in AAAI Spring Symposium: Intelligent Narrative Technologies II (2009), 44–52.

9. For more, see Benjamin Nicoll and Brendan Keogh, The Unity Game Engine and the Circuits of Cultural Software (Cham: Palgrave Pivot, 2019), 4; Robert Nideffer, "Game Engines as Creative Frameworks," in Context Providers: Conditions of Meaning in Media Arts, ed. Margot Lovejoy, Christiane Paul, and Victoria Vesna (Chicago, IL: University of Chicago Press, 2011), 175–197; and Conor McKeown, "Playing with Materiality: An Agential-Realist Reading of SethBling's Super Mario World Code-Injection," Information, Communication & Society 21, no. 9 (2018): 1234–1245.

10. Alayna Cole, "Connecting Player and Character Agency in Videogames," Text 22, no. 49 (Special 2018): 1–14.

11. Amanda Phillips, Gillian Smith, Michael Cook, and Tanya Short, "Feminism and Procedural Content Generation: Toward a Collaborative Politics of Computational Creativity," Digital Creativity 27, no. 1 (2016): 82–97.

12. Casey O'Donnell, Developer's Dilemma: The Secret World of Videogame Creators (Cambridge, MA: MIT Press, 2014).

13. John Banks, Co-Creating Videogames (London: Bloomsbury Publishing, 2013).

14. Jennifer R. Whitson, "Voodoo Software and Boundary Objects in Game Development: How Developers Collaborate and Conflict with Game Engines and Art Tools," New Media & Society 20, no. 7 (2018): 2315–2332.

15. Nick Dyer-Witheford and Greig De Peuter, Games of Empire: Global Capitalism and Video Games (Minneapolis: University of Minnesota Press, 2009); and Aleena Chia, "The Artist and the Automaton in Digital Game Production," Convergence 28, no. 2 (2022): 389-412.

16. Brendan Keogh, "Situating the Videogame Maker's Agency through Craft," Convergence 28, no. 2 (2022): 374–388.

17. Keogh, "Situating the Videogame Maker's Agency," 388.

18. Felan Parker, "Canonizing BioShock: Cultural Value and the Prestige Game," Games and Culture 12, no. 7–8 (2017): 739–763.

19. Stefan Schubert, "Objectivism, Narrative Agency, and the Politics of Choice in the Video Game BioShock," in Poetics of Politics: Textuality and Social Relevance in

Contemporary American Literature and Culture, ed. Timo Müller and Sascha Pöhlmann (Würzburg: Königshausen & Neumann, 2015), 271.

20. Lev Manovich, *The Language of New Media* (Cambridge, MA: MIT Press, 2002).

21. Jennings, "A Meta-Synthesis of Agency."

22. Diana Adesola Mafe, "Race and the First-Person Shooter: Challenging the Video Gamer in BioShock Infinite," *Camera Obscura: Feminism, Culture, and Media Studies* 30, no. 2 (2015): 89–123.

23. Cole "Connecting Player and Character Agency."

24. Andrew Goldfarb, "BioShock Infinite Cosplayer Becomes Official Face of Elizabeth," *IGN*, December 3, 2012, https://www.ign.com/articles/2012/12/03 /bioshock-infinite-cosplayer-becomes-official-face-of-elizabeth.

25. See, for example, Ian Bogost, *Unit Operations: An Approach to Videogame Criticism* (Cambridge, MA: MIT Press, 2008); Ian Bogost, *Persuasive Games: The Expressive Power of Videogames* (Cambridge, MA: MIT Press, 2010).

26. See, N. Katherine Hayles, "Print Is Flat, Code Is Deep: The Importance of Media-Specific Analysis," *Poetics Today* 25, no. 1 (2004): 67–90; N. Katherine Hayles, "Traumas of Code," *Critical Inquiry* 33, no. 1 (2006): 136–157.

27. Aubrey Anable, "Platform Studies," *Feminist Media Histories* 4, no. 2 (2018): 135–140.

28. Aubrey Anable, *Playing with Feelings: Video Games and Affect* (Minneapolis: University of Minnesota Press, 2018), viii.

29. Anable, *Playing with Feelings*.

30. For more, see, Christopher M. Kelty, *Two Bits: The Cultural Significance of Free Software* (Durham, NC: Duke University Press, 2008), Carys J. Craig, Joseph F. Turcotte, and Rosemary J. Coombe, "What Is Feminist about Open Access?: A Relational Approach to Copyright in the Academy," *Feminists@law* 1, no. 1 (2011): 1-35.

31. Jesse Schell, *The Art of Game Design: A Book of Lenses* (Boca Raton, FL: CRC Press, 2008).

32. Jennifer Whitson, "Voodoo Software and Boundary Objects in Game Development: How Developers Collaborate and Conflict with Game Engines and Art Tools," *New Media & Society* 20, no. 7 (2018): 2315–2332.

33. Anable, *Playing with Feelings*, xviii.

34. Gilles Deleuze and Félix Guattari, *Anti-Oedipus: Capitalism and Schizophrenia* (London: Penguin, 2009).

35. Anable, *Playing with Feelings*, 5, summarizing Raymond Williams, "Structures of Feeling," in *Structures of Feeling: Affectivity and the Study of Culture*, ed. Devika Sharma and Frederik Tygstrup (Berlin: De Gruyter, 2015), 20–28.

36. Karen Barad, *Meeting the Universe Halfway: Quantum Physics and the Entanglement of Matter and Meaning* (Durham, NC: Duke University Press, 2007).

37. Benjamin Nicoll and Brendan Keogh, *The Unity Game Engine and the Circuits of Cultural Software* (London: Palgrave Pivot, 2019).

38. Nick Montfort and Ian Bogost, *Racing the Beam: The Atari Video Computer System* (Cambridge, MA: MIT Press, 2009).

39. Murray, *Hamlet on the Holodeck*.

40. Russworm, "Dystopian Blackness."

41. Sociologist Roger Caillois originally uses the term to demarcate one of four kinds of rule-structured play, an analytic move that sets a foundation for later, more

strict, demarcations of "games" and "play"; see, Roger Caillois, *Man, Play, and Games* (Champaign: University of Illinois Press, 1991). Bernard Suits' *The Grasshopper* would more formally define rules, order, and competition as fundamental elements of a game; see, Bernard Suits, *The Grasshopper: Games, Life and Utopia* (Peterborough, ON: Broadview Press, 2014).

42. Suzanne Keen, "Reader's Temperaments and Fictional Character," *New Literary History* 42 (2011): 295–314, 295.

43. Espen Aarseth, "Genre Trouble, Narrativism and the Art of Simulation," in *First Person: New Media as Story, Performance and Game*, ed. Noah Wardrip-Fruin and Pat Harrigan (Cambridge, MA: MIT Press, 2004), 45–55.

44. Suzanne Keen, "A Theory of Narrative Empathy," *Narrative* 14, no. 3 (2006): 207–236.

45. Ken Levine, interview by Kevin VanOrd, "We Can Kill the Industry with Cynicism—Ken Levine—Bioshock," *The Break Room*, YouTube by Gamespot, March 20, 2013, http://www.youtube.com/watch?v=JwsjALh2vYA.

46. James W. Malazita and Korryn Resetar, "Infrastructures of Abstraction: How Computer Science Education Produces Anti-Political Subjects," *Digital Creativity* 30, no. 4 (2019): 300–312.

47. Ranjodh Singh Dhaliwal, "On Addressability, or What Even Is Computation?" *Critical Inquiry* 49, no. 1 (2022): 1–27.

48. Dhaliwal, "On Addressability," *Cultural Theory: An Anthology* (2010), 204–222; citing Louis Althusser, *Ideology and ideological state apparatuses (Notes towards an investigation)*, in Lenin and Philosophy and Other Essays, trans. Ben Brewster (New York and London: Monthly Review Press, 1971), 142–7, 166–76.

49. Susan Leigh Star, "This Is Not a Boundary Object: Reflections on the Origin of a Concept," *Science, Technology, & Human Values* 35, no. 5 (2010): 601–617.

50. Ken Levine, "Irrational Interviews 6: Randy Pitchford," *Inside Irrational Podcast*, February 3, 2011, https://irrationalgames.ghoststorygames.com/insider/irrational-interviews-6-randy-pitchford/.

51. Anable, *Playing with Feelings*.

52. Margaret Burnett, "Software Engineering for Visual Programming Languages," in *Handbook of Software Engineering and Knowledge Engineering*, vol. 2, ed. S.K. Chang. (Singapore: World Scientific, 2001), 1.

53. Roland Barthes, *S/Z: An Essay* (Mexico City: Siglo XXI, 1980); Algirdas J. Greimas and François Rastier, "The Interaction of Semiotic Constraints," *Yale French Studies* 41 (1968): 86–105.

54. George P. Landow and Paul Delany, (eds.), *Hypermedia and Literary Studies*, (Cambridge, Massachusetts: The MIT Press, 1991), 3–50, cited in Ilana Ariela Snyder, *Hypertext: The Electronic Labyrinth* (New York: New York University Press, 1996).

55. Bruno Latour, *Reassembling the Social: An Introduction to Actor-Network-Theory* (Oxford: Oxford University Press, 2007).

56. Bruno Latour, "Anti-zoom," in *Scale in Literature and Culture*, ed. Michael Tavel Clarke and David Wittenberg, 93–101 (London: Palgrave Macmillan, 2017).

57. James Malazita, "Critique Is the Steam: Reorienting Critical Digital Humanities across Disciplines," in *Debates in the Digital Humanities 2023*, ed. Lauren F. Klein and Matthew Gold (Minneapolis: University of Minnesota Press, 2023), 367.

58. Shawn Robertson, "Creating BioShock Infinite's Elizabeth," *GDC 2014* (2014); archived at the GCD Vault, accessed August 22, 2022, https://www.gdcvault.com/play/1020545/Creating-BioShock-Infinite-s.

59. VanOrd, quoting Ken Levine, "We Can Kill the Industry."
60. Amanda Phillips, *Gamer Trouble: Feminist Confrontations in Digital Culture* (New York: New York University Press, 2020).
61. John Abercrombie, "Bringing Elizabeth to Life," *GDC 2014*, https://www.gdcvault.com/play/1020831/Bringing-BioShock-Infinite-s-Elizabeth.
62. VanOrd, "We Can Kill the Industry."
63. VanOrd, "We Can Kill the Industry."
64. VanOrd, "We Can Kill the Industry."
65. Andrew Goldfarb, "How Playing as Elizabeth Changes BioShock Infinite," *IGN*, August 7, 2013, http://www.ign.com/articles/2013/08/07/how-playing-as-elizabeth-changes-BioShock-infinite.
66. Goldfarb, "How Playing as Elizabeth Changes."
67. Anita Sarkeesian, "Ms. Male Character—Tropes vs. Women," *Feminist Frequency*, November 18, 2013, https://feministfrequency.com/video/ms-male-character-tropes-vs-women/.
68. James Malazita, "The Material Undermining of Magical Feminism in BioShock Infinite: Burial at Sea," in *Feminism in Play*, ed. Kishonna Gray, Gerald Vorhees, and Emma Vossen (London: Palgrave Macmillan, 2018), 37–50.
69. Goldfarb, quoting Amanda Jeffrey, "Playing as Elizabeth."
70. Lois McNay, *Gender and Agency: Reconfiguring the Subject in Feminist and Social Theory* (Hoboken, NJ: John Wiley & Sons, 2013).

Chapter 4

1. Steve Clarke, "Conspiracy Theories and Conspiracy Theorizing," *Philosophy of the Social Sciences* 32, no. 2 (2002): 131–150.
2. John Moffet. *Conspiracy Theory: Did We Land on the Moon?* (2001), aired on *Fox News*, February 15, 2001.
3. Henry Jenkins, "Transmedia Storytelling and Entertainment: An Annotated Syllabus," *Continuum* 24, no. 6 (2010): 943–958.
4. John Berger, *Ways of Seeing* (London: Penguin, 1972).
5. Dominic Kao and D. Fox Harrell, "Embellishment & Effects: Seduction by Style," in *Avatars, Assembled: The Sociotechnical Anatomy of Digital Bodies*, ed. Jaime Banks (Bern: Peter Lang, 2017), 235–246.
6. Steve Swink, *Game Feel: A Game Designer's Guide to Virtual Sensation* (Boca Raton, FL: CRC Press, 2008).
7. Gillian Rose, *Visual Methodologies: An Introduction to Researching with Visual Materials* (Newbury Park, CA: Sage, 2016), quoted in Kao and Harrell, "Embellishment & Effects," 242–243.
8. André Brock Jr,. *Distributed Blackness: African American Cybercultures* (New York: New York University Press, 2020), 35.
9. NVIDIA, "Over the Moon: NVIDIA RTX-Powered Apollo 11 Spectacle Lands at SIGGRAPH," *NVIDIA* blog, July 30, 2019, https://blogs.nvidia.com/blog/2019/07/30/nvidia-rtx-apollo-11-demo/.
10. James W. Carey, "Historical Pragmatism and the Internet," *New Media & Society* 7, no. 4 (2005): 443–455.
11. Brock, *Distributed Blackness*, 34; Dinerstein's figuration can be found in Joel Dinerstein, "Technology and Its Discontents: On the Verge of the Posthuman,"

American Quarterly 58, no. 3 (2006): 569–595; Brock's reference to Carey's technological sublime can be found in Carey, "Historical Pragmatism."

12. Luce Irigaray and Edith Oberle, "Is the Subject of Science Sexed?" *Cultural Critique* 1 (1985): 73–88, 78 (emphasis in the original).

13. Chanda Prescod-Weinstein, "Making Black Women Scientists under White Empiricism: The Racialization of Epistemology in Physics," *Signs: Journal of Women in Culture and Society* 45, no. 2 (2020): 421–447.

14. T. L. Taylor, "The Assemblage of Play," *Games and Culture* 4, no. 4 (2009): 331–339.

15. Stephanie Boluk and Patrick LeMieux, *Metagaming: Playing, Competing, Spectating, Cheating, Trading, Making, and Breaking Videogames* (Minneapolis: University of Minnesota Press, 2017).

16. Casey O'Donnell, "Engines & Platforms: Functional Entanglements," in *Avatar, Assembled*, ed. Jaime Banks (Bern: Peter Lang, 2017), 265–273.

17. Ken Levine, "Irrational Interviews Episode 4: Cliff Bleszinski," *Inside Irrational Podcast*, November 3, 2010, https://irrationalgames.ghoststorygames.com/insider/irrational-interviews-episode-4/.

18. "Unreal," *NEXT Generation Magazine* (February 1997), no. 26.

19. "Unreal," *NEXT Generation Magazine*, 71.

20. "Unreal," *NEXT Generation Magazine*, 70.

21. Eric Freedman, "Engineering Queerness in the Game Development Pipeline," *Game Studies* 18, no. 3 (2018), citing Boluk and LeMieux, *Metagaming*, 129.

22. Freedman, "Engineering Queerness."

23. Julie A. Turnock, *Plastic Reality: Special Effects, Technology, and the Emergence of 1970s Blockbuster Aesthetics* (New York: Columbia University Press, 2015), 11.

24. Turnock, *Plastic Reality*, 11.

25. Julie A. Turnock, *The Empire of Effects: Industrial Light and Magic and the Rendering of Realism* (Austin: University of Texas Press, 2022), 10.

26. Turnock, *Empire of Effects*, 11, quoting George Lucas.

27. Turnock, *Plastic Reality*, 212.

28. Theodore Kim, "Histories and Counter-Histories of CGI in Movies," talk given at Rensselaer Polytechnic Institute's "Critical Game Design" Colloquium Speaker Series, September 28, 2022.

29. Turnock, *Plastic Reality*, 100.

30. In vanilla Unreal, at least. Individual developers can compile the engine from source and can modify things as they wish/have technical capacity.

31. Noah Wardrip-Fruin and Michael Mateas, "Defining Operational Logics," DiGRA Conference 2009, "Breaking New Ground: Innovation in Games, Play, Practice and Theory," September 1–4, West London, UK.

32. Gillies Deleuze and Félix Guattari, *A Thousand Plateaus: Capitalism and Schizophrenia* (London: Bloomsbury Publishing, 1988).

33. Aleena Chia, Brendan Keogh, Dale Leorke, and Benjamin Nicoll, "Platformisation in Game Development," *Internet Policy Review* 9, no. 4 (2020): 1–28.

34. Benjamin Nicoll and Brendan Keogh, *The Unity Game Engine and the Circuits of Cultural Software* (London: Palgrave Pivot, 2019).

35. Even here, "universality" is broadly variable.

36. Sébastien Lagarde and Charles de Rousiers, "Siggraph 2014," July 14, 2014, *Sébastien Lagarde* blog https://seblagarde.wordpress.com/2015/07/14/siggraph-2014-moving-frostbite-to-physically-based-rendering/.

37. Richard Dyer, *White: Essays on Race and Culture* (New York: Routledge, 1997), 47.

38. Matt Pharr, Wenzel Jakob, and Greg Humphreys, *Physically Based Rendering: From Theory to Implementation, Third Edition* (San Francisco, CA: Morgan Kaufmann Press, 2017).

39. Adrian Mackenzie, "Distributive Numbers: A Post-Demographic Perspective on Probability," in *Modes of Knowing: Resources from the Baroque*, ed. John Law and Evelyn Ruppert (Manchester, UK: Mattering Press, 2016), 115–135, 115.

40. Pharr, Jakob, and Humphreys, *Physically Based Rendering*.

41. Brent Burley and Walt Disney Animation Studios, "Physically-Based Shading at Disney," in *ACM SIGGRAPH* 2012: 1–7.

42. Jeff Russell, "Basic Theory of Physically Based Rendering," *Marmoset*, accessed July 6, 2021, https://marmoset.co/posts/basic-theory-of-physically-based-rendering/.

43. Semi-conductive materials also exist in the physical world, but are considered too rare to be worth correctly modeling by PBR developers.

44. J. Wilson, "Physically Based Rendering and You Can Too," *Marmoset*, accessed July 6, 2021, https://marmoset.co/posts/physically-based-rendering-and-you-can-too/.

45. Jacob Gaboury, "Hidden Surface Problems: On the Digital Image as Material Object," *Journal of Visual Culture* 14, no. 1 (2015): 40–60.

46. Karl Marx and Serge L. Levitsky, *Das Kapital: A Critique of Political Economy* (Washington, DC: H. Regnery, 1965).

47. Heinrich Wölfflin, *Principles of Art History: The Problem of the Development of Style in Early Modern Art: One Hundredth Anniversary Edition* (Los Angeles, CA: Getty Publications, 2015).

48. Interview with Karen Barad, in Iris van der Tuin and Rick Dolphijn, *New Materialism: Interviews & Cartographies* (London: Open Humanities Press, 2012).

49. Interview with Karen Barad, in van der Tuin and Dolphijn, *New Materialism*.

50. Nancy Cartwright, *How the Laws of Physics Lie* (Oxford: Oxford University Press, 1983), 153.

51. Cartwright, *How the Laws of Physics Lie*.

52. Cartwright, *How the Laws of Physics Lie*, 153.

53. Stephen R. Marschner, Stephen H. Westin, Eric P. F. Lafortune, and Kenneth E. Torrance, "Image-Based Bidirectional Reflectance Distribution Function Measurement," *Applied Optics* 39, no. 16 (2000): 2592–2600.

54. "PxrDisney," *RenderMan*, accessed July 6, 2021, https://renderman.pixar.com/resources/RenderMan_20/PxrDisney.html.

55. Gérard Genette and Marie Maclean, "Introduction to the Paratext," *New Literary History* 22, no. 2 (1991): 261–272.

56. Sébastien Lagarde, "DONTNOD Physically Based Rendering Chart for Unreal Engine 4," *Sébastien Lagarde* blog, April 14, 2014, https://seblagarde.wordpress.com/2014/04/14/dontnod-physically-based-rendering-chart-for-unreal-engine-4/.

57. James Baxter, post on *Unreal Engine Forum*, April 2014, https://forums.unrealengine.com/t/dontnod-physically-based-rendering-chart-for-unreal-engine-4/2926.

58. Marschner "Image-Based Bidirectional Reflectance," 14.

59. Joseph D. Martin, "Prestige Asymmetry in American Physics: Aspirations, Applications, and the Purloined Letter Effect," *Science in Context* 30, no. 4 (2017): 475–506.

60. Chanda Prescod-Weinstein, *The Disordered Cosmos: A Journey into Dark Matter, Spacetime, & Dreams Deferred* (New York: Bold Type Books, 2021), 64.

61. Sandra Harding, "Rethinking Standpoint Epistemology: What Is 'Strong Objectivity?'" *Centennial Review* 36, no. 3 (1992): 437–470.

62. Patricia Hill Collins, *Black Feminist Thought: Knowledge, Consciousness, and the Politics of Empowerment* (New York: Routledge, 2002).

63. Luce Irigaray, "Is the Subject of Science Sexed?" in *Feminism and Science*, ed. Nancy Tuana and Sandra Morgen (Bloomington: Indiana University Press, 1989), 58–68, 78.

64. Irigaray, "Is the Subject of Science Sexed?", 78 (emphasis in the original).

65. Aleena Chia, "The Artist and the Automaton in Digital Game Production," *Convergence* 28, no. 2 (2022): 389–412.

66. Aleena Chia, "The Metaverse, but Not the Way You Think: Game Engines and Automation beyond Game Development," *Critical Studies in Media Communication* 39, no. 3 (2022): 191-200.

Chapter 5

1. Aleena Chia, "The Artist and the Automaton in Digital Game Production," *Convergence* 28, no. 2 (2022): 389-412.

2. Julie A. Turnock, *Plastic Reality: Special Effects, Technology, and the Emergence of 1970s Blockbuster Aesthetics* (New York: Columbia University Press, 2015).

3. Julie A. Turnock, *The Empire of Effects: Industrial Light and Magic and the Rendering of Realism* (Austin: University of Texas Press, 2022), 10.

4. Turnock, *Empire of Effects*.

5. Theodore Kim, "Histories and Counter-Histories of CGI in Movies," talk given at Rensselaer Polytechnic Institute's "Critical Game Design" Colloquium Speaker Series, September 28, 2022.

6. Luce Irigaray and Edith Oberle, "Is the Subject of Science Sexed?" *Cultural Critique* 1 (1985): 73–88, 78.

7. Aleena Chia, "The Metaverse, but Not the Way You Think: Game Engines and Automation beyond Game Development," *Critical Studies in Media Communication* 39, no. 3 (2022): 191-200.

8. Patrick Wolfe, *Traces of History: Elementary Structures of Race* (New York: Verso Books, 2016).

9. Wendy Hui Kyong Chun, "Race and/as Technology, or How to Do Things to Race," in *Race after the Internet*, ed. Lisa Nakamura and Peter A. Chow-White (New York: Routledge, 2013), 44–66.

10. Chia, "The Metaverse."

11. Mel Y. Chen, *Animacies: Biopolitics, Racial Mattering, and Queer Affect* (Durham, NC: Duke University Press, 2012).

12. Amanda Phillips, *Gamer Trouble: Feminist Confrontations in Digital Culture* (New York: New York University Press, 2020).

13. Evan Narcisse, "The Natural: The Trouble Portraying Blackness in Video Games," *Kotaku*, February 13, 2017, https://kotaku.com/the-natural-the-trouble-portraying-blackness-in-video-1736504384.

14. Theodore Kim, "The Racist Legacy of Computer-Generated Humans," *Scientific American*, August 18, 2020, https://www.scientificamerican.com/article/the-racist-legacy-of-computer-generated-humans/.

15. Chia, "The Metaverse."

16. Alison Reed and Amanda Phillips, "Additive Race: Colorblind Discourses of Realism in Performance Capture Technologies," *Digital Creativity* 24, no. 2 (2013): 130–144, 130.

17. André Brock, *Distributed Blackness: African American Cybercultures* (New York: New York University Press, 2020).

18. Brock, *Distributed Blackness*, 31.

19. André Brock and J. Khadijah Abdurahman, "(Dis)Info Studies: André Brock, Jr. on Why People Do What They Do on the Internet," in *Logic Magazine*, no. 15, December 25, 2021.

20. Donna Haraway, "Situated Knowledges: The Science Question in Feminism and the Privilege of Partial Perspective," *Feminist Studies* 14, no. 3 (1988): 575–599.

21. Brock, *Distributed Blackness*, 35.

22. Reed and Phillips "Additive Race," 137.

23. Reed and Phillips, "Additive Race," 137–138, citing Jessica Aldred, "From Synthespian to Avatar: Reframing the Digital Human in Final Fantasy and The Polar Express," *Mediascape* (Winter 2011): 4, http://www.tft.ucla.edu/mediascape/Winter 2011_Avatar.pdf.

24. Eric Freedman, "Non-Binary Binaries and Unreal MetaHumans," in *Race/Gender/Class/Media: Considering Diversity across Audiences, Content, and Producers*, 5th ed., ed. R. A. Lind (New York: Routledge, forthcoming, 2023), 2.

25. Epic Games, "MetaHuman Documentation," Unrealengine.com, accessed November 15, 2022, https://docs.metahuman.unrealengine.com/en-US/.

26. Freedman, "Non-Binary Binaries and Unreal MetaHumans," 7.

27. Freedman, "Non-Binary Binaries and Unreal MetaHumans," 8.

28. Freedman, "Non-Binary Binaries and Unreal MetaHumans," 8. For a more in-depth look at game industry claims of racialized empathy production, see Lisa Nakamura, "Feeling Good about Feeling Bad: Virtuous Virtual Reality and the Automation of Racial Empathy," *Journal of Visual Culture* 19, no. 1 (2020): 47–64.

29. "Low Resolution," or the combination of 3D models with aesthetically lower polygonal counts than often seen in contemporary game design with lighting and shading models that mimic the flatter or simpler rendering models of older computer graphics technologies, such as those seen on the PlayStation.

30. Joshua D. Miner, "Biased Render: Indigenous Algorithmic Embodiment in 3D Worlds," *Screen Bodies* 4, no. 1 (2019): 48–71.

31. Evan Narcisse, "The Natural: The Parameters of Afro," in *The State of Play: Creators and Critics on Video Game Culture*, ed. Daniel Goldberg and Linus Larsson (New York: Seven Stories Press, 2015), 53–74.

32. Narcisse, "The Natural."

33. This intra-active reading of Aveline's agency as a distributed body across narrative and engine mimics my reading of Elizabeth's agency in *BioShock Infinite*, as seen in chapter 3.

34. Sara Ahmed, "The Phenomenology of Whiteness," *Feminist Theory* 8, no. 2 (2007): 149–168, 149.

35. Ahmed, "Phenomenology of Whiteness."

36. Ahmed, "Phenomenology of Whiteness," citing Michelle Fine, Lois Weis, Linda Powell Pruitt, and April Burns, *Off White: Readings on Power, Privilege, and Resistance* (New York: Routledge, 2012), xi.

37. Tania Murray Li and David Mosse, "Rendering Society Technical," *Adventures in Aidland: The Anthropology of Professionals in International Development* 6 (2011): 57.

38. Technically "albedo" and "diffuse" are different ways of mapping light, but the results are so similar and the maps so interchangeable that materials artists now mostly use the terms interchangeably.

39. For more detail on the generative adversarial networks (GANs) used by Meta-Humans to generate new characters, please see Eric Freedman, "Non-Binary Binaries and Unreal MetaHumans," in *Race/Gender/Class/Media*, 5th ed., ed. R. A. Lind (New York: Routledge, 2023).

40. Freedman "Non-Binary Binaries and Unreal MetaHumans," 3.

41. Phillips, *Gamer Trouble*.

42. Chia, "The Metaverse," 191-200.

43. For an extended discussion of the interrelations between cinematic special effects, chroma keying, and Blackness, see Charu Maithani, "Blan/ck Screens: Chroma Screens Performing Race," *Media-N* 18, no. 1 (2022): 121-142.

44. Bradford Young, "Q&A with Bradford Young," *American Cinematographer*, February 2015, https://theasc.com/ac_magazine/February2015/QandAwithBradfordYoung/page1.html.

45. See Meghan Collie, "Here's How the Woman behind the Camera on Insecure Properly Lights Its Black Actors," *Flare*, August 11, 2017, https://fashionmagazine.com/flare/insecure-lighting/; and Xavier Harding, "Keeping 'Insecure' Lit: HBO Cinematographer Ava Berkofsky on Properly Lighting Black Faces," *Mic*, September 6, 2017, https://www.mic.com/articles/184244/keeping-insecure-lit-hbo-cinematographer-ava-berkofsky-on-properly-lighting-black-faces#.IrdY52aFu.

46. Young, "Q&A."

47. Collie, "Why 'Insecure' Needs to Be Properly Lit." interview by Ava Berkofsky.

48. Krista A. Thompson, *Shine: The Visual Economy of Light in African Diasporic Aesthetic Practice* (Durham, NC: Duke University Press, 2015).

49. Thompson, *Shine*, 112.

50. Thompson, *Shine*, 114.

51. Chen, *Animacies*.

52. Svetlana Alpers, "Describe or Narrate? A Problem in Realistic Representation," *New Literary History* 8, no. 1 (1976): 15–41, cited in Thompson, *Shine*, 227.

53. Thompson, *Shine*, 232.

54. National Humanities Center, "Slave Auctions, an Eyewitness Account," *National Humanities Center Resource Toolbox: The Making of African American Identity: Vol. I, 1500–1865*, 2007, http://nationalhumanitiescenter.org/pds/maai/enslavement/text2/slaveauctions.pdf.

55. Thompson, *Shine*, 22.

56. Genevieve Yue, *Girl Head: Feminism and Film Materiality* (New York: Fordham University Press, 2020).

57. Yue, *Girl Head*, 53.

58. Lorna Roth, "Looking at Shirley, the Ultimate Norm: Colour Balance, Image Technologies, and Cognitive Equity," *Canadian Journal of Communication* 34, no. 1 (2009): 111-136.

59. Mandalit del Barco, "How Kodak's Shirley Cards Set Photography's Skin-Tone Standard," *Color Decoded: Stories That Span the Spectrum*, NPR, November 13, 2014,

https://www.npr.org/2014/11/13/363517842/for-decades-kodak-s-shirley-cards
-set-photography-s-skin-tone-standard.

60. Tayyab Mahmud, "Review Essay: Genealogy of a State-Engineered Model Minority: Not Quite/Not White South Asian Americans," *Denver Law Review* 78, no. 4 (2001): 657–686.

61. For more on the historical and aesthetic framing of the Asian woman through the white eye, see Anne Anlin Cheng, "Ornamentalism: A Feminist Theory for the Yellow Woman," *Critical Inquiry* 44, no. 3 (2018): 415–446.

62. Theodore Kim, Holly Rushmeier, Julie Dorsey, Derek Nowrouzezahrai, Raqi Syed, Wojciech Jarosz, and A. M. Darke, "Countering Racial Bias in Computer Graphics Research," arXiv preprint arXiv:2103.15163 (2021).

63. Haiwen Feng, Timo Bolkart, Joachim Tesch, Michael J. Black, and Victoria Abrevaya, "Towards Racially Unbiased Skin Tone Estimation via Scene Disambiguation," in *European Conference on Computer Vision*, (Cham: Springer, 2022), 72–90.

64. Kim, "Racist Legacy of Computer Generated Humans."

65. Kim, "Racist Legacy of Computer Generated Humans."

66. Kim, "Racist Legacy of Computer Generated Humans."

67. Kim et al., "Countering Racial Bias."

68. Chanda Prescod-Weinstein, *The Disordered Cosmos: A Journey into Dark Matter, Spacetime, & Dreams Deferred* (New York: Bold Type Books, 2021).

69. djelly, "Physically Modeling Skin Tones," *Half4.xyz*, August 18, 2020, https://half4.xyz/index.php/2020/08/18/introduction-physically-modeling-skin-tones/.

70. Theodore Kim, "Countering Bias in Graphics Research," presentation at the SIGGRAPH "Birds of a Feather" sessions, 2021.

71. Tania Murray Li, *The Will to Improve: Governmentality, Development, and the Practice of Politics* (Durham, NC: Duke University Press, 2007).

72. "UnWhiteWash the Bad Batch," accessed November 15, 2021, https://unwhitewashthebadbatch.carrd.co/#abttbb.

73. Nathanial Eker, "'Bad Batch' Reportedly Being Edited Following Whitewashing Controversy," *Inside the Magic*, May 11, 2021, https://insidethemagic.net/2021/05/the-bad-batch-star-wars-whitewashing-controversy-ne1/.

74. James Whitbrook, "Why Star Wars Fans Are Concerned about 'The Bad Batch' and Whitewashing," *Gizmodo*, May 6, 2021, https://gizmodo.com/why-star-wars-fans-are-concerned-about-the-bad-batch-an-1846831469.

75. Imani Perry, *More Beautiful and More Terrible* (New York: New York University Press, 2011).

76. Young, "Q&A."

77. Here "actor" is used in Unreal Engine's sense, that each discrete object in an Unreal scene is identified as an "actor." For more details, see Chapter 2.

78. "Rect Lights," Unreal Engine.com, accessed November 11, 2022, https://docs.unrealengine.com/4.26/en-US/BuildingWorlds/LightingAndShadows/LightTypes/RectLights/; "Can You Increase Specular Scale on Directional Light Past 1.0? Wet Road Sun Glare," *Unreal Engine Forums*, September 2018, https://forums.unrealengine.com/t/can-you-increase-specular-scale-on-directional-light-past-1-0-wet-road-sun-glare/116511/11.

79. Jeryce Dianingana, Twitter, May 17, 2022, https://twitter.com/JeryceDia/status/1605787514400186369?s=20&t=8H6G1hgg9bWJ5osb2slT7Q.

80. Jan-Bart Van Beek, Twitter, May 17, 2022, https://twitter.com/janbartvanbeek/status/1606041079098118144?s=20&t=8H6G1hgg9bWJ50sb2slT7Q.

81. Emma Vossen, Twitter, June 12, 2019, https://twitter.com/emmahvossen/status/1138841342921060354?s=20&t=8H6G1hgg9bWJ50sb2slT7Q.

Conclusion

1. Tara McPherson, "Designing for Difference," *Differences* 25, no. 1 (2014): 177–188.

2. John Law, *Aircraft Stories: Decentering the Object in Technoscience* (Durham, NC: Duke University Press, 2002).

3. Malou Juelskjær and Nete Schwennesen, "Intra-active Entanglements: An Interview with Karen Barad," *Kvinder, Køn & Forskning* 1–2 (2012): 10–23.

4. Adele E. Clarke, "From Grounded Theory to Situational Analysis: What's New? Why? How?" in *Developing Grounded Theory*, ed. Kathy Charmaz (New York: Routledge, 2021), 223–266.

5. See, for example, Thomas Poell, David B. Nieborg, and Brooke Erin Duffy, *Platforms and Cultural Production* (Cambridge, UK: Polity, 2021); Jean-Christophe Plantin et al., "Infrastructure Studies Meet Platform Studies in the Age of Google and Facebook," *New Media & Society* 20, no. 1 (2018): 293–310.

6. Nick Srnicek, *Platform Capitalism* (Hoboken, NJ: John Wiley & Sons, 2017).

7. Michele Willson and Tama Leaver, "Zynga's FarmVille, Social Games, and the Ethics of Big Data Mining," *Communication Research and Practice* 1, no. 2 (2015): 147–158.

8. See, Benjamin Nicoll and Brendan Keogh, *The Unity Game Engine and the Circuits of Cultural Software* (Cham: Palgrave Pivot, 2019); and Maxwell Foxman, "United We Stand: Platforms, Tools and Innovation with the Unity Game Engine," *Social Media + Society* 5, no. 4 (2019).

9. Nicoll and Keogh, *Unity Game Engine*.

10. Poell et al., *Platforms and Cultural Production*.

11. Tanya Richardson and Gisa Weszkalnys, "Introduction: Resource Materialities," *Anthropological Quarterly* 87, no. 1 (2014): 5–30.

12. Will Hershey, Twitter, December 26, 2019, 3:00 pm, https://twitter.com/maybebullish/status/1210289415991578625?s=20&t=9NnqLRn4_wSOXwGo6IRUsQ.

13. David Taylor, "Fortnite Creative, Meet Unreal Engine 5," *Naavik*, September 11, 2022, https://naavik.co/digest/fortnite-creative-meet-unreal-engine-five.

14. Tim Sweeney, Twitter, December 26, 2019, 3:11 pm, https://twitter.com/TimSweeneyEpic/status/1210291961904730114?s=20&t=9NnqLRn4_wSOXwGo6IRUsQ; Sweeney, Twitter, December 26, 2020, 12:04 am, https://twitter.com/TimSweeneyEpic/status/1342697699179700224?s=20&t=9NnqLRn4_wSOXwGo6IRUsQ; Sweeney, Twitter, December 27, 2021, 4:40 pm, https://twitter.com/TimSweeneyEpic/status/1475582484356153349?s=20&t=9NnqLRn4_wSOXwGo6IRUsQ.

15. Sweeney 2020, December 26, 2020, 12:04, Twitter.

16. Stephen Kline, Nick Dyer-Witheford, and Greig De Peuter, *Digital Play: The Interaction of Technology, Culture, and Marketing* (Montreal: McGill-Queen's Press, 2003).

17. David Golumbia, *The Politics of Bitcoin: Software as Right-wing Extremism* (Minneapolis: University of Minnesota Press, 2016).

18. Tim Sweeney, "Epic's CEO on Fortnite on Android, Skipping Google Play, and the Open Metaverse," *RocketNews*, August 6, 2018, https://www.rocketnews.com

/2018/08/tim-sweeney-epics-ceo-on-fortnite-on-android-skipping-google
-play-and-the-open-metaverse/.

19. Liam Mackay, "Unreal Editor for Fortnite: Release Date, Features, Leaks, Creative 2.0, More," *CharlieIntel*, March 17, 2023, https://charlieintel.com/fortnite
-creative-2-0/184245/.

20. "The LEGO Group and Epic Games Team Up to Build a Place for Kids to Play in the Metaverse," Epic Games.com, April 7, 2022, https://www.epicgames
.com/site/en-US/news/the-lego-group-and-epic-games-team-up-to-build-a
-place-for-kids-to-play-in-the-metaverse.

21. Henry Jenkins and Mizuko Ito, *Participatory Culture in a Networked Era: A Conversation on Youth, Learning, Commerce, and Politics* (Hoboken, NJ: John Wiley & Sons, 2015).

22. Aleena Chia and James Malazita, "The Plumbing of the Metaverse," preconstituted panel, DiGRA 2022, Krakow, Poland, July 7-11 2022.

23. Lorraine Daston, ed., *Biographies of Scientific Objects* (Chicago, IL: University of Chicago Press, 2000).

24. Abby J. Kinchy, Roopali Phadke, and Jessica M. Smith, "Engaging the Underground: An STS Field in Formation," *Engaging Science, Technology, and Society* 4 (2018): 22–42, citing Tanya Richardson and Gisa Weszkalnys, "Introduction: Resource Materialities," *Anthropological Quarterly* 87, no. 1 (2014): 5–30.

25. T. L. Taylor, "Living Digitally: Embodiment in Virtual Worlds," in *The Social Life of Avatars*, ed. Ralph Schroeder (London: Springer, 2002), 40–62.

26. See, Sara Hendren, *What Can a Body Do?: How We Meet the Built World* (New York: Penguin, 2020); and Brendan Keogh, *A Play of Bodies: How We Perceive Videogames* (Cambridge, MA: MIT Press, 2018).

27. See, Lisa Nakamura, *Digitizing Race: Visual Cultures of the Internet* (Minneapolis: University of Minnesota Press, 2007); Amanda Phillips, *Gamer Trouble: Feminist Confrontations in Digital Culture* (New York: New York University Press, 2020); and Jennifer DeWinter, Carly A. Kocurek, and Randall Nichols, "Taylorism 2.0: Gamification, Scientific Management and the Capitalist Appropriation of Play," *Journal of Gaming & Virtual Worlds* 6, no. 2 (2014): 109–127.

28. Mary F. E. Ebeling, *Afterlives of Data: Life and Debt under Capitalist Surveillance* (Oakland: University of California Press, 2022).

29. Aleena Chia, "The Artist and the Automaton in Digital Game Production," *Convergence* 28, no. 2. (2022): 389-412.

30. Chia and Malazita, "The Plumbing of the Metaverse."

31. Thomas N. Theis and H-S. Philip Wong, "The End of Moore's Law: A New Beginning for Information Technology," *Computing in Science & Engineering* 19, no. 2 (2017): 41–50.

32. Nicole Starosielski, "Thermocultures of Geological Media," *Cultural Politics* 12, no. 3 (2016): 293–309.

33. Adreas Jungherr and Damien B. Schlarb, "The Extended Reach of Game Engine Companies: How Companies Like Epic Games and Unity Technologies Provide Platforms for Extended Reality Applications and the Metaverse," *Social Media+Society* 8, no. 2 (2022): 20563051221107641.

34. United States District Court, Northern District of California. Case No. 4:20-cv-05 640-YGR. "Epic Games, Inc. v. Apple Inc./Apple Inc. v. Epic Games, Inc," filed September 9, 2021, p. 21, https://www.documentcloud.org/documents/21060631
-apple-epic-judgement.

Bibliography

Aarseth, Espen. "Genre Trouble, Narrativism and the Art of Simulation." In *First Person: New Media as Story, Performance and Game*, edited by Noah Wardrip-Fruin and Pat Harrigan. Cambridge, MA: MIT Press, 2004.

Ahmed, Sara. *Queer Phenomenology: Orientations, Objects, Others*. Durham, NC: Duke University Press, 2006.

Ahmed, Sara. "The Phenomenology of Whiteness." *Feminist Theory* 8, no. 2 (August 2007): 149–168.

Aldred, Jessica. "From Synthespian to Avatar: Reframing the Digital Human in Final Fantasy and The Polar Express." *Mediascape* (Winter 2011). http://www.tft.ucla.edu/mediascape/Winter2011_Avatar.pdf.

Allen, Robertson. *America's Digital Army: Games at Work and War*. Lincoln: University of Nebraska Press, 2017.

Alpers, Svetlana. "Describe or Narrate? A Problem in Realistic Representation." *New Literary History* 8, no. 1 (1976): 15–41.

Althusser, Louis. "Ideology and Ideological State Apparatuses (Notes towards an Investigation)." *Cultural Theory: An Anthology* (2010): 204–222.

Anable, Aubrey. "Platform Studies." *Feminist Media Histories* 4, no. 2 (2018): 135–140.

Anable, Aubrey. *Playing with Feelings: Video Games and Affect*. Minneapolis: University of Minnesota Press, 2018.

Apperley, Thomas H., and Darshana Jayemane. "Game Studies' Material Turn." *Westminster Papers in Communication and Culture* 9, no. 1 (2012): 5–25. doi: http://doi.org/10.16997/wpcc.145.

Apperley, Thomas, and Jussi Parikka. "Platform Studies' Epistemic Threshold." *Games and Culture* 13, no. 4 (2018): 349–369.

Åsberg, Cecilia. "Enter Cyborg: Tracing the Historiography and Ontological Turn of Feminist Technoscience Studies." *International Journal of Feminist Technoscience* 1, no. 1 (2010): 1–25.

Ash, James. "Technologies of Captivation: Videogames and the Attunement of Affect." *Body & Society* 19, no. 1 (2013): 27–51.

Banks, John. *Co-creating Videogames*. New York: Bloomsbury, 2013.

Barad, Karen. "Posthumanist Performativity: Toward an Understanding of How Matter Comes to Matter." *Signs: Journal of Women in Culture and Society* 28, no. 3 (2003): 801–831.

Barad, Karen. *Meeting the Universe Halfway: Quantum Physics and the Entanglement of Matter and Meaning*. Durham, NC: Duke University Press, 2007.

Barthes, Roland. *S/Z: An Essay*. New York: Hill and Wang, 1974.

Baudrillard, Jean. *Simulacra and Simulation*. Ann Arbor: University of Michigan, 1994.

Baudrillard, Jean. *The Gulf War Did Not Take Place*. Bloomington: Indiana University Press, 1995.

Benjamin, Ruha. *Race after Technology: Abolitionist Tools for the New Jim Code*. Medford, OR: Polity Press, 2019.

Berger, John. *Ways of Seeing*. London: Penguin, 1972.

Bogost, Ian. *Unit Operations: An Approach to Videogame Criticism*. Cambridge, MA: MIT Press, 2008.

Bogost, Ian. *Persuasive Games: The Expressive Power of Videogames*. Cambridge, MA: MIT Press, 2010.

Bogost, Ian, and Nick Montfort. "Platform Studies: Frequently Questioned Answers." Digital Arts and Culture conference, December 12–15, 2009, Irvine, California. http://bogost.com/writing/platform_studies_frequently_qu_1/

Bolter, J. David, and Richard A. Grusin. "Remediation." *Configurations* 4, no. 3 (1996): 311–358.

Boluk, Stephanie, and Patrick LeMieux. *Metagaming: Playing, Competing, Spectating, Cheating, Trading, Making, and Breaking Videogames*, vol. 53. Minneapolis: University of Minnesota Press, 2017.

Brock, André. *Distributed Blackness: African American Cybercultures*. New York: New York University Press, 2020.

Brock, A., and J. Khadijah Abdurahman, 2021."(Dis)Info Studies: André Brock, Jr. on Why People Do What They Do on the Internet." *Logic Magazine* (no. 15), December 25, 2021.

Burgess, Jean, and Nancy K. Baym. *Twitter: A Biography*. New York: New York University Press, 2020.

Burley, Brent, and Walt Disney Animation Studios. "Physically-Based Shading at Disney." *ACM SIGGRAPH* (2012): 1–7.

Burnett, Margaret. "Software Engineering for Visual Programming Languages." In *Handbook of Software Engineering and Knowledge Engineering*, vol. 2, edited by Shi Kuo Chang. Singapore: World Scientific, 2001.

Butler, Judith. *Bodies That Matter: On the Discursive Limits of "Sex."* New York: Routledge, 1993.

Caffrey Jr., Matthew J. *On Wargaming*. Newport, RI: US Naval War College Press, 2019.

Caillois, Roger. *Man, Play, and Games*. Champaign: University of Illinois Press, 1991.

Carey, James W. "Historical Pragmatism and the Internet." *New Media & Society* 7, no. 4 (2005): 443–455.

Cartwright, Nancy. *How the Laws of Physics Lie*. Oxford: Oxford University Press, 1983.

Cheah, Pheng. "Mattering." *Diacritics* 26, no. 1 (1996):108-139.

Chen, Mel Y. *Animacies: Biopolitics, Racial Mattering, and Queer Affect*. Durham, NC: Duke University Press, 2012.

Cheng, Anne Anlin. "Ornamentalism: A Feminist Theory for the Yellow Woman." *Critical Inquiry* 44, no. 3 (2018): 415–446.

Chia, Aleena. "The Artist and the Automaton in Digital Game Production." *Convergence* 28, no. 2 (2022): 389-412.

Chia, Aleena. "The Metaverse, but Not the Way You Think: Game Engines and Automation Beyond Game Development." *Critical Studies in Media Communication* 39, no. 2 (2022): 191–200.

Chia, Aleena, Brendan Keogh, Dale Leorke, and Benjamin Nicoll. "Platformisation in Game Development." *Internet Policy Review* 9, no. 4 (2020): 1–28.

Chia, Aleena, and James Malazita. "The Plumbing of the Metaverse." *DiGRA* (2022).

Chun, Wendy Hui Kyong. "Race and/as Technology, or How to Do Things to Race." In *Race after the Internet*, edited by Lisa Nakamura and Peter Chow-White, 44–66. Milton Park, UK: Routledge, 2013.

Clarke, Adele E. "From Grounded Theory to Situational Analysis: What's New? Why? How?" In *Developing Grounded Theory*, edited by Janice M. Morse, Barbara J. Bowers, Kathy Charmaz, Adele E. Clarke, Juliet Corbin, Caroline Jane Porr, and Phyllis Noerager Stern, 223–266. Milton Park, UK: Routledge, 2021.

Clarke, Steve. "Conspiracy Theories and Conspiracy Theorizing." *Philosophy of the Social Sciences* 32, no. 2 (2002): 131–150.

Cole, Alayna. "Connecting Player and Character Agency in Videogames." *Text* 22, Special Issue 49 (2018): 1–14.

Collins, Patricia Hill. *Black Feminist Thought: Knowledge, Consciousness, and the Politics of Empowerment*. Milton Park, UK: Routledge, 2002.

Craig, Carys J., Joseph F. Turcotte, and Rosemary J. Coombe. "What Is Feminist about Open Access?: A Relational Approach to Copyright in the Academy." *Feminists@ Law* 1, no. 1 (2011): 1-35.

Crary, Jonathan. *Techniques of the Observer: On Vision and Modernity in the Nineteenth Century*. Cambridge, MA: MIT Press, 1992.

Cross, Nigel. "Designerly Ways of Knowing: Design Discipline versus Design Science." *Design Issues* 17, no. 3 (2001): 49–55.

Csikszentmihalyi, Mihaly, Sami Abuhamdeh, and Jeanne Nakamura. "Flow." In *Handbook of Competence and Motivation*, edited by Andrew J. Elliot and Carol S. Dweck, 598–608. New York: Guilford Publications, 2005.

Custodio, Alex. *Who Are You?: Nintendo's Game Boy Advance Platform*. Cambridge, MA: MIT Press, 2020.

Daston, Lorraine, ed. *Biographies of Scientific Objects*. Chicago, IL: University of Chicago Press, 2000.

Deleuze, Gilles, and Félix Guattari. *Anti-Oedipus: Capitalism and Schizophrenia*. London: Penguin, 2009.

Deleuze, Gilles, and Félix Guattari. *A Thousand Plateaus: Capitalism and Schizophrenia*. London: Bloomsbury, 1988.

Derian, James Der. "Cyberspace as Battlespace: The New Virtual Alliance of the Military, the Media, and the Entertainment Industry." *Living with Cyberspace: Technology & Societies in the 21st Century*, edited by John Armitage and Joanne Roberts, 61–71. London: Continuum, 2002.

DeWinter, Jennifer, Carly A. Kocurek, and Randall Nichols. "Taylorism 2.0: Gamification, Scientific Management and the Capitalist Appropriation of Play." *Journal of Gaming & Virtual Worlds* 6, no. 2 (2014): 109–127.

Dhaliwal, Ranjodh Singh. "On Addressability, or What Even Is Computation?" *Critical Inquiry* 49, no. 1 (2022): 1–27.

Dinerstein, Joel. "Technology and Its Discontents: On the Verge of the Posthuman." *American Quarterly* 58, no. 3 (2006): 569–595.

Dourish, Paul. "What We Talk about When We Talk about Context." *Personal and Ubiquitous Computing* 8, no. 1 (2004): 19–30.

Dourish, P. *The Stuff of Bits: An Essay on the Materiality of Information*. Cambridge, MA: The MIT Press, 2017.

Downey, Gary Lee. *The Machine in Me: An Anthropologist Sits among Computer Engineers*. Milton Park, UK: Routledge, 1998.

Dyer, Richard. *White: Essays on Race and Culture*. Milton Park, UK: Routledge, 1997.

Dyer-Witheford, Nick, and Greig De Peuter. *Games of Empire: Global Capitalism and Video Games*. Minneapolis: University of Minnesota Press, 2009.

Ebeling, Mary F. E. *Afterlives of Data: Life and Debt under Capitalist Surveillance*. Oakland: University of California Press, 2022.

Emmerich, Katharina, Patrizia Ring, and Maic Masuch. "I'm Glad You Are on My Side: How to Design Compelling Game Companions." In *Proceedings of the 2018 Annual Symposium on Computer-Human Interaction in Play*, 141–152. New York: Association for Computing Machinery, 2018.

Feng, Haiwen, Timo Bolkart, Joachim Tesch, Michael J. Black, and Victoria Abrevaya. "Towards Racially Unbiased Skin Tone Estimation via Scene Disambiguation." In *European Conference on Computer Vision*, 72–90. Cham: Springer, 2022.

Fine, Michelle, Lois Weis, Linda Powell Pruitt, and April Burns. *Off White: Readings on Power, Privilege, and Resistance*. Milton Park, UK: Routledge, 2012.

Foxman, Maxwell. "United We Stand: Platforms, Tools and Innovation with the Unity Game Engine." *Social Media + Society* 5, no. 4 (2019).

Freedman, Eric. "Engineering Queerness in the Game Development Pipeline." *Game Studies* 18, no. 3 (2018).

Freedman, Eric. *The Persistence of Code in Game Engine Culture*. Milton Park, UK: Routledge, 2020.

Freedman, Eric. "Non-Binary Binaries and Unreal MetaHumans." In *Race/Gender/Class/Media: Considering Diversity across Audiences, Content, and Producers*, 5th ed., edited by R. A. Lind. New York: Routledge, 2023.

Friedberg, Anne. *The Virtual Window: From Alberti to Microsoft*. Cambridge, MA: MIT Press, 2009.

Gaboury, Jacob. "Hidden Surface Problems: On the Digital Image as Material Object." *Journal of Visual Culture* 14, no. 1 (2015): 40–60.

Galloway, Alexander R. *Gaming: Essays on Algorithmic Culture*. Minneapolis: University of Minnesota Press, 2006.

Gass, Arianna. *The Body in Play: Performance in and through Video Games*. PhD diss., University of Chicago, 2022.

Genette, Gérard, and Marie Maclean. "Introduction to the Paratext." *New Literary History* 22, no. 2 (1991): 261–272.

Golumbia, David. *The Politics of Bitcoin: Software as Right-Wing Extremism*. Minneapolis: University of Minnesota Press, 2016.

Gray, Kishonna L. *Intersectional Tech: Black Users in Digital Gaming*. Baton Rouge, LA: LSU Press, 2020.

Greimas, Algirdas J., and François Rastier. "The Interaction of Semiotic Constraints." *Yale French Studies* 41 (1968): 86–105.

Guins, Raiford, and Henry Lowood. "Atari's Army Battlezone Project." *ROMchip* 2, no. 1 (2020).

Halberstam, Jack. *The Queer Art of Failure*. Durham, NC: Duke University Press, 2011. https://doi.org/10.2307/j.ctv11sn283.

Halter, Ed. *From Sun Tzu to Xbox: War and Video Games*. New York: Thunder's Mouth Press, 2006.

Haraway, Donna. "Situated Knowledges: The Science Question in Feminism and the Privilege of Partial Perspective." *Feminist Studies* 14, no. 3 (1988): 575–599.

Haraway, Donna. "A Game of Cat's Cradle: Science Studies, Feminist Theory, Cultural Studies." *Configurations* 2, no. 1 (1994): 59–71.

Haraway, Donna J. *Staying with the Trouble: Making Kin in the Chthulucene*. Durham, NC: Duke University Press, 2016.

Harding, Sandra. "Rethinking Standpoint Epistemology: What Is 'Strong Objectivity'?" In *Feminist Epistemologies*, edited by Linda Alcoff and Elizabeth Potter, 49–82. New York: Routledge, 2013.

Harrell, D. Fox, and Jichen Zhu. "Agency Play: Dimensions of Agency for Interactive Narrative Design." In *AAAI Spring Symposium: Intelligent Narrative Technologies II* (2009): 44–52. http://groups.csail.mit.edu/icelab/sites/default/files/pdf/Harrell-Zhu-aaai2009.pdf.

Harrigan, P., and M. G. Kirschenbaum. *Zones of Control. Perspectives on Wargaming*. Cambridge, MA: MIT Press, 2016.

Hayles, N. Katherine. "Print Is Flat, Code Is Deep: The Importance of Media-Specific Analysis." *Poetics Today* 25, no. 1 (2004): 67–90.

Hayles, N. Katherine. "Traumas of Code." *Critical Inquiry* 33, no. 1 (2006): 136–157.

Hendren, Sara. *What Can a Body Do?: How We Meet the Built World*. London: Penguin, 2020.

Herman, Edward S., and Noam Chomsky. *Manufacturing Consent: The Political Economy of the Mass Media*. New York: Random House, 2010.

Hersh, Seymour. *Chain of Command*. London: Penguin Books, 2005.

Irigaray, Luce, and Edith Oberle. "Is the Subject of Science Sexed?" *Cultural Critique* 1 (1985): 73–88.

Jenkins, Henry. "Transmedia Storytelling and Entertainment: An Annotated Syllabus." *Continuum* 24, no. 6 (2010): 943–958.

Jennings, Stephanie C. "A Meta-Synthesis of Agency in Game Studies: Trends, Troubles, Trajectories." *G|A|M|E: Games as Art, Media, Entertainment* 1, no. 8 (2019): 85–106.

Jennings, Stephanie C. "Only You Can Save the World (of Videogames): Authoritarian Agencies in the Heroism of Videogame Design, Play, and Culture." *Convergence* 28, no. 3 (2022): 320–344.

Jones, Steven E., and George K. Thiruvathukal. *Codename Revolution: The Nintendo WII Platform*. Cambridge, MA: MIT Press, 2012.

Juelskjær, Malou, and Nete Schwennesen. "Intra-Active Entanglements—An Interview with Karen Barad." *Kvinder, Køn & Forskning* 1-2(2012): 10–23.

Jungherr, Andreas, and Damien B. Schlarb. "The Extended Reach of Game Engine Companies: How Companies Like Epic Games and Unity Technologies Provide

Platforms for Extended Reality Applications and the Metaverse." *Social Media+ Society* 8, no. 2 (2022).

Kao, Dominic, and D. Fox Harrell. "Embellishment & Effects: Seduction by Style." In *Avatars, Assembled: The Sociotechnical Anatomy of Digital Bodies*, edited by Jaime Banks, 235–246. Bern: Peter Lang, 2017.

Keen, Suzanne. "A Theory of Narrative Empathy." *Narrative* 14, no. 3 (2006): 207–236.

Keen, Suzanne. "Reader's Temperments and Fictional Character." *New Literary History* 42 (2011): 295–314.

Kellner, Douglas. The Persian Gulf TV War Revisited," in *Reporting War*, edited by Stuart Allan, Barbie Zelizer, 146–164. New York: Routledge, 2004.

Kelty, Christopher M. *Two Bits: The Cultural Significance of Free Software*. Durham, NC: Duke University Press, 2008.

Keogh, Brendan. *A Play of Bodies: How We Perceive Videogames*. Cambridge, MA: MIT Press, 2018.

Keogh, Brendan. "Situating the Videogame Maker's Agency through Craft." *Convergence* 28, no. 2 (2022): 374–388.

Kim, Theodore. "The Racist Legacy of Computer-Generated Humans." *Scientific American*, August 18, 2020. https://www.scientificamerican.com/article/the-racist-legacy-of-computer-generated-humans/.

Kim, Theodore. "Countering Bias in Graphics Research." Presentation at the 2021 SIGGRAPH "Birds of a Feather" sessions, Vancouver, CA.

Kim, T., H. Rushmeier, J. Dorsey, D. Nowrouzezahrai, R. Syed, W. Jarosz, and A. Darke. "Countering Racial Bias in Computer Graphics Research." arXiv preprint arXiv:2103.15163 (2021).

Kim, Theodore. "Histories and Counter-Histories of CGI in Movies." Talk given at Rensselaer Polytechnic Institute's "Critical Game Design" Colloquium Speaker Series, September 28, 2022. Troy, NY.

Kinchy, Abby J., Roopali Phadke, and Jessica M. Smith. "Engaging the Underground: An STS Field in Formation." *Engaging Science, Technology, and Society* 4 (2018): 22–42.

Kline, Stephen, Nick Dyer-Witheford, and Greig De Peuter. *Digital Play: The Interaction of Technology, Culture, and Marketing*. Montreal: McGill-Queen's University Press, 2003.

Konzack, Lars. "Computer Game Criticism: A Method for Computer Game Analysis." Proceedings of Computer Games and Digital Cultures Conference, ed. Frans Mäyrä. Tampere: Tampere University Press, 2002.

Landow, George P., and Paul Delany. "Hypertext, Hypermedia and Literary Studies: The State of the Art." In *Hypermedia and Literary Studies*, edited by Paul Delany and George Landow, 3–50. Cambridge, MA: MIT Press, 1991.

Latour, Bruno. "Visualization and Cognition." *Knowledge and Society* 6, no. 6 (1986): 1–40.

Latour, Bruno. *Reassembling the Social: An Introduction to Actor-Network Theory*. Oxford: Oxford University Press, 2007.

Latour, Bruno. "Drawing Things Together." In *The Map Reader: Theories of Mapping Practice and Cartographic Representation*, edited by Martin Dodge, Rob Kitchin, and Chris Perkins, 65–72. Hoboken, NJ: John Wiley and Sons, 2011.

Latour, Bruno. "Anti-Zoom." In *Scale in Literature and Culture*, edited by Michael Tavel Clarke and David Wittenberg, 93–101. London: Palgrave Macmillan, 2017.

Law, John. *Aircraft Stories: Decentering the Object in Technoscience.* Durham, NC: Duke University Press, 2002.

Law, John, and Annemarie Mol. "Notes on Materiality and Sociality." *Sociological Review* 43, no. 2 (1995): 274–294.

Law, John, and Marianne Elisabeth Lien. "Slippery: Field Notes in Empirical Ontology." *Social Studies of Science* 43, no. 3 (2013): 363–378.

Leigh Star, Susan. "This Is Not a Boundary Object: Reflections on the Origin of a Concept." *Science, Technology, & Human Values* 35, no. 5 (2010): 601–617.

Lenoir, Tim. "All but War Is Simulation: The Military-Entertainment Complex." *Configurations* 8, no. 3 (2000): 289–335.

Lenoir, Tim, and Luke Caldwell. *The Military-Entertainment Complex.* Cambridge, MA: Harvard University Press, 2018.

Leorke, Dale. "Rebranding the Platform: The Limitations of 'Platform Studies.'" *Digital Culture and Education* 4, no. 3 (2012): 257–268.

Li, Tania Murray. *The Will to Improve: Governmentality, Development, and the Practice of Politics.* Durham, NC: Duke University Press, 2007.

Li, Tania Murray, and David Mosse. "Rendering Society Technical." *Adventures in Aidland: The Anthropology of Professionals in International Development* 6 (2011): 57.

Mackenzie, Adrian. "Distributive Numbers: A Post-Demographic Perspective on Probability." In *Modes of Knowing: Resources from the Baroque*, edited by John Law and Evelyn Ruppert, 115–135. Manchester, UK: Mattering Press, 2016.

Mafe, Diana Adesola. "Race and the First-Person Shooter: Challenging the Video Gamer in BioShock Infinite." *Camera Obscura: Feminism, Culture, and Media Studies* 30, no. 2 (2015): 89–123.

Maithani, Charu. "Blan/ck Screens: Chroma Screens Performing Race." *Media-N* 18, no. 1 (2022): 121–142.

Malazita, James. "The Material Undermining of Magical Feminism in BioShock Infinite: Burial at Sea." In *Feminism in Play*, edited by Kishonna Gray, Gerald Vorhees, and Emma Vossen, 37–50. London: Palgrave Macmillan, 2018.

Malazita, James. "Critique Is the Steam: Reorienting Critical Digital Humanities across Disciplines." In *Debates in the Digital Humanities 2023*, edited by Lauren F. Klein and Matthew Gold, 367–381. Minneapolis: University of Minnesota Press, 2023.

Malazita, James, Alexander Nikolaev, and Douglas Porpora. "Moral Argument in the Public Sphere: The Case of Bosnia." *Review of Communication* 14, no. 3–4 (2014): 229–244.

Malazita, James W., Dominic Francis Gelfuso, and Dean Nieusma. "Contextualizing 3D Printing's and Photosculpture's Contributions to Techno-Creative Literacies." In *Proceedings of the 2016 ASEE Annual Conference & Exposition*, 2016. https://peer.asee.org/contextualizing-3d-printing-s-and photosculpture-s-contributions-to-techno-creative-literacies

Malazita, James W., and Korryn Resetar. "Infrastructures of Abstraction: How Computer Science Education Produces Anti-political Subjects." *Digital Creativity* 30, no. 4 (2019): 300–312.

Malkowski, Jennifer, and TreaAndrea M. Russworm. *Gaming Representation: Race, Gender, and Sexuality in Video Games.* Bloomington: Indiana University Press, 2017.

Malviya, Saumya. "Symbol as Metonymy and Metaphor: A Sociological Perspective on Mathematical Symbolism." *Science, Technology and Society* 24, no. 1 (2019): 53–72.

Manovich, Lev. *The Language of New Media*. Cambridge, MA: MIT Press, 2002.

Marschner, Stephen R., Stephen H. Westin, Eric PF Lafortune, and Kenneth E. Torrance. "Image-Based Bidirectional Reflectance Distribution Function Measurement." *Applied Optics* 39, no. 16 (2000): 2592–2600.

Martin, Joseph D. "Prestige Asymmetry in American Physics: Aspirations, Applications, and the Purloined Letter Effect." *Science in Context* 30, no. 4 (2017): 475–506.

Marx, Karl, and Serge L. Levitsky. *Das Kapital: A Critique of Political Economy*. Washington, DC: H. Regnery, 1965.

Matamoros-Fernández, Ariadna. "Platformed Racism: The Mediation and Circulation of an Australian Race-Based Controversy on Twitter, Facebook and YouTube." *Information, Communication & Society* 20, no. 6 (2017): 930–946.

McKeown, Conor. "Playing with Materiality: An Agential-Realist Reading of Seth-Bling's Super Mario World Code-Injection." *Information, Communication & Society* 21, no. 9 (2018): 1234–1245.

McKittrick, Katherine. *Dear Science and Other Stories*. Durham, NC: Duke University Press, 2020.

McNay, Lois. *Gender and Agency: Reconfiguring the Subject in Feminist and Social Theory*. Hoboken, NJ: John Wiley & Sons, 2013.

McPherson, Tara. "US Operating Systems at Mid-century: The Intertwining of Race and UNIX." In *Race after the Internet*, edited by Lisa Nakamura and Peter Chow-White, 21–37. Milton Park, UK: Routledge, 2013.

McPherson, Tara. "Designing for Difference." *Differences* 25, no. 1 (2014): 177–188.

Miner, Joshua D. "Biased Render: Indigenous Algorithmic Embodiment in 3D Worlds." *Screen Bodies* 4, no. 1 (2019): 48–71.

Mol, Annemarie. *The Body Multiple: Ontology in Medical Practice*. Durham, NC: Duke University Press, 2002.

Montfort, Nick. "Combat in Context." *Game Studies* 6, no. 1 (2006): 1.

Montfort, Nick. "Platform Studies at 10." *Post Position* blog, July 26, 2018. https://nickm.com/post/2018/07/platform-studies-at-10/.

Montfort, Nick, and Ian Bogost. *Racing the Beam: The Atari Video Computer System*. Cambridge, MA: MIT Press, 2009.

Mulvin, Dylan. *Proxies: The Cultural Work of Standing In*. Cambridge, MA: MIT Press, 2021.

Murray, Janet H. *Hamlet on the Holodeck, Updated Edition: The Future of Narrative in Cyberspace*. Cambridge, MA: MIT Press, 2017.

Nakamura, Lisa. *Digitizing Race: Visual Cultures of the Internet*. Minneapolis: University of Minnesota Press, 2007.

Nakamura, Lisa. "Indigenous Circuits: Navajo Women and the Racialization of Early Electronic Manufacture." *American Quarterly* 66, no. 4 (2014): 919–941.

Nakamura, Lisa. "Feeling Good about Feeling Bad: Virtuous Virtual Reality and the Automation of Racial Empathy." *Journal of Visual Culture* 19, no. 1 (2020): 47–64.

Narcisse, Evan. "The Natural: The Parameters of Afro." *The State of Play: Creators and Critics on Video Game Culture*, edited by Daniel Goldberg and Linus Larsson, 53–74. New York: Seven Stories Press, 2015.

Narcisse, Evan. "The Natural: The Trouble Portraying Blackness in Video Games." *Kotaku* 2017. https://kotaku.com/the-natural-the-trouble-portraying-blackness-in-video-1736504384.

Nicoll, Benjamin. "A Dialectic of Obsolescence? The Sega Saturn as a Residual Plat-form." In *Minor Platforms in Videogame History*, 133–156. Amsterdam: Amsterdam University Press, 2019.

Nicoll, Benjamin, and Brendan Keogh. *The Unity Game Engine and the Circuits of Cultural Software*. London: Palgrave Pivot, 2019.

Nideffer, Robert F. "Game Engines as Creative Frameworks." In *Context Providers: Conditions of Meaning in Media Arts*, edited by Margot Lovejoy, Christiane Paul, and Victoria Vesna, 175–197. Chicago, IL: University of Chicago Press, 2011.

Nieborg, David B. "Empower Yourself, Defend Freedom!: Playing Games during Times of War." In *Digital Material: Tracing New Media in Everyday Life and Technology*, edited by M. van den Boomen, S. Lammes, A.-S. Lehmann, J. Raessens, and M. T. Schäfer, 35–47. Amsterdam: Amsterdam University Press, 2009.

Nieborg, David. "From Premium to Freemium: The Political Economy of the App." In *Social, Casual and Mobile Games: The Changing Gaming Landscape*, edited by Tama Leaver and Michele Willson, 225–240. London: Bloomsbury, 2016.

Nieusma, Dean, and James W. Malazita. "'Making' a Bridge: Critical Making as Synthesized Engineering/Humanistic Inquiry." In *Proceedings of the 2016 ASEE Annual Conference & Exposition*, 2016. https://peer.asee.org/making-a-bridge-critical -making-as-synthesized-engineering-humanistic-inquiry

Noble, Safiya Umoja. *Algorithms of Oppression: How Search Engines Reinforce Racism*. New York: New York University Press, 2018.

Nooney, Laine. "A Pedestal, a Table, a Love Letter: Archaeologies of Gender in Videogame History." *Game Studies* 13, no. 2 (2013).

Nooney, Laine. "Let's Begin Again: Sierra On-Line and the Origins of the Graphical Adventure Game." *American Journal of Play* 10, no. 1 (2017): 71–98.

O'Donnell, Casey. *Developer's Dilemma: The Secret World of Videogame Creators*. Cambridge, MA: MIT Press, 2014.

O'Donnell, Casey. "Platforms in the Cloud: On the Ephemerality of Platforms." *Digital Culture & Education* 8 (2016): 185–190.

O'Donnell, Casey. "Engines & Platforms: Functional Entanglements," In *Avatars, Assembled: The Sociotechnical Anatomy of Digital Bodies*, edited by Jaime Banks, 265–273. Bern: Peter Lang, 2018.

Parker, Felan. "Canonizing BioShock: Cultural Value and the Prestige Game." *Games and Culture* 12, no. 7–8 (2017): 739–763.

Patterson, Zabet. *Peripheral Vision: Bell Labs, the SC 4020, and the Origins of Computer Art*. Cambridge, MA: MIT Press, 2015.

Penley, Constance. *The Future of an Illusion: Film, Feminism, and Psychoanalysis*. Minneapolis: University of Minnesota Press, 1989.

Penley, Constance, Andrew Ross, and Donna Haraway. "Cyborgs at Large: Interview with Donna Haraway." *Social Text* 25/26 (1990): 8–23.

Perry, Imani. *More Beautiful and More Terrible*. New York: New York University Press, 2011.

Pharr, Matt, Wenzel Jakob, and Greg Humphreys. *Physically Based Rendering: From Theory to Implementation*. Burlington, MA: Morgan Kaufmann, 2017.

Phillips, Amanda. *Gamer Trouble: Feminist Confrontations in Digital Culture*. New York: New York University Press, 2020.

Phillips, Amanda, Gillian Smith, Michael Cook, and Tanya Short. "Feminism and Procedural Content Generation: Toward a Collaborative Politics of Computational Creativity." *Digital Creativity* 27, no. 1 (2016): 82–97.

Plantin, Jean-Christophe, Carl Lagoze, Paul N. Edwards, and Christian Sandvig. "Infrastructure Studies Meet Platform Studies in the Age of Google and Face-book." *New Media & Society* 20, no. 1 (2018): 293–310.

Poell, Thomas, David B. Nieborg, and Brooke Erin Duffy. *Platforms and Cultural Production*. Hoboken, NJ: John Wiley & Sons, 2021.

Power, Marcus. "Digitized Virtuosity: Video War Games and Post-9/11 Cyber-Deterrence." *Security Dialogue* 38, no. 2 (2007): 271–288.

Prescod-Weinstein, Chanda. "Making Black Women Scientists under White Empiricism: The Racialization of Epistemology in Physics." *Signs: Journal of Women in Culture and Society* 45, no. 2 (2020): 421–447.

Prescod-Weinstein, Chanda. *The Disordered Cosmos: A Journey into Dark Matter, Space-time, & Dreams Deferred*. New York: Bold Type Books, 2021.

Reed, Alison, and Amanda Phillips. "Additive Race: Colorblind Discourses of Realism in Performance Capture Technologies." *Digital Creativity* 24, no. 2 (2013): 130–144.

Richardson, Tanya, and Gisa Weszkalnys. "Introduction: Resource Materialities." *Anthropological Quarterly* 87, no. 1 (2014): 5–30.

Rocha, J., and F. Snelting, "Dis-orientation and Its Aftermath." In *Volumetric Regimes: Material Cultures of Quantified Presence*, edited by Jara Rocha and Femke Snelting, 57–75. London: Open Humanities Press, 2022.

Rose, Gillian. *Visual Methodologies: An Introduction to Researching with Visual Materials*. Newbury Park, CA: SAGE, 2016.

Roth, Lorna. "Looking at Shirley, the Ultimate Norm: Colour Balance, Image Technologies, and Cognitive Equity." *Canadian Journal of Communication* 34, no. 1 (2009): 111–136.

Russell, Legacy. "Elsewhere, after the Flood: Glitch Feminism and the Genesis of the Glitch Body Politic." *Rhizome*, March 12, 2013. http://rhizome.org/editorial/2013/mar/12/glitch-body-politic/.

Russworm, TreaAndrea. "Dystopian Blackness and the Limits of Racial Empathy in The Walking Dead and The Last of Us." In *Gaming Representation: Race, Gender, and Sexuality in Video Games*, edited by Jennifer Malkowski and TreaAndrea Russworm, 109–128. Bloomington: Indiana University Press, 2017.

Salter, Anastasia, and John Murray. *Flash: Building the Interactive Web*. Cambridge, MA: MIT Press, 2014.

Schell, Jesse. *The Art of Game Design: A Book of Lenses*. Boca Raton, FL: CRC Press, 2008.

Schubert, Stefan. "Objectivism, Narrative Agency, and the Politics of Choice in the Video Game BioShock." In *Poetics of Politics: Textuality and Social Relevance in Contemporary American Literature and Culture*, edited by Sebastian M. Herrmann, Carolin Alice Hofmann, Katja Kanzler, Stefan Schubert, and Frank Usbeck, 271–290. Heidelberg: Universitätsverlag, 2015.

Snyder, Ilana Ariela. *Hypertext: The Electronic Labyrinth*. New York: New York University Press, 1996.

Sobchack, Vivian. *The Address of the Eye: A Phenomenology of Film Experience*. Princeton, NJ: Princeton University Press, 1992.

Soderman, Braxton. *Against Flow: Video Games and the Flowing Subject*. Cambridge, MA: MIT Press, 2021.

Srnicek, Nick. *Platform Capitalism*. Hoboken, NJ: John Wiley & Sons, 2017.

Starosielski, Nicole. "Thermocultures of Geological Media." *Cultural Politics* 12, no. 3 (2016): 293–309.

Steele, Catherine Knight. *Digital Black Feminism*. New York: New York University Press, 2021.

Steinberg, Marc. "From Automobile Capitalism to Platform Capitalism: Toyotism as a Prehistory of Digital Platforms." *Organization Studies* 43, no. 7 (2022): 1069–1090.

Strathern, Marilyn. "On Space and Depth." In *Complexities: Social Studies of Knowledge Practices*, edited by John Law and Annemarie Mol, 88. Durham, NC: Duke University Press, 2002.

Suits, Bernard. *The Grasshopper: Games, Life and Utopia*. Peterborough, ON: Broadview Press, 2014.

Sundén, Jenny. "On Trans-, Glitch, and Gender as Machinery of Failure." *First Monday* 20, no. 4–6 (2015).

Svelch, J. "Platform Studies, Computational Essentialism, and Magic: The Gathering." *Analog Game Studies* 3, no. 5 (2016).

Swink, Steve. *Game Feel: A Game Designer's Guide to Virtual Sensation*. Boca Raton, FL: CRC Press, 2008.

Tasker, Yvonne. *Spectacular Bodies: Gender, Genre, and the Action Cinema*. New York: Routledge, 1993.

Taylor, T. L. "Living Digitally: Embodiment in Virtual Worlds." In *The Social Life of Avatars: Presence and Interaction in Shared Virtual Environments*, edited by Ralph Schroeder, 40–62. London: Springer, 2002.

Taylor, T. L. "The Assemblage of Play." *Games and Culture* 4, no. 4 (2009): 331–339.

Tayyab Mahmud. "Review Essay: Genealogy of a State-Engineered Model Minority: Not Quite/Not White South Asian Americans." *Denver Law Review* 78, no. 4. (2001): 657-686.

Theis, Thomas N., and H.-S. Philip Wong. "The End of Moore's Law: A New Beginning for Information Technology." *Computing in Science & Engineering* 19, no. 2 (2017): 41–50.

Thompson, Krista A. *Shine: The Visual Economy of Light in African Diasporic Aesthetic Practice*. Durham, NC: Duke University Press, 2015.

Tuin, Iris van der, and Rick Dolphijn. *New Materialism: Interviews & Cartographies*. London: Open Humanities Press, 2012.

Turnock, Julie A. *Plastic Reality: Special Effects, Technology, and the Emergence of 1970s Blockbuster Aesthetics*. New York: Columbia University Press, 2015.

Turnock, Julie A. *The Empire of Effects: Industrial Light and Magic and the Rendering of Realism*. Austin: University of Texas Press, 2022.

Van der Graaf, Shenja, and David B. Nieborg. "Together We Brand: America's Army." In *Level Up: Digital Games Research Conference*, edited by Marinka Copier and Joost Raessens. 324-328. Utrecht, Holland: Universiteit Utrecht, 2003.

Wajcman, Judy. *Feminism Confronts Technology*. University Park, PA: Penn State Press, 1991.

Wajcman, Judy. "Feminist Theories of Technology." *Cambridge Journal of Economics* 34, no. 1 (2010): 143–152.

Wardrip-Fruin, Noah, and Michael Mateas. "Defining Operational Logics." *DiGRA Conference 2009*, "Breaking New Ground: Innovation in Games, Play, Practice and Theory," September 1–4, West London, UK.

Werning, Stefan. *Making Games: The Politics and Poetics of Game Creation Tools*. Cambridge, MA: MIT Press, 2021.

Whitson, Jennifer R. "Voodoo Software and Boundary Objects in Game Development: How Developers Collaborate and Conflict with Game Engines and Art Tools." *New Media & Society* 20, no. 7 (2018): 2315–2332.

Williams, Raymond. "Structures of Feeling." In *Structures of Feeling: Affectivity and the Study of Culture*, edited by Devika Sharma and Frederik Tygstrup, 20–28. Berlin: De Gruyter, 2015.

Willson, Michele, and Tama Leaver. "Zynga's FarmVille, Social Games, and the Ethics of Big Data Mining." *Communication Research and Practice* 1, no. 2 (2015): 147–158.

Wolf, Mark J. P. "Z-Axis Development in the Video Game." In *The Video Game Theory Reader 2*, edited by Bernard Perron and Mark Wolf, 173–190. New York: Routledge, 2008.

Wolfe, Patrick. *Traces of History: Elementary Structures of Race*. Brooklyn, NY: Verso Books, 2016.

Wölfflin, Heinrich. *Principles of Art History: The Problem of the Development of Style in Early Modern Art: One Hundredth Anniversary Edition*. Los Angeles, CA: Getty Publications, 2015.

Woolgar, Steve. "Configuring the User: The Case of Usability Trials." *Sociological Review* 38, no. 1 supplemental (1990): 58–99.

Yue, Genevieve. *Girl Head: Feminism and Film Materiality*. New York: Fordham University Press, 2020.

Index